THE WORKS OF

WITTER BYNNER

GENERAL EDITOR, JAMES KRAFT

SELECTED POEMS

Edited, and with a critical introduction, by Richard Wilbur;
biographical introduction by James Kraft

LIGHT VERSE AND SATIRES

Edited, and with an introduction, by William Jay Smith

THE CHINESE TRANSLATIONS

THE JADE MOUNTAIN

Introduction by Burton Watson

THE WAY OF LIFE ACCORDING TO LAOTZU

Introduction by David Lattimore

PROSE PIECES

Edited, and with an introduction, by James Kraft

LETTERS

Edited, and with an introduction, by James Kraft

THE CHINESE TRANSLATIONS

WITTER BYNNER AND KIANG KANG-HU

IN 1929

THE WORKS OF
WITTER BYNNER

GENERAL EDITOR, JAMES KRAFT

THE CHINESE
TRANSLATIONS

· ❧❧❧ ·

FARRAR · STRAUS · GIROUX / NEW YORK

This edition copyright © 1978 by The Witter Bynner Foundation
The Jade Mountain copyright 1929,
copyright renewed 1957 by Alfred A. Knopf, Inc.
The Way of Life According to Laotzu copyright © 1944
by Witter Bynner; copyright renewed 1972
by Dorothy Chauvenet and Paul Horgan
All rights reserved
First printing, 1978
Printed in the United States of America
Published simultaneously in Canada by
McGraw-Hill Ryerson Ltd., Toronto
Designed by Cynthia Krupat

Library of Congress Cataloging in Publication Data
Main entry under title: The Chinese translations.
(The Works of Witter Bynner)
The jade mountain is a translation of T'ang shih san
pai shou, compiled by C. Sun. The way of life according
to Laotzu is a translation of Tao tê ching.
Includes bibliographical references and indexes.
CONTENTS: Bynner, W. Remembering a gentle scholar.
—Watson, B. Introduction to The jade mountain.
—The jade mountain. [etc.]
1. Chinese poetry—Translations into English.
2. English poetry—Translations from Chinese.
I. Bynner, Witter, 1881–1968. / II. Bynner, Witter, 1881–1968.
Remembering a gentle scholar. 1978.
III. Sun, Chu, 1711–1778, comp. T'ang shih san pai shou.
English. 1978. / IV. Lao-tzǔ. Tao tê ching. English. 1978.
V. Series: Bynner, Witter, 1881–1968. Works.
PL2658.E3C59 / 895.1'1'308 / 78–482

This book is published with the aid of a grant from
The Witter Bynner Foundation for Poetry

Contents

Remembering a Gentle Scholar,
by Witter Bynner / 3

Introduction to
THE JADE MOUNTAIN,
by Burton Watson / 15

THE JADE MOUNTAIN / 33

Introduction to
THE WAY OF LIFE
ACCORDING TO LAOTZU,
by David Lattimore / 309

THE WAY OF LIFE
ACCORDING TO LAOTZU / 329

Remembering
a Gentle Scholar

BY WITTER BYNNER

This essay by Bynner appeared in the Winter 1953 issue of The Occident, *the undergraduate literary publication of the University of California at Berkeley. In it Bynner explains how he came to meet Kiang Kang-hu and to translate the two Chinese works in this volume,* The Jade Mountain *(1929) and* The Way of Life According to Laotzu *(1944).*

In suggesting that, after an interval of many years, I again contribute to *The Occident,* its editor wrote me that the autumn issue "is to focus upon Asiatic literature" and added that "this theme was given impetus by a sense of its necessity in our present Western thought."

With more time and space, I should have liked to dwell on the theme as it relates to that necessity, our present political involvement with Asia making acutely necessary our understanding of the Oriental spirit; but I hope that a brief factual account of my connection with Chinese poetry and philosophy will not only record experience pertinent to the theme and to the impetus prompting it—as well as incidentally pertinent to the University of California—but will help to indicate the fact that human emotion and thought are of sympathetic kinship the world over and that such thought in Chinese philosophy as has lasted from the 6th century B.C. and in Chinese poetry from the 6th, 7th and 8th centuries A.D. is basically close to what is likely to last of "present Western thought."

In 1918, when I was a member of the faculty at Berkeley, I met a fellow member, Dr. Kiang Kang-hu, to whom I was at once drawn. What he had recently done as a man of principle and brave action was enough to evoke my interest even before I learned to know him as a gentle scholar and stimulating companion. He had been secretary to Yüan Shih-k'ai, China's first president after Sun Yat-sen's provisional presidency and patriotic withdrawal. When in 1916, Yüan schemed to make himself emperor, Dr. Kiang, denouncing the plot and instrumental in blocking it, had to flee for his life and, landing in the United States, speedily learned enough English to become an able and popular teacher at the University of California. Like most Americans, I had been trained exclusively in the European culture which stems from Athens, Rome and Jerusalem. Until 1917, the best part of which year I spent in Japan and China, I had known next to nothing of the world's Asiatic background; and now at Berkeley I was finding myself moved by it as it reflected in Dr. Kiang, especially by fragments of Chinese poetry with which he would now and then illuminate his conversation. I had been superficially familiar with the ethical teachings of Confucius, had respected his sense of order, his successful rejection of divine attributes, and his intelligent concern with one world at a time, but had been a bit chilled by his preoccupation with domestic and social etiquette, his elaborate anticipation of Emerson's findings that in some respects manners are morals. Through glimpses of the calm, kind, almost democratic thinking, the intuitional sense of oneness in man, nature and eternity, which permeates many of the T'ang poems, I began seeing for the first time into an ancient society of individual spirits not shackled by dogma, by fixed commandment or code, not shadowed by jealous deity. Against the burdens and buffets of life, these poets had found an inner peace and a good will toward men at least as sure and sweet, it seemed to me, as any peace or good will found in a later world.

Jesus says, Leave all else and follow Me, which no all-powerful God would need to say and no man, impotent against change, should assume to say. His followers say, God died for us. It's the Me and the me. T'ang poets, living their Taoism, had eased meship into the whole current of life itself, no god or man intervening. They acknowledged the melancholy natural to man over his predicaments, but had not let it become anything like the morbidly mystical egotism in which Christianity has mythologized it. Wang Wêi says, I shall

> some day meet an old wood-cutter
> And talk and laugh and never return.

Han Hung asks,

> Who need be craving a world beyond this one?
> Here, among men, are the Purple Hills!

Mêng Chiao asks,

> What troubling wave can arrive to vex
> A spirit like water in a timeless well?

Liu Chang-ch'ing confesses,

> Mingling with Truth among the flowers,
> I have forgotten what to say.

A wisdom was here, I thought, relaxed and open, of which Christian civilization—perhaps Buddhist civilization also—stood in need for a simplifying and cleansing and strengthening of life; a wisdom which, I felt, some unnecessary screen had been hiding from us of the West. Perhaps the screen was the fact that, through priesthood and pathetic credulity, Taoism had degenerated from a pure philosophic faith into superstition and claptrap, much as the teachings of Jesus have done; some of the Christian mythology seeming to me as savage as that of Greece but less engaging. Perhaps Jesus needs Laotzu over here, I wondered, and Laotzu needs Jesus over there. I tried to find Laotzu in translations of his sayings; but the translations only clouded him for me, whereas Kiang's oral Anglicizing of T'ang poets, and of their Taoism, illumined him. So I asked Kiang if he and I might

not try collaborating in translating poems by Wang Wêi. I wish
we had then thought of trying to translate the source, the *Tao
Teh Ching* itself. But Kiang proposed an 18th century anthology,
Three Hundred Pearls of the T'ang Dynasty (618 to 906 A.D.)
the compiler of which had remarked in his preface, "This is but
a family reader for children, but it will hold good until our hair
is white": a collection of far wider popularity in China than,
say, *The Golden Treasury* here. *170 Chinese Poems*, the first
book of translations by Arthur Waley, Britain's distinguished
Sinologist, had not then appeared and resounded, or I might have
quit my project; and earlier translations, except a few by Helen
Waddell, had not held what I wanted. Ezra Pound's small sheaf,
Cathay, printed in London three years before, contained passages
arrestingly fine, as well as prophetic of Waley's direct manner;
but Kiang, wondering why the American poet should call Li Po
only by his Japanese name, Rihaku, recited off-hand versions of
the same poems Pound had chosen, which I found, even in
Kiang's halting English, still finer.

So we went to work, believing that in a year's time we could
string the three hundred Chinese pearls on English thread. Two
years later we sailed for China together, planning continuance
through the summer of our far from finished task. By a freak of
fortune we lost each other. He was to spend a fortnight with
relatives and on business in Shanghai. He had given me as his
address a Chinese hotel there; but he had advised my going
ahead with the Arthur Davison Fickes, our travelling companions, to Si Wu, the lake resort near Hangchow where he would
join us later, for escape from Shanghai's terrific heat. When we
still had to flee heat, we wrote giving him our address on Mokan-
shan, a comparatively cool mountain, still farther from Shanghai.
His hotel, being full as we learned afterwards, not only had no
room for him but apparently took no interest in his mail, though
he called there again and again and I wrote there again and again
all summer, he thinking as ill of an American as I of a Chinese.
In the autumn, we met by accident on a Shanghai street. Since
he had left with me his rough literal texts of the poems and I

had been hard at work on them, we were able to go over them for accuracy, as we had done before and were to do again many times.

The publishers' announcement of *The Jade Mountain* for 1921, when we had expected it to be ready, led to an amusing literary panic of which I knew nothing until 1946 when, asked to review a volume of correspondence between Amy Lowell and Florence Ayscough, I discovered how hard Miss Lowell had driven her collaborator in order to issue their translations from the Chinese ahead of ours. As it happened, *Fir-Flower Tablets* appeared in 1921 and *The Jade Mountain*—after eight more years of work on it—in 1929.

Meanwhile the popular welcome given Arthur Waley's and Shigeyoshi Obata's translations, as well as magazine publication of nearly all our three hundred "pearls," had shown a marked Western interest in Chinese poetry, not as something exotic or picturesque but as a record of human feeling and thought so simply and rightly expressed as almost to conceal its artistry. I often wish that among our own contemporary poets there were more of the T'ang awareness that "a poem can be tipped over by one heavy word." In poetry, apart from political comments, officially commanded tributes or playful literary games, those old boys used no ponderous or intricate symbolism, no foppish babble, but the grace of an art in which a man's mind never grows childish and a child's heart never dies.

It is of course gratifying to me that Dr. Kiang's work and mine, as translators, stays alive; and I attribute its vitality to the fact that in spirit and expression the poems remain as close as we could keep them to what the originals mean in China. Mr. Waley, who knows Chinese, greeted the book warmly and took generous pains to point out a number of initial errors which have been corrected in later editions. I trust that the vogue of flashy, deliberately false translations, like those of Powys Mathers in *Colored Stars*, is past. I used to argue with Miss Lowell and Mrs. Ayscough against their exaggerated use of root-meanings in Chinese characters, so that under their hands what was natural, direct, every-day expression in the Orient would become in English odd or complex or literary. The temptation to dart toward such glitter is easy to understand; but I early agreed with Kiang that for translators the bright fly concealed a hook. I quote from one of Mrs. Ayscough's letters: "Take, for instance, *yu*, formed of the two radicals 'the wind' and 'to speak'; instead of just saying 'a gale,' Miss Lowell has rendered this 'shouts on the clearness of a gale.' One must be careful not to exaggerate," continues her collaborator, "but it makes lovely poems." Though it may gratify Mrs. Ayscough's weakness for "lovely poems" and though Chinese scholars may have sensitive feelers for the roots of their written characters, such translation does not give the reader or auditor in English the equivalent of what a Chinese reads or hears in the original. Poets write for people, not for etymologists. Whether or not Po Chü-yi, as is said, tested his poems by reading them to his cook, they are as human and simple as if he had done so and can be finally as appealing in Canton, Ohio, as in Canton, Kwangtung. On Second Avenue in New York I noticed years ago a Chinese restaurant called *The Jade Mountain* and, told by a waiter that the owner had taken the title from a book of translated poems, I hoped it was because they were well translated. But it was more probably because of magic in the name, Kiang Kang-hu. I had already been shown respect by the proprietor of a Chinese restaurant in Santa Fe due to my connection with "a great scholar." These days when Kiang is mentioned in The New Canton Cafe, my friend there shakes his head sadly and observes, "Maybe he was too ambitious, but he is still a great scholar."

It happened that, during the Sino-Japanese war, Dr. Kiang joined the puppet government at Nanking as Minister of Education. He wrote me that he considered his act not political but a means of serving his people in captivity, as a scholar should. Unfortunately, when he became later a captive of the Nationalists, they did not relish his explanation and sentenced him to death. Because of appeals from many sources, including two American generals who had met and admired him, the sentence was commuted to life imprisonment. There had to be more appeals before he was permitted brush and paper for writing.

It was after his imprisonment that, still unsatisfied with English versions of the *Tao Teh Ching,* even with Arthur Waley's and Lin Yutang's which were published after my earlier research, I decided that I must attempt one by myself, must try to uncover in Laotzu's book the secret of his profound influence on China's loftiest thinkers and doers. Without Kiang's help, except for the general perception due to our eleven years of collaborating, I pondered and worked for many months, digging out from a dozen or so translations in English what I felt Laotzu must have meant; and for better or worse the resultant "American version" has maintained remarkable popularity in the United States through the past decade. Innumerable letters have certified a readiness among all sorts and conditions of Americans to add Laotzu's wisdom to the wisdom of the West.

Partly because Arthur Waley had thought my turns of expression too smooth and had questioned some of my interpretations, partly because I feared that I had been presumptuous, but finally because I would rather have my readings in *The Way of Life* approved by Kiang than by anyone else, I needed most the letter which came from his Nanking prison, dated August 13, 1948, four years after I had sent him the book. I have heard nothing from him since; and for several years his wife and children have received no answer concerning him from Chinese authorities. But through the silence I hear again, in his letter, the gentle scholar I first heard in Berkeley thirty-five years ago.

"As to your interpretation of Lao-tse" (he uses the older English spelling, instead of my Anglicized form, comparable to our spelling Kung Fu-tze, Confucius) "I can only say that it was entirely your insight of a 'fore-Nature' understanding that rendered it so simple and yet so profound. Lao-tse's text is direct, and we have to go around about it. It is impossible to translate it without an interpretation. Most of the former translations were based on the interpretations of certain commentators, but you chiefly took its interpretation from your own insight, which I term the 'fore-Nature' understanding or, in Chinese, Hsien-T'ien. This Hsien-T'ien understanding is above and beyond words. As the Chinese say, 'All human beings are of the same heart, and all human hearts are for the same reason.' If this reason was not sidetracked by anything of an 'after-Nature,' then everyone would come to an identical or similar understanding. So the translation could be very close to the original text, even without knowledge of the words. I am grateful to you indeed for your kind dedication, but rather shameful for not being able to assist you in any way."

Though he does not commit himself to my interpretation, this gentle comment from Kiang Kang-hu has assisted me in more ways than one. I have tried to thank him in China, and I thank him here.

It is a warming phenomenon that our having been to all purposes at war with the present government of China's mainland—this fact has not turned our people against the Chinese as people. Russia, behind China, has been our real dread. And I doubt that the Chinese people will long be docile to foreign-inspired masters. Docility to any master is not in their nature nor in their history. Although the Soviet system, insofar as it means local government by guilds, originated in China, the Soviet system as developed by Russia into a police state is alien to Chinese character and tradition. From earliest times scholars and poets have held high place in Chinese government and, though often punished for individualism and candor, have seldom feared to criticize and to oppose and undo tyranny, as Dr. Kiang opposed and helped to thwart the attempted tyranny of Yüan Shih-k'ai. It is notable today that not only a statesman like Syngman Rhee but many thousands of Korean and Chinese soldiers are gallantly, stoutly opposing both Communist tyranny and our own powerful, disgraceful and unprecedented tyranny in imprisoning and tormenting our declared friends. I have a feeling that our own people at large are ashamed of our captains and bargainers. At least there is no surging popular sentiment among us favoring assault on the people of China. And I am convinced that under similar circumstances our feeling would have been less civilized fifty years ago, that among people in the Occident an understanding of people in the Orient has subtly and surely arisen and that this understanding is due more than we realize to the fact that Asian thought and art has reached and touched the West, that we now know Chinese civilization, for instance, to be not only the oldest civilization still vigorous but to be a civilization profoundly informed as to lasting values.

At the moment the element which controls China would seem to have set its face against the wisdom of philosophers and poets who have made China great in the past and who have lately come alive anew in conveying a sense of its greatness to a wider world. But are we less fluctuant, we in the West?

Three years ago I was calling on the Minister of War in London. He had recently returned from an official trip in the Orient and said that during his stay there he had written a poem which was to have been published in *The London Observer.* The Prime Minister, happening to notice a proof of it on the War Minister's desk, had to ask and be told what it was. He advised that it be withdrawn, since poetry writing was beneath the dignity of a Cabinet Member. He probably did not even know that for centuries Chinese Emperors, Premiers and Generals had been proud to write poetry, nor had he any suspicion that his own successor as Prime Minister in Britain would receive a Nobel award for literature.

Cabinet Members come and go. But Li Shang-yin, a gentle scholar, continues saying, as he said in the 9th century:

Literature endures, like the universal spirit,
And its breath becomes a part of the vitals of all men.

And Kiang Kang-hu continues quoting, even in prison: "All human beings are of the same heart, and all human hearts are for the same reason."

Kiang Kang-hu is believed to have died in prison in Shanghai on December 6 or 7, 1954. Bynner wrote to a friend, Mabel Mac-

Donald Carver, on June 12, 1962, about this final period of his friend's life: "Poor Kiang made the grave error of accepting the secretaryship of education in the cabinet of Henry Pu Yi in the Manchukuo, called the Puppet Government. Kiang insisted to the end that he merely wished to keep the youngsters in his country educated, while subject to Japan, and that he never was in the least politically active. Unfortunately, the Nationalists did not take it that way and put the man in jail where later the Communists kept him until his tragic death there. I am amazed that my inscribed copy of The Way of Life was allowed to reach the prisoner and his note about it allowed to reach me. The sad end was when a note of his did reach his daughter living in China, asking her if she could bring him some candy. She did, only to be told by an official at the prison: 'Your father died last night of malnutrition.' They did not even return her the candy."

INTRODUCTION TO

The Jade Mountain

BY BURTON WATSON

Fifty years have passed since the American poet Witter Bynner began making translations of Chinese poetry, at first publishing them piecemeal in various magazines and in 1929 collecting them in a volume entitled *The Jade Mountain* (Alfred A. Knopf). It is an appropriate time to inquire how well his works have stood up over the years, both as translations from the Chinese and as English poetry.

Bynner read no Chinese. In making his translations he relied entirely upon the assistance of the eminent Chinese scholar and educator Kiang Kang-hu (Chiang K'ang-hu), who taught for a time at the University of California at Berkeley. Bynner had met him in 1918, when he himself taught for a year at the same university. Kiang supplied him with literal versions of the poems from which to work and aided him in shaping the translations and in preparing notes and biographical information. Bynner made two trips to China, the second when he was already at work on his translations, and thus he had the opportunity to become personally familiar with the life and landscape of the country whose poetry he translated.

No doubt on Dr. Kiang's advice, Bynner chose to translate a standard Chinese anthology rather than poems selected at random. The anthology, entitled *T'ang-shih san-pai-shou*, or *Three Hundred Poems of the T'ang*, was compiled by a Ch'ing scholar named Sun Chu and bears a preface dated 1763. Though apparently intended mainly for elementary students, it has enjoyed tremendous popularity among readers of all ages over the centuries since its appearance. It consists of some three hundred poems in *shih* form dating from the T'ang dynasty (618–906) and arranged by subdivisions of the form. The original anthology contained 310 poems, but later editors have made various additions, so that the exact number differs with the particular edition. The *shih* was the most popular form in use during this period, and the T'ang poets are widely regarded as having raised it to its highest level of artistic excellence. Bynner was thus presenting works that the Chinese consider to be among their very finest.

Any anthology inevitably reflects the particular tastes and interests of the compiler and his era, and may not accord exactly with those of later periods. The *Three Hundred Poems of the T'ang* contains almost no poems dating from the early decades of the dynasty, but, as I shall have occasion to remark on later, this is quite defensible, since these works for the most part employ the florid and shallow style inherited from the preceding Sui and late Six Dynasties era and, in terms of literary history, belong to that earlier period. Stylistically, true T'ang poetry begins around the close of the seventh century and is represented by such illustrious names as Li Po, Tu Fu, Po Chü-yi, and Han Yü. Sun Chu's anthology presents a judicious sample of their works, though it may not coincide precisely with the selection a present-day compiler would choose. Sun Chu also includes many poems by less prominent figures, introducing the reader to a wisely balanced variety of themes, genres, and metrical forms.

Like all anthologies, Sun Chu's has had its critics. Many Chinese scholars, apart from decrying specific omissions, appear to be offended essentially by the brevity of the selection, pointing out that there are close to 49,000 extant T'ang poems from which a compiler might choose. Since one of the main purposes of anthologies is to condense a large body of literature to manageable proportions, this criticism would seem to be irrelevant at best. It reflects, however, the frequent tendency to equate mere bigness with greatness, and to be founded upon the assumption that one who reads 3,000 T'ang poems necessarily has ten times as fine an aesthetic experience as one who reads only 300, and so on, by mathematical progression. Such an assumption, needless to say, ignores the fact that in literature it is the quality of the reading that counts, the sympathy and insight with which the reader approaches his material, rather than the quantity he covers. Thus a thoughtful and sensitive appreciation of 300 T'ang poems may well impart a far deeper understanding of the real worth of T'ang poetry than a superficial acquaintance with the entire corpus. The very brevity of Sun Chu's anthology, in fact, is what made it so appropriate a choice for introduction to English readers in Bynner's time, when they had little or no knowledge of Chinese poetry, presenting them with a sample they could savor and digest without being overwhelmed.

One suspects that many traditionally trained Chinese scholars manifest an instinctive aversion to the *Three Hundred Poems of the T'ang* mainly because they have wearied of its contents through constant exposure from childhood on. They react to it the way many Western listeners of classical music react to Beethoven's Fifth. But, understandable as the reaction may be, it is hardly a legitimate gauge of aesthetic value, and in any event is of little relevance to the Western reader who has had no such background. If the latter is to comprehend and appreciate traditional Chinese literature and culture properly, he must perforce begin in school, acquainting himself with the works that every Chinese schoolchild knows by heart before venturing on to rarer fare. For this reason as well, Kiang and Bynner's decision to translate the *Three Hundred Poems* may be said to have been a wise one.

Bynner translated the entire anthology, appending notes to explain allusions and rearranging the poems by author, since the prosodic differences that distinguish the various categories of the original are largely obscured in translation. He also provided an introductory essay, "Poetry and Culture," eloquently setting forth his views on the worth of Chinese poetry and apprising the reader of certain liberties taken in the translations in an effort to make them more acceptable to Western tastes. Dr. Kiang supplied a second introductory essay outlining the history of Chinese poetry and describing the prosody of the *shih* form. Some of the information in his essay is now obsolete, since he accepted dates and attributions for certain works that are no longer held to be valid, and readers might do well to consult more recent treatments of the subject in English such as James J. Y. Liu's *The Art of Chinese Poetry* (University of Chicago Press, 1962), or my *Chinese Lyricism: Shih Poetry from the Second to the Twelfth Century* (Columbia University Press, 1971).

·

Before discussing problems of translation and Bynner's own methods of dealing with them, it may be well to comment in brief on the general nature and importance of T'ang poetry, though in doing so I will to some extent be going over ground already covered by Bynner and Kiang in their respective essays.

China in the long centuries of its history before the T'ang had several remarkable flowerings of the poetic spirit. The first took place around the years 1000–600 B.C. and is represented by the hymns, folk songs, and celebrations of the lives of the feudal aristocracy contained in the *Shih ching,* or *Book of Odes.* A second outstanding period of poetic activity occurred around A.D. 200–500, when many distinguished literati-officials produced works of great power and beauty in both the *shih* and the *fu,* or rhyme-prose, forms. During the intervening centuries, though poetry by no means ceased to be written, it generally displayed less vitality than prose, resulting in only sporadic works of distinction, or, as in the sixth century, dwindled into lifeless mannerism.

Though the T'ang was founded in 618, its poetry, as I have noted, did not begin to display genuine vigor and originality until the latter years of the seventh century. Thereafter it evolved with astonishing rapidity, reaching its height with the works of men such as Wang Wei, Li Po, and Tu Fu in the eighth century. These were succeeded by poets of only slightly less imposing stature, such as Han Yü, Po Chü-yi, and Li Shang-yin in the late eighth and early ninth centuries.

What occasioned this unprecedented outburst of creativity in the *shih* form? One is tempted to link it to the vigor of the dynasty itself. The T'ang, infused with new blood from the non-

Chinese peoples of the north, displayed great military prowess, extending Chinese power and influence eastward in the Korean peninsula, southward into Vietnam, and deep into Central Asia. At the same time, it established firm control over its far-reaching domains through a complex and tightly regulated bureaucracy. Cultural life flourished under the peace and prosperity that resulted, encouraged by the patronage of the court and aristocracy and enriched by foreign influences, particularly those entering the country from Central Asia. Moreover, the civil service examination system, elevated to a position of importance it had not known in earlier times, opened up to men of learning and literary ability avenues of advancement that had previously been largely reserved to members of the aristocracy.

All these factors may indeed have helped to foster the T'ang poetic renaissance by engendering a resurgent sense of national and cultural pride and inspiring men to create a new style of poetry liberated from the stereotypes of the past, vital and broad-visioned like the dynasty itself. It is significant that nearly all the major T'ang poets were government officials, many of them selected for office through the examination system, and their personal fortunes were thus intimately tied to those of the dynasty.

And yet, although something of the brilliance of the court and the grandeur of empire are mirrored in T'ang poetry, these represent only one facet of its varied makeup. The dynasty, even in its brightest days, was never free from palace intrigues and factional struggles. Moreover, just as the new poetic movement was gaining momentum, civil war broke out in 755, the ruler and his court were forced to flee from the capital, and the nation was plunged into prolonged chaos and suffering. Though order was eventually restored, the dynasty never recovered full control of the country, and the remaining years of its rule were marked by repeated shifts of power at court, growing anarchy in the provinces, and in time outright rebellion.

In another sense, therefore, the greatness of T'ang poetry may be seen as a response less to the richness and glory of the T'ang era than to its sorrows and uncertainties, particularly the uncertainties of political life. The finest T'ang poetry, one notes immediately, is almost without exception the product of the dynasty's darker days. Men like Wang Wei, Li Po, and Tu Fu, who had grown up when the nation was affluent and well ordered, had lived through the harrowing years of the civil war, and could see the tragic changes it had wrought, no doubt felt the sense of shock and loss most poignantly. Those who came after them could only struggle to maneuver through the perilously fluctuating political environment, ponder what measures might be taken to restore the nation to health, or brood upon the doom that seemed to be overtaking it.

Yet China had had similar dark and troubled periods in the past, and these were not necessarily accompanied by any outflowing of poetic spirit such as the T'ang witnessed. Perhaps the relationship between the history of an age and its artistic creativity is too obscure and problematical ever to be susceptible to clear analysis. At least there is no way to determine a precise causal relationship between the history of the T'ang period and the extraordinary outburst of creativity in its poetry.

·

The first thing that will probably strike the reader when he approaches the T'ang poems in Bynner's selection is their remarkable accessibility. Though T'ang poetry has its literary conventions, particularly in works dealing with the court and the women of the palace, these are seldom of the kind that requires elaborate explanation to be understood by readers not acquainted with the culture of the period. For the most part, Chinese poetry in the *shih* form, including that of the T'ang, impresses one with its directness, moderation, and great visual clarity. Though the Chinese *shih* poet employs a certain number of allusions to the past, usually drawn from history and referring to men whose lives resemble his own, he seldom, unlike his counterpart in many periods of Western poetry, draws upon mythology, or indulges in extravagant flights of rhetoric or fancy. Likewise absent from his works are those personifications of abstract qualities such as Justice, Love, or Freedom which, like haughty goddesses, parade through so much of the traditional poetry of the West. At first glance at least, the T'ang works appear to be strikingly realistic and personal, in many ways like the poetry of our own time.

This appearance, however, is to some degree deceptive. Though a great many of the finest T'ang poems are occasional in nature and describe the poet's own experiences or the landscapes that confront him, they are seldom as genuinely realistic as they may at first appear. The poet does not simply record what is before his eyes, but is highly selective in his choice of images, repeatedly focusing upon certain trees, birds, or other objects in the natural scene that in the Chinese tradition are endowed with rich symbolic associations. His treatment is carefully calculated to expand the scene or experience beyond its normal proportions, to endow it with a connotative depth and resonance that transcends actual life. His works, for all their simplicity and apparent realism, move almost always in the direction of the mythic, the timeless.

This is evident in the poet's revelation of himself as a person. If his mood is one of melancholy or apprehension, as is usually the case in T'ang poetry, he will customarily relate the emotion to a particular event in his life—parting from a friend, frustration in his career, the loneliness of a journey, or the pain of exile. His poem of grief will typically be given up almost entirely to a depiction of the scene of his sorrowing, the physical surroundings at the time he experiences the emotion, presenting what we now term objective correlatives of his inner state. And in the closing lines, when he comes to describe the emotion itself, he almost never seeks to analyze or philosophize upon it, much less exploit it for a display of individualism. Instead his statement is deliberately couched in language that is conventionalized, self-effacing, and low-keyed, ending the poem on a note that will often strike the present-day reader as anticlimactic.

"Look what is happening to *me!*" seems to be the message of much modern poetry, delivered in a tone shrill with personal outrage. "Look what happens to man" is, by contrast, the subdued suggestion of the T'ang poet. Poetry for him is a means not of asserting ego but of shedding it, of merging himself in the context of mankind as a whole, and in the still larger context of nature. Hence his gaze focuses so often upon the eternal mountains, the endlessly flowing rivers, the cycle of the seasons, which represent for him a realm where individual pain and frustration are in the end annulled and shorn of meaning.

Such, then, is the typical T'ang poem, which describes the immediate and the momentary but seeks always to see beyond them to the timeless. Not all T'ang poems, of course, fit this category, and not all T'ang poets were capable of sustaining this lofty tone, or desired to do so. Some, notably Po Chü-yi, began to experiment with a style more genuinely realistic and personal, and these tendencies became increasingly pronounced in the succeeding Sung period (960–1279). As a result, Sung poetry is varied, intimate, and expressive of the poet's individuality to a degree previously unknown. But in reducing the aesthetic distance between the poet and his creation, it in most cases loses the tone of transcendence that characterizes T'ang poetry at its finest.

The Chinese of later ages at times sought to imitate the T'ang style, at other times preferred to make the Sung their model. But nearly all agreed that, though much fine poetry had been written both before and after the T'ang, none of it could rival the sustained grandeur and universality of the T'ang masters. In terms of *shih* poetry, they stand at the pinnacle.

·

Let us turn now to the question of translation. I have listened to and read numberless discussions of the topic of how to translate Chinese poetry. Sifted of technical terminology and the jargon of criticism, they usually come down to the assertion that the translator should be faithful to the original and at the same time produce a rendering that reads like a genuine work of literature.

These, needless to say, are the Two Noble Truths of all translators, dicta as old as the art of translation itself. No one would question that they should guide the translator, any more than one would doubt that a pianist should strive to play the notes as they are written and at the same time present an interpretation that is musically intelligent and moving. Pious reiteration of ideals, however, takes neither the translator nor the pianist very far along the road to attaining them. Only artistic sensibility and a prodigious amount of hard work will do that.

Nearly anyone with a keen ear for language and some knowledge of the original can recognize a superior translation when he sees one. But the process by which such a translation is achieved, involving as it does an almost infinite amount of testing and rejecting, tinkering and adjusting, is so complex and elusive as to defy lucid formulation. As in the case of original works of literature, of which translations are the unglamorous and often-maligned cousins, one can lay down no rules of procedure beforehand but only examine the finished product and try to discover how and why it succeeds or fails.

Much has been made of the fact that some translators of Chinese such as Bynner and Pound had little knowledge of the language they were translating from, relying upon notes or the assistance of collaborators, while others such as Waley had almost complete control of the originals. This, however, strikes me as a relatively minor consideration. Some splendid translations have been produced through collaboration, and countless dreadful ones by individuals who could read the original language to perfection. What matters is the end result. Let us turn, therefore, to Bynner's renditions and attempt to determine where they excel and where they fall short.

I would define as an inaccuracy not a minor departure from the exact wording or syntax of the original but a rendering that radically distorts or misrepresents the writer's intention. By this definition, Bynner's translations are almost miraculously free of basic error. The credit for this of course belongs largely to Kiang.

In a letter written to Kiang in 1928 that accompanied the final version of the manuscript (both Bynner and Kiang moved around a good deal during their collaboration and conducted much of it by mail), Bynner requests Kiang to make a last thorough check of the translations, adding, "Do not . . . let me be incorrect." It is a plea perennially on the lips of translators, though most of us, lacking a consultant of Dr. Kiang's authority upon whose time and patience we may presume without restraint, must more often address it to the Fates.

In spite of precautions and the finest of intentions, a few serious errors have nevertheless found their way into Bynner's translations, presumably the result of imperfect communication between the collaborators. An example occurs in the final couplet of Li Po's famous "Drinking Alone with the Moon," where the poet, addressing the moon, says:

> *Let us pledge forever a friendship without feeling*
> *and meet again in the far-off Milky Way.*

Bynner—or possibly Kiang—failed to understand that Li Po's ideal was the kind of blithe, unobligating companionship he enjoyed with the moon and other objects of nature, as contrasted to entangling and emotion-filled human ties—hence his unconventional call for a "friendship without feeling." Out of bafflement, one supposes, Bynner resorts to a highly uncharacteristic fuzziness, rendering the lines:

> *. . . Shall goodwill ever be secure?*
> *I watched the long road of the River of Stars.*

Another faintly amusing example of error, which probably came about through a misreading of Kiang's notes, occurs in Meng Hao-jan's "On Climbing Yen Mountain with Friends," the fifth line of which reads in the original:

> *The water has fallen, fish weirs stand in shallows.*

The term *yü-liang*, "fish weirs," was apparently not explained to Bynner, and he failed to realize that the words *shui lo*, "water falls," mean that the water level of the river has fallen. These misunderstandings, always a potential danger in works of collaboration, compounded to produce the following rather surprising rendition:

Where a fisher-boat dips by a waterfall

Leaving aside those passages in the original that are ambiguous and the subject of debate even among experts, however, outright misinterpretations such as those cited above are rare in Bynner's renditions. Also rare are those gratuitous flourishes and elaborations on the original into which translators, particularly those of a literary bent, are so often beguiled—presumably in the conviction that, by improving on the original where they can, they are in a sense making up for beauties believed lost elsewhere in the process of translation. Bynner shows almost impeccable restraint in this respect, and I find only one minor example where his integrity faltered. In his translation of Ts'uei T'u's "On New Year's Eve," line four reads:

A stranger with a lonely lantern shaken in the wind.

The Chinese says simply: "Lone lantern, a man from a different land." Bynner evidently felt the line needed filling out in English and could not resist the beautiful but unjustified addition, "shaken in the wind."

When Bynner began making translations from Chinese poetry around 1920, the only previously published examples of Chinese poetry in English free verse were those of Ezra Pound's *Cathay* (1915) and Arthur Waley's *170 Chinese Poems* (1918). These were followed shortly by those of Florence Ayscough and Amy Lowell, *Fir-Flower Tablets* (1921). Free verse itself was still highly controversial, and its application to Chinese translation was deplored by many, as it continues to be in some quarters today.* Although Bynner was not the innovator in this respect, and wrote often in traditional verse forms himself, he showed acute judgment and foresight in adopting the new form in his translations—it is one of the principal reasons why they remain readable and exciting even today. But free verse, despite its deceptive title, is an extremely difficult form to handle, particularly when applied to translation. When the old mechanical devices of rhyme and meter are jettisoned, they must be compensated for by more inventive and varied beauties of rhythm and euphony, by a greater tautness and clarity of language, if the verse line is not to slacken into prose. In undertaking to translate an entire Chinese anthology into free verse, rather than to select merely those poems that he felt would come across well in English, Bynner set himself a formidable task.

I have already touched upon the matter of outright mistranslations in Bynner's work. We approach now the question of renditions which, though basically quite correct, take certain liberties with the precise wording and syntax of the original. This is the great gray area in translation where what one critic would condone as justifiable license, another brands as shocking infidelity.

At the time when Bynner first produced his translations, English readers, as noted above, had little familiarity with Chinese poetry. In his eagerness to have it properly appreciated, he adopted, as he explains in his introduction, certain practices that he felt would make it more palatable, such as at times substituting more general geographical terms for specific place names in the original or sliding over allusions (though he almost always

---

* See the spirited remarks by the late Jesuit priest John Turner in the introduction to his *A Golden Treasury of Chinese Poetry* (Hong Kong: The Chinese University of Hong Kong, 1976), pp. 9–22. Father Turner's own rhymed-verse translations, for all their ingenuity, strike me as contrived and cloyingly old-fashioned in tone, and in the end, I think, serve to vindicate the course which Pound, Waley, and Bynner chose.

explains the latter in notes). Translators of Chinese poetry nowadays, more confident of their audience, may view such expedients as needless or even indefensible, though before censuring Bynner too severely they would do well to consider that Western readers in the twenties were far less receptive toward Asian literature than they are today.

Another practice that Bynner frequently resorted to was that of weaving together lines that are in the original usually end-stopped, supplying logical and syntactical connectives that are at best merely implied in the Chinese. This at times creates a pleasant flowing effect, one that Bynner no doubt felt would be more nearly consonant with traditional English poetic taste. But it obscures the stark, deliberately disjointed quality so intrinsic to Chinese poetry in the *shih* form, and at times seriously distorts the meaning. For example, one such forced splicing of lines in Po Chü-yi's "Song of Unending Sorrow" is quite inexcusable:

> *And later when he turned to look, the place of blood and tears*
> *Was hidden in a yellow dust blown by a cold wind.*

This violates a boundary at which the poem shifts in both rhyme and locale. In the original, the first line, "When he turned to look, blood and tears flowed together," concludes the death scene of Yang Kuei-fêi; the following line, "Yellow dust spread abroad, winds sighed coldly," introduces the section on the imperial flight to Szechwan.

Most present-day translators would reject the use of such connectives, preferring to let the lines stand in the same purity of isolation they so often possess in the original. Once again they can choose this course with greater assurance because in the years since Bynner's time English readers have become acclimated to this choppy quality and accept it as characteristic of most Chinese poetry.

Again, Bynner often juggles the syntax of the original, preserving all the ideas of the Chinese line but assigning them slightly different grammatical functions. By permitting himself this freedom, which a more fastidious translator might feel compelled to forgo, he succeeds in creating many interesting and even arresting effects—effects that, because of their sheer beauty, one is inclined to say justify the means. In particular, the strength and vividness of his verbs serve to keep the translation constantly alive. A purist might object that his verbs in fact display greater range and vigor than those of the original, which is often more subdued and static in tone. But Bynner would probably argue that he is merely exploiting the strong points of English, whose verbs are its crowning glory, albeit these may not correspond exactly to the strong points of classical Chinese.

Because Chinese and English happen to resemble each other in construction and word order, it is possible—and proper, I think—to stick close to the syntax of the original when translating from classical Chinese. But one should keep in mind that such fidelity is possible only through an accident of language. The English translator from classical Japanese, for example, must depart constantly from the word order of the original if he is to make sense, and yet we would hardly be justified in accusing him of infidelity or excessive license. One should, I feel, avoid making a fetish of mere literalism and succumbing to the "more-accurate-than-thou" attitude that prevails among some translators today.

Finally, Bynner indulges at times in a practice quite different from those pointed out above, one which might be described as undertranslation. This is evident particularly in his handling of short poems, especially those employing a seven-character line, in which he simply omits an adjective or other qualifying word here and there, apparently out of a desire to achieve a sparer, cleaner effect. The results are often very lovely as English poems—in fact, among the loveliest in the collection—and yet, for all their lyric grace, they usually seem less sharply or fully realized than the originals.

Bynner, we may be certain, did not supply connectives,

tamper with syntax, or venture the other liberties I have described without knowing what he was doing or without feeling that through such liberties he could better convey to the English reader the true impact of the originals. He was far too good a poet, too sincere in his approach and modest by nature, to indulge in verbal opportunism or mere displays of cleverness, as lesser translators have often done. The way in which we judge him must rest upon how sympathetically we respond to the results. The following rather extreme example may serve to point up the dilemmas involved in arriving at such a judgment. In his translation of Li Po's "On Hearing Chün the Buddhist Monk from Shu Play His Lute," there occurs the following couplet:

I hear him in the cleansing brook,
I hear him in the icy bells.

Li Po's couplet is dense and obscure, the first line containing an allusion to a famous lute player whose music suggested the flowing of water, the second an allusion to some legendary bells that toll of themselves when frost falls. Joseph J. Lee in a recently published translation renders the couplet as follows:

The flowing stream cleanses a traveler's heart,
*Its dying strains fade into the first bells of frost.**

This is already more explicit than Li Po's original, and requires two footnotes to explain it. At the same time it fails to convey the most important fact—which *does* come across in Bynner's much freer version—that the sounds of the stream and the bells exist in or blend with the music that the monk is playing. (It is the dying strains of the lute, not those of the flowing stream, as Lee's translation suggests, that fade into the bells.)

* Wu-chi Liu and Irving Yucheng Lo, eds., *Sunflower Splendor: Three Thousand Years of Chinese Poetry* (New York: Anchor Books, 1975), p. 110.

Lee's translation is conscientious, reasonably literal, and doesn't really convey the point; Bynner's departs from Li Po's wording, suppresses the allusions, but achieves superb poetry. How should we judge between them?

·

Bynner never gave in to the fashion, still widely prevalent in his time, of patronizing his material by investing it with a deliberately quaint or exotic tone. He stuck faithfully both to the spirit and form of the originals, making one line of English correspond to one line of Chinese, and in almost all cases rendering the titles just as they are, though Pound had often substituted titles of his own—his renowned "River-Merchant's Wife: A Letter," for example, is Bynner's "Song of Ch'ang-kan." Pound also on occasion condensed several lines of the original into a single English line, or, where he found the Chinese particularly intractable, simply substituted a line of his own invention.

The recently published anthology *Sunflower Splendor*, cited in a previous note, demonstrates just how far we have advanced in Chinese poetry translation in terms of accuracy and strict conformity to the wording of the original since the time of Pound and Bynner. The fifty translators presented in it, while following Bynner's general practices, prefer to work much closer to the Chinese than he did and, partly as a result of meticulous supervision by the editors, have succeeded in avoiding the minor errors and misunderstandings that mar Bynner's work. Regrettably, the anthology also demonstrates that, with certain notable exceptions, there are not many translators of Chinese poetry in America today who can equal the kind of sonority and brilliance of language that Bynner achieved. To revert to my piano-playing analogy above, we have many people who can hit all the notes but few who are great interpreters of the music.

Paradoxically, this is probably in part because more Americans read Chinese now than in Bynner's time, and they consequently tend to take greater care with their Chinese than with their English. In translating Chinese poetry, it is a constant temptation, and one I myself have given in to often enough, to reach for the first word that comes to mind and then to excuse oneself from the labor of reconsidering the choice or casting about for a better word on the grounds that, after all, "that's what the text says." Because of the fortuitous similarity of Chinese and English syntax, this will very likely result in translations that are generally accurate and readable. As A. C. Graham remarks in the introduction to his *Poems of the Late T'ang* (Penguin Books, 1965), "partial successes are unexpectedly easy." It is when we try to rise above the level of partial success—of mere readability—that we encounter real difficulty. Rightly, I think, we deny ourselves the kind of liberties that Bynner often invoked to give his renderings variety and force. But for that very reason we must work harder than ever to produce genuinely distinguished results within the limitations we set for ourselves. We must take the pains to keep questioning each word and phrase until we are satisfied that we have achieved the most effective cadence, the cleanest and brightest diction possible. These clearly were the pains Bynner took with his renderings. He was never content to sit back and say, "That will have to do," and it is for this reason that we keep turning back to him for tutelage and inspiration. And it is precisely because he took such pains that, fifty years later, his works, though they are dated as translations, remain amazingly alive as poetry.

The following, Bynner's rendering of the first of Yüan Chen's elegies on the death of his wife, glides over the allusions in the first couplet and takes certain freedoms with the wording of the original. Yet how many other translations from Chinese poetry produced during the half century since its appearance can begin to match it in power and poignancy?

> *O youngest, best-loved daughter of Hsieh,*
> *Who unluckily married this penniless scholar,*
> *You patched my clothes from your own wicker basket,*

And I coaxed off your hairpins of gold, to buy wine with;
For dinner we had to pick wild herbs—
And to use dry locust-leaves for our kindling.
. . . Today they are paying me a hundred thousand—
And all that I can bring to you is a temple sacrifice.

THE JADE MOUNTAIN

MOUNTAIN

A CHINESE ANTHOLOGY

Being Three Hundred Poems
of the T'ang Dynasty
618–906

T R A N S L A T E D   B Y

Witter Bynner

F R O M   T H E   T E X T S   O F

Kiang Kang-hu

We join in dedicating our translations to

A L B E R T   M .   B E N D E R

————————————

"Literature endures, like the universal spirit,
And its breath becomes a part of the vitals of all men."

L I   S H A N G - Y I N

Contents

INTRODUCTION

I · Poetry and Culture by Witter Bynner / 39

II · Chinese Poetry by Dr. Kiang Kang-hu / 44

TRANSLATIONS / 59

APPENDICES

Historical Chronology / 245

Chronology of the Poets / 247

Topography / 251

Notes on the Poems / 257

Acknowledgments / 287

INDICES

Index of Titles / 291

Index of First Lines / 299

Introduction

· ❦❧❦❧❦ ·

I · POETRY AND CULTURE

BY WITTER BYNNER

Like most of us who have been schooled in this Western world,
I was afforded in my youth a study of culture flowing mainly
from two sources, the Greek and the Hebrew. I had come to feel
that poetic literature must contain streams from one or the other
of these two sources: on the one hand the clean, objective, sym-
metrical, athletic beauty of the Greek; on the other hand the
turgid, subjective, distorted, elaborated beauty of the Hebrew.
Like my fellow students, I had been offered nothing of the litera-
tures of the Far East. I am still doubtful that I could ever feel any
real adherence to the ornate and entranced literature of India;
but I have come by accident into as close touch with Chinese
poetry as a Westerner is able to come without a knowledge of
the Chinese tongue. And I feel with conviction that in the matter
of poetry I have begun to receive a new, finer, and deeper education than ever came to me from the Hebrew or the Greek.

Centuries ago cultivated Chinese had reached the intellectual saturation which has tired the mind of the modern European.
The Chinese gentleman knew the ancient folk-songs, compiled
by Confucius. He knew also, all around him, a profoundly rich
civilization, a more poised and particularized sophistication than
we Westerners have yet attained. Through the Asian centuries
everyone has written verse. In fact, from early imperial days
down to these even worse disordered days of the Republic, the
sense of poetry as a natural and solacing part of life has lasted
among the Chinese people. Whether or not the individual may
form or enjoy his poetry in metrical shape, he is constantly aware
of the kinship between the beauty of the world and the beauty

of imaginative phrase. On any Chinese mountain-climb toward a temple, rock after rock with its terse and suggestive inscription will bear witness to his temper. So will the street cries of the peddlers, or the names of the tea-houses, and on many hill-tops and lake-sides the casual but reverent jottings of this or that anonymous appreciator of natural beauty. When Whitman said: "To have great poets there must be great audiences too," he must have had in the back of his mind enriched generations like the Elizabethan in England or like almost any generation in China. In those great audiences each man, to the limit of his capacity and with natural ease, was a poet.

There is a simple secret in these generations. It is told in a pamphlet by a venerable Chinese scholar who, until his death two years ago, was still with infinite passion adhering to the precepts of his ancestors, and with infinite patience, acceptably expressed by the way among foreigners, adhering to his conviction that foreigners impair the health of China. His name is Ku Hung-ming. His pamphlet, written in English, one of the five languages which he could use, is called *The Spirit of the Chinese People*. In it he advances, as reason for the eternal youth of the Chinese people, the fact that the average Chinese has managed to maintain within himself the head of a man and the heart of a child. On this brief he is absorbingly interesting, explaining the continuance of Chinese culture, the only ancient culture still racially existent. My immediate concern with his brief is more special. I detect in it something that he does not specify: a reason for the continuance of poetry as a live factor among his people and, more than that, the best reason I know of for the persistence of poetry anywhere among cultured races.

Music may be the most intimate of the arts, I am not sure. Except for simple melodies, music is beyond the reach of any individual who is not a technician. Painting and sculpture are obviously arts expressing themselves in single given objects, which, although they may be copied and so circulated, are for the most part accessible only to the privileged or to those who make pilgrimages. Poetry more than any other of the arts may be carried about by a man either in his own remembering heart or else in compact and easily available printed form. It belongs to anyone. It is of all the arts the closest to a man; and it will so continue to be, in spite of the apparent shocks given it by the noises of modern commerce and science and jazz.

It has been a common occurrence in China that poets, even the best of them, devote their earlier years to some form of public service. Century after century, Chinese poems reflect this deep devotion of their authors to the good of the State—their unwavering allegiance to righteousness, even when it meant demotion or exile or death. In modern Western times there have been periods when poetry has seemed to be a candle-lit and thin-blooded occupation. I venture to surmise that poetry written in that sort of atmosphere grows with time less and less valid, less and less noticed. As a matter of fact, the outstanding English poets have been acutely concerned with the happiness of their fellow men and have given themselves warmly to public causes in which they believed. Similarly, present-day poets in America, with amazingly few exceptions, have clustered to the defence of noble souls at bay like Eugene Debs, or have been quick to protest against doubtful justice, as in the case of Sacco and Vanzetti. This sort of zeal may not result in poetry of a high order immediately connected with the specific cause; but there is no question that but for this bravery, this heat on behalf of man's better nature, there would not be in the hearts of the poets so fine a crucible for their more personal alchemies.

Let me say a more general word than Dr. Kiang's as to the characteristic method of the best Chinese poetry. I am not referring to the technical means by which a Chinese poet makes his words balanced and melodious. The discovery which has largely undone my previous convictions as to the way of writing poetry has rather to do with use of substance than with turns of expression. Mencius said long ago, in reference to the Odes collected by Confucius: "Those who explain the Odes must not insist on one term so as to do violence to a sentence, nor on a sentence so as to do violence to the general scope. They must try with their thoughts to meet that scope, and then they will apprehend it." In the poetry of the West we are accustomed to let our appreciative minds accept with joy this or that passage in a poem—to prefer the occasional glitter of a jewel to the straight light of the sun. The Chinese poet seldom lets any portion of what he is saying unbalance the entirety. Moreover, with the exception of a particular class of writing—adulatory verse written for the court—Chinese poetry rarely trespasses beyond the bounds of actuality. Whereas Western poets will take actualities as points of departure for exaggeration or fantasy, or else as shadows of contrast against dreams of unreality, the great Chinese poets accept the world exactly as they find it in all its terms, and with profound simplicity find therein sufficient solace. Even in phraseology they seldom talk about one thing in terms of another, but are able enough and sure enough as artists to make the ultimately exact terms become the beautiful terms. If a metaphor is used, it is a metaphor directly relating to the theme, not something borrowed from the ends of the earth. The metaphor must be concurrent with the action or flow of the poem; not merely superinduced, but an integral part of both the scene and the emotion.

Wordsworth, of our poets, comes closest to the Chinese; but their poetry cleaves even nearer to nature than his. They perform the miracle of identifying the wonder of beauty with common sense. Rather, they prove that the simplest common sense, the most salutary, and the most nearly universal, is the sense of the beauty of nature, quickened and yet sobered by the wistful warmth of human friendship.

For our taste, used as we are to the operatic in poetry, the substance of Chinese poems seems often mild or even trivial; but if we will be honest with ourselves and with our appreciation of what is lastingly important, we shall find these very same poems to be momentous details in the immense patience of beauty. They are the heart of an intimate letter. They bring the true, the beautiful, the everlasting, into simple, easy touch with the human, the homely, and the immediate. And I predict that future Western poets will go to school with the masters of the T'ang Dynasty, as well as with the masters of the golden age of Greece, or with the Hebrew prophets, or with the English dramatists or romanticists—to learn how best may be expressed, for themselves and others, that passionate patience which is the core of life.

It is not necessary that culture bring about the death of poetry, as it did in the Rome of Virgil. The cynics are wrong who see in our future no place for an art which belongs, they say, to the childhood of the race. The head of a man and the heart of a child working together as in the Chinese have made possible with one race and may make possible with any race, even in the thick of the most intricate culture, the continuance of the purest poetry.

Because of the absence of tenses, of personal pronouns and of connectives generally, the translator of Chinese poetry, like the Chinese reader himself, has considerable leeway as to interpretation. If even in English, so much more definite a language, there may be varying interpretations of a given poem, it is no wonder that critics and annotators have differed as to the meaning of poems in Chinese. There have been frequent instances in this volume where Dr. Kiang and I have discussed several possible meanings of a poem and have chosen for translation into the more definite language the meaning we preferred.

With his sanction I have decided that for readers in English it is better to eliminate or use only seldom the names of places and persons not highly important to the sense of a poem: to use "southern" or "eastern," for instance, instead of regional names unfamiliar in the Occident; to indicate the person meant when the poem, according to Chinese custom, employs the name and attributes of some other similar well-known person, and to embody in the English text something of the significance which would be conveyed to any Chinese reader, but not to Western readers, by historical or literary allusions.

At the risk of criticism, I have made certain reasonable compromises. I have used the sometimes inaccurate term "Tartar" instead of "Hun" or "barbarian," the term "China" instead of "Han," the term "Turkestan" when it roughly corresponded to the ancient term. There are many other approximations which have seemed advisable. Once in a while, for good reason, I have changed a title. And there are occasional unimportant omissions. I have omitted, for instance, the "ninth-born" or "eleventh-born," frequently added in the original to names of persons, and meaning the ninth or eleventh child in a family. Whenever possible, I have avoided phraseology which, natural and familiar in Chinese, would be exotic or quaint in English; I have hoped rather to accent in these T'ang masterpieces the human and universal qualities by which they have endured.

Santa Fe, New Mexico

II · CHINESE POETRY

BY KIANG KANG-HU

Poems of the Early Period

Chinese poetry began with our written history about 5500 years ago. The oldest poems now extant were written by the Emperor Yao (2357 B.C.); and one of them was adopted as the Chinese national song in the beginning of the Republic, because Yao was in reality a life president of the most ancient republic in the world, and this poem expresses the republican spirit. Shun and Yü, the other two sagacious presidents, left with us also some poems. Their works, together with other verses by following emperors and statesmen, may be found in our classics and official histories.

In the Chou Dynasty (1121–256 B.C.) poetry became more important, not only to individual and social life, but also to the government. Emperors used to travel over all the feudal states and to collect the most popular and typical poems or songs. The collection being then examined by the official historians and musicians, public opinion and the welfare of the people in the respective states would thus be ascertained and attested. In the ceremonies of sacrifice, inter-state convention, official banquet, and school and military exercises, various poems were sung and harmonized with music. Poetry in this period was not a special literary task for scholars, but a means of expression common to both sexes of all classes.

The Classical Poems

One of the five Confucian classics is the *Book of Poetry*. It is a selection of poems of the Chou Dynasty, classified under different types. This selection was made by Confucius out of the governmental collections of many states. It contains three hundred and eleven poems, all of high standard, both as literature and as music. Since the loss of the Confucian *Book of Music* during the period of the Great Destruction (221–211 B.C.) the musical significance of this classic can hardly be traced, but its literary value remains and the distinction of the classical poems, which can never be duplicated.

Poems Since the Han Dynasty

The classical poems were usually composed of lines of four characters, or words, with every other line rhymed. Lines were allowed, however, of more or fewer words. Under the reign of the Emperor Wu (140–87 B.C.) of the Western Han Dynasty new types of poetry were introduced; and the five-character and seven-character poems became popular and have dominated ever since. The Emperor himself invented the latter; while Li Ling and Su Wu, two of his statesmen-generals, wrote their verses in the former type. The number of characters of each line was uniform; no irregular line might occur. These two types were afterwards named the "ancient" or "unruled" poems. Nearly all poems before the T'ang Dynasty were in this form. The Emperor Wu introduced also the Po Liang style, which is a seven-character poem with every line rhyming in the last word. Po Liang was the name of a pavilion in the Emperor's garden where, while he banqueted his literary attendants, each wrote one line to complete a long poem. This has been a favourite game among Chinese poets.

The Poems of the T'ang Dynasty

As many a dynasty in Chinese history is marked by some phase of success representing the thought and life of that period, the T'ang Dynasty is commonly recognized as the golden age of poetry. Beginning with the founder of the dynasty, down to the last ruler, almost every one of the emperors was a great lover and patron of poetry, and many were poets themselves. A special tribute should be paid to the Empress Wu-chao or the "Woman-Emperor" (690–704), through whose influence poetry became a requisite in examinations for degrees and an important course leading to official promotion. This made every official as well as every scholar a poet. The poems required in the examination, after long years of gradual development, followed a formula, and many regulations were established. Not only must the length of a line be limited to a certain number of characters, usually five or seven, but also the length of a poem was limited to a certain number of lines, usually four or eight or twelve. The maintenance of rhymes, the parallelism of characters, and the balance of tones were other rules considered essential. This is called the "modern" or "ruled" poetry. In the Ch'ing or Manchu Dynasty the examination poem was standardized as a five-character-line poem of sixteen lines with every other line rhymed. This "eight-rhyme" poem was accompanied by the famous "eight-legged" literature (a form of literature divided into eight sections) as a guiding light for entrance into mandarin life.

The above-mentioned rules of poetry applied first only to examination poems. But afterwards they became a common exercise with "modern" or "ruled" poems in general. Chinese poetry since the T'ang Dynasty has followed practically only two forms, the "modern" or "ruled" form and the "ancient" or "unruled" form. A poet usually writes both. The "eight-rhyme" poem, however, was practised for official examinations only.

The progress of T'ang poetry may be viewed through a

division into four periods, as distinguished by different styles and a differing spirit. There were, of course, exceptional works, especially at the transient points, and it is difficult to draw an exact boundary-line between any two periods. The first period is approximately from A.D. 620 to 700, the second from 700 to 780, the third from 780 to 850, and the fourth from 850 to 900. The second period, corresponding to the summer season of the year, is regarded as the most celebrated epoch. Its representative figures are Li Po (705–762), the genie of poetry; Tu Fu (712–720), the sage of poetry; Wang Wêi (699–759) and Mêng Hao-jan (689–740), the two hermit-poets, and Ts'ên Ts'an (given degree, 744) and Wêi Ying-wu (about 740–830), the two magistrate-poets. The first period is represented by Chang Yüeh (667–730) and Chang Chiu-ling (673–740), two premiers, and by Sung Chih-wên (died 710) and Tu Shên-yen (between the seventh and the eighth centuries); the third, by Yüan Chên (779–832) and Po Chü-yi (772–846), two cabinet ministers, and by Han Yü (768–824) and Liu Tsung-yüan (773–819), two master *literati* more famous for their prose writing than for their verse; and the fourth, by Wên T'ing-yun (ninth century) and Li Shang-yin (813–858), the founders of the Hsi K'un school, and by Hsü Hun (given degree, 832) and Yao Hê (A.D. 9th century). All these poets had their works published in a considerable number of volumes. Secondary poets in the T'ang Dynasty were legion.

Poems after the T'ang Dynasty

Since the T'ang Dynasty, poetry has become even more popular. Its requirement as one of the subjects in the governmental examinations has continued, for a thousand years, to the end of the last century, through all changes of dynasty. Many great poets have arisen during this time. Su Shih (1036–1101), Huang T'ing-chien (1050–1110), Ou-yang Hsiu (1007–1072) and Lu Yu (1125–1209), of the Sung Dynasty, are names as celebrated as those great names of the second period of the T'ang Dynasty. But people still honour the works of the T'ang poets as the model for ever-coming generations, though many of more varied literary taste prefer the Sung works.

Chao Mêng-fu (1254–1322) of the Yüan Dynasty and Yüan Hao-wên (1190–1258) of the Kin Dynasty were the shining stars of that dark age. Many poets of the Ming Dynasty, such as Liu Chi (1311–1375), Sung Lien (1310–1381), Li Tung-yang (1447–1516), and Ho Ching-ming (1483–1521) were very famous. Still greater poets lived in the Ch'ing Dynasty. Ch'ien Ch'ien-yi (1581–1664), Wu Wêi-yeh (1609–1671), Wang Shih-chêng (1526–1593), Chao Yi (1727–1814), Chiang Shih-ch'üan (1725–1784), Yuan Mêi (1715–1797), Huang Ching-jên (1749–1783), and Chang Wên-t'ao (1764–1814) are some of the immortals. Their works are by no means inferior to those in the previous dynasties.

Literature differs from science. It changes according to times and conditions, but shows, on the whole, neither rapid improvement nor gradual betterment. Later writings might appear to be more expressive and therefore more inspiring, but the dignity and beauty of ancient works are inextinguishable and even unapproached. This is especially true of poetry and of the T'ang poems, for the reason that during those three hundred years the thinking capacity and the working energy of all excellent citizens in the Empire were encouraged and induced to this single subject. Neither before nor after has there been such an age for poetry.

Selections of the T'ang Poems

Hundreds of collections and selections of T'ang poems have been published during the succeeding dynasties. Two compiled in the Ch'ing Dynasty are considered the best. One is the *Complete Collection of T'ang Poems* and the other is the *Three Hundred T'ang Poems*. These two have no similarity in nature and in purpose. The first is an imperial edition aiming to include every line of existing T'ang poetry: which amounts to 48,900 poems by 2,200 poets in 900 volumes. The second is but a small text-book for elementary students, giving only 311 better-known works by 77 of the better-known writers, the same number of poems as in the Confucian Classic of Poetry. This selection was made by an anonymous editor who signed himself "Hêng T'ang T'uêi Shih" or "A Retired Scholar at the Lotus Pool," first published in the reign of the Emperor Ch'ien Lung (1735–1795). The title of this selection was based upon a common saying: "By reading thoroughly three hundred T'ang poems, one will write verse without learning."

In the preface the compiler assures us that "this is but a family reader for children; but it will hold good until our hair is white." This statement, as years have passed, has proved true. The collection has always stood in China as the most popular volume of poetry, for poets and for the mass of the people alike. Even illiterates are familiar with the title of the book and with lines from it. Other selections may be of a higher standard and please scholars better, but none can compare with this in extensive circulation and accessible influence.

The anthology in Chinese is in two volumes. The first contains all "ancient" or "unruled" poems, and the second all "modern" or "ruled" poems. The former is again divided into two parts of five-character lines and seven-character lines, the latter into four parts: (1) eight five-character lines, (2) eight seven-character lines, (3) four five-character lines, and (4) four seven-character lines. In learning Chinese poems the order is always reversed. The shorter line of fewer characters should come first. We have, however, rearranged the volume in English, according to poets rather than to poetic technique, the poets following one another in the alphabetical order of their surnames. (The surname in Chinese comes first.) Under each poet we have kept the following order of poems:

1. Modern poems of four five-character lines.
2. Modern poems of four seven-character lines.
3. Modern poems of eight five-character lines.
4. Modern poems of eight seven-character lines.
5. Ancient poems of five-character lines.
6. Ancient poems of seven-character lines.

Various Poetic Regulations and Forms

There are more strict regulations in writing poems in Chinese than in any other language. This is because Chinese is the only living language governed by the following rules: First, it is made of individual hierographic characters; second, each character or word is monosyllabic; and third, each character has its fixed tone. Hence certain very important regulations in Chinese poetry are little considered or even unknown to the poetry of other languages. For instance, the avoidance of using a word twice, the parallelism of words of the same nature and the balancing of words of different tones, all need special preliminary explanation.

The first of these regulations is possible only in Chinese poetry. We find many long poems with hundreds or even thousands of characters, and not a single one repeated, as in the form of *p'ai-lü* or "arranged rule." The second means that all the characters of one line should parallel as parts of speech those of the next line; thus noun with noun, adjective with adjective, verb with verb, etc. Even in the same parts of speech, nouns designating animals should be parallel, adjectives of colour, numbers, etc. The third means that all the characters of a line should balance, in the opposite group of tones, those of the next line. There are five tones in the Chinese written language. The first is called the upper even tone; the second, the lower even tone; the third, the upper tone; the fourth, the departing tone; and the fifth, the entering tone. The first two are in one group, named "even tones," and the last three are in the other group and named "uneven tones." Thus, if any character in a line is of the even group, the character which balances with it in the next line should be of the uneven group, and vice versa.

These strict regulations, though very important to "modern" or "ruled" poems, do not apply to "ancient" or "unruled" poems. The ancient form is very liberal. There are but two regulations for it—namely, a limit to the number of characters in each line, five or seven; and rhyme on the last character of every other line.

The seven-character "ancient" poem gives even more leeway. It may have irregular lines of more or fewer characters, and every line may rhyme as in the Po Liang style.

There are also, as in English, perfect rhymes and allowable rhymes. The perfect rhymes are standardized by an Imperial Rhyming Dictionary. In this dictionary all characters are arranged, first according to the five tones, and then to different rhymes. The two even tones have 30 rhymes; the third, 29; the fourth, 30; and the fifth, a very short sound, only 17. These rhymes are so grouped, following the old classical pronunciation, that some rhyming words may seem to the modern ear discordant. The allowable rhymes include words that rhymed before the standard was made. The "modern" poem must observe perfect rhymes; the "ancient" poem is permitted allowable rhymes. Again, the former should use only one rhyme of the even tones; the latter may use many different rhymes of different tones in one poem.

The "modern" poem has also its fixed pattern of tones. There are four patterns for the five-character poems and four for the seven-character poems. The signs used in the following charts are commonly adopted in Chinese poetry: — indicates an even tone; I indicates an uneven tone; ⊤ indicates that the character should be of an even tone, but that an uneven is permitted; ⊥ indicates the reverse; ⊖ indicates the rhyme.

TONE PATTERNS FOR FIVE-CHARACTER

MODERN POEMS

A

```
8 7 6 5 4 3 2 1
⊥ T T ⊥ ⊥ T T ⊥
| - - | | - - |
| - | - | - | -
- | | - - | | -
⊖ | ⊖ | ⊖ | ⊖ |
```

B

```
8 7 6 5 4 3 2 1
T ⊥ ⊥ T T ⊥ ⊥ T
- | | - - | | -
| - | - | - | -
| - - | | - - |
⊖ | ⊖ | ⊖ | ⊖ |
```

C

```
8 7 6 5 4 3 2 1
⊥ T T ⊥ ⊥ T T ⊥
| - - | | - - |
| - | - | - | |
- | | - - | | -
⊖ | ⊖ | ⊖ | ⊖ ⊖
```

D

```
8 7 6 5 4 3 2 1
T ⊥ ⊥ T T ⊥ ⊥ T
- | | - - | | -
| - | - | - | |
| - - | | - - |
⊖ | ⊖ | ⊖ | ⊖ ⊖
```

First line ⎫ First pair ⎫
Second line ⎭   ⎪ First group
Third line ⎫ Second pair ⎭
Fourth line ⎭

Fifth line ⎫ Third pair ⎫
Sixth line ⎭   ⎪ Second group
Seventh line ⎫ Fourth pair ⎭
Eighth line ⎭

TONE PATTERNS FOR

SEVEN-CHARACTER

MODERN POEMS

A

```
8 7 6 5 4 3 2 1
⊥ T T ⊥ ⊥ T T ⊥
|  − − |  |  − − |
T ⊥ ⊥ T T ⊥ ⊥ T
− |  |  − − |  |  −
|  − |  − |  − |  −
|  − − |  |  − − |
⊖ |  ⊖ |  ⊖ |  ⊖ |
```

B

```
8 7 6 5 4 3 2 1
T ⊥ ⊥ T T ⊥ ⊥ T
− |  |  − − |  |  −
⊥ T T ⊥ ⊥ T T ⊥
|  − − |  |  − − |
|  − |  − |  − |  −
− |  |  − − |  |  −
⊖ |  ⊖ |  ⊖ |  ⊖ |
```

C

```
8 7 6 5 4 3 2 1
⊥ T T ⊥ ⊥ T T ⊥
|  − − |  |  − − |
T ⊥ ⊥ T T ⊥ ⊥ T
− |  |  − − |  |  −
|  − |  − |  − |  |
|  − − |  |  − − |
⊖ |  ⊖ |  ⊖ |  ⊖ ⊖
```

D

```
8 7 6 5 4 3 2 1
T ⊥ ⊥ T T ⊥ ⊥ T
− |  |  − − |  |  −
⊥ T T ⊥ ⊥ T T ⊥
|  − − |  |  − − |
|  − |  − |  − |  −
− |  |  − − |  |  −
⊖ |  ⊖ |  ⊖ |  ⊖ |
```

For further and clearer explanation I use as an example the following poem:

Surname 杜 Tu[4]		Cabinet 閣 Kê[5]	
given name 甫 Fu[3]		night 夜 yeh[4]	
(Author)		(Title)	

Heaven's 天 T'ien[1]	year 歲 Suêi[4]
limit 涯 ya[2]	late 暮 mu[4]
frost (and) 霜 shuang[1]	(the) negative force 陰 yin[1]
snow 雪 hsüeh[5]	(and) positive force 陽 yang[2]
brighten 霽 chi[4]	urge 催 ts'uêi[1]
(the) cold 寒 han[2]	(the) short 短 tuan[3]
night. 宵 hsiao[1]	daylight. 景 ching[3]

(Upon the) three 三 San[1]	(At the) fifth 五 wu[3]
mountains 峽 hsia[5]	watch 更 kêng[1]
(the) stars (and) 星 hsing[1]	(the) drum (and) 鼓 ku[3]

milky way's	河	he²		bugle's	角	chüeh⁵
shadows	影	ying³		sound	聲	shêng¹
move (and)	動	tung⁴		sad (and)	悲	pêi¹
wave.	搖	yao²		brave.	壯	chuang⁴

Barbarian	夷	i²		Wild	野	yeh³
songs	歌	kê¹		sobs (of)	哭	k'u⁵
every	是	shih⁴		many	幾	chi³
place	處	ch'u⁴		homes	家	chia¹
arise (from)	起	ch'i³		(are) heard (in)	聞	wên²
fishers (and)	漁	yü²		fighting (and)	戰	chan⁴
woodcutters.	樵	ch'iao²		attacking.	伐	fa⁵

Human	人	Jên²		(The) Lying	臥	Wo⁴
affairs (in)	事	shih⁴		Dragon (and)	龍	lung²
messages (and)	音	yin¹		(the) Jumping	躍	yüeh⁵
letters	書	shu¹		Horse	馬	ma³
(may) let it be	漫	man⁴		finally (became)	終	chung¹
silent (and)	寂	chi⁵		yellow	黃	huang²
solitude.	寥	liao²		dusts.	土	t'u³

The first group of a "ruled poem" is named the "rising pair"; the second, the "receiving pair"; the third, the "turning pair"; and the fourth, the "concluding pair."

This example shows us that in writing a "modern" or "ruled" poem many essential regulations are involved. They may be summed up in six rules:

1. Limitation of lines (four or eight, though the *p'ai lü* or "arranged rule" poem may have as many lines as the writer likes).
2. Limitation of characters in each line (five or seven).
3. Observation of the tone pattern (the five-character four-line poems in old times did not observe this rule strictly).
4. Parallelism of the nature of words in each couplet (though the first and the last couplets may be exempted).
5. Selection of a single rhyme from the even tones and rhyming the last characters of alternate lines (the second, the fourth, the sixth, and the eighth lines; sometimes the first line also). The five-character four-line poems in the old days, however, were allowed rhymes from the uneven tones.
6. Avoidance of using a character twice unless deliberately repeated for effect.

Thus we see the great difficulty in writing a "modern" poem. But poets have always believed that the "modern" poem, though difficult to learn, is easy to write, while the "ancient" poem, though easy to learn, is very difficult to write well. Besides, the "modern" poem is constructed in a very convenient length. It enables the poet to finish his whole work while his thought is still fresh and inspiring; and, if necessary, he can express it in a series, either connected or separated. We find, ever since the T'ang Dynasty, most of the poets writing most of their poems in the "modern" forms.

Chinese Poetry in General

All the above statements treat only poems which are in Chinese called *shih*. This word is too narrow to correspond to the English word "poetry," which is more like the Chinese word *"yün-wên,"* or rhythmic literature, and yet *"yün-wên"* has a broader content, for it includes also drama. There are, however, many other kinds of *yün-wên* besides *shih*, not only drama, but poetry in general. I will give a brief explanation of each; my idea being that the works we present in this volume, though the most common type of Chinese poetry, are but one of many types.

In the later part of the Chou Dynasty two new types of poetry were originated; one is the *ch'u-ts'ŭ*, by Ch'ü Yüan (fourth century, B.C.), and the other *fu*, by Hsün K'uang (fourth century, B.C.). They are both, though rhymed, called rhythmic prose, and have been much practised ever since. The latter is more popular and used to be a subject in the official examinations. Since the Han Dynasty, the *yüeh-fu*, or poem "written for music," has been introduced into literature. We have a few examples in this volume in different forms. Because we do not sing them with their old music, which has vanished, they have practically lost their original quality, though still distinguished by title and style.

Another type of poetry, named *ts'ŭ*, was formulated in the second period of the T'ang Dynasty, but was not commonly practised until the last, or fourth, period. The Sung Dynasty is the golden age of the *ts'ŭ* poems and Li Ch'ing-chao and Chu Shu-chêng, two woman poets, are the most famous specialists. This form is composed of lines irregular, but according to fixed patterns. There are hundreds of patterns, each regulated as to the number of characters, group of tones, etc. In the same dynasty the *ch'ü*, or dramatic song, the *t'an-ts'ŭ*, or string song, and the *ku-shu*, or drum tale, were also brought into existence. The next dynasty, the Yüan or Mongol Dynasty, is known as the golden age of these forms of literature. Professional story-tellers or readers are found everywhere singing them with string instruments or drums. Besides these, the *ch'uan-ch'i*, or classical play, the *chiao-pên*, or common play, and the *hsiao-tiao*, or folk-song, are all very popular.

There are numberless Chinese poems written in the revolving order, to be read back and forth. The most amazing poems in human history are the *Huêi-wên-t'ü* or the revolving chart, by Lady Su Huêi, of the Chin Dynasty (265–419), and the *Ch'ien-tzŭ-wên*, or thousand-character literature, by Chou Hsing-ssŭ, (fifth century A.D.). The former is composed of eight hundred characters, originally woven in five colors on a piece of silk, being a love-poem written and sent to her husband, General Tou T'ao, who was then guarding the northern boundary against the Tartar invasion. The characters can be read from different ends in different directions and so form numerous poems. Four hundred have already been found, some short and some very long. It is believed that there are still more undiscovered. The latter, made of a thousand different characters, was a collection of stone inscriptions left by the master calligrapher, Wang Hsi-chih. They had been but loose characters in no order and with no connexion, but were arranged and rhymed as a perfect poem by Chou Hsing-ssŭ. The same thousand characters have been made into poems by ten or more authors; and these marvels in the poetical world can never be dreamed of by people who speak language other than Chinese!

All these various forms under various names are not *shih* in the Chinese sense, but are poetry in the English sense. Each of them possesses its own footing in the common ground of Chinese poetry. To make any remarks on Chinese poetry at large, or to draw any conclusions from it, one must take into consideration not only the *shih*, but all the various forms. I sometimes hear foreigners, as well as young Chinese students, blaming Chinese poems as being too stiff or confined. They do not realize that some forms of Chinese poetry are even freer than English free verse. They also criticize the Chinese for having no long poems, as other races have, ignoring the fact that many *fu* poems are thousands of lines long, with tens of thousands of characters, and that many rhythmic historical tales fill ten or more volumes, each volume following a single rhyme.

Kiang Kang-hu

Peking, China

THREE HUNDRED POEMS OF THE

T'ANG DYNASTY

618–906

ANONYMOUS

氏名無

The Day of No Fire

As the holiday approaches, and grasses are bright after rain,
And the causeway gleams wtih willows, and wheatfields wave in
    the wind,
We are thinking of our kinsfolk, far away from us.
O cuckoo, why do you follow us, why do you call us home?

(1, 1a)

CHANG CHI

張 繼

A Night-Mooring Near Maple Bridge

While I watch the moon go down, a crow caws through the frost;
Under the shadows of maple-trees a fisherman moves with his
  torch;
And I hear, from beyond Su-chou, from the temple on Cold
  Mountain,
Ringing for me, here in my boat, the midnight bell.

CHANG CHI

籍 張

Thinking of a Friend
Lost in the Tibetan War

Last year you went with your troops to Tibet;
And when your men had vanished beyond the city-wall,
News was cut off between the two worlds
As between the living and the dead.
No one has come upon a faithful horse guarding
A crumpled tent or torn flag, or any trace of you.
If only I knew, I might serve you in the temple,
Instead of these tears toward the far sky.

CHANG CH'IAO

喬 張

On the Border

Though a bugle breaks the crystal air of autumn,
Soldiers, in the look-out, watch at ease today
The spring wind blowing across green graves
And the pale sun setting beyond Liang-chou.
For now, on grey plains done with war,
The border is open to travel again;
And Tartars can no more choose than rivers:
They are running, all of them, toward the south.

CH'ANG CHIEN

建 常

A Buddhist Retreat
Behind Broken-Mountain Temple

In the pure morning, near the old temple,
Where early sunlight points the tree-tops,
My path has wound, through a sheltered hollow
Of boughs and flowers, to a Buddhist retreat.
Here birds are alive with mountain-light,
And the mind of man touches peace in a pool,
And a thousand sounds are quieted
By the breathing of a temple-bell.

At Wang Ch'ang-ling's Retreat

Here, beside a clear deep lake,
You live accompanied by clouds;
Or soft through the pine the moon arrives
To be your own pure-hearted friend.
You rest under thatch in the shadow of your flowers,
Your dewy herbs flourish in their bed of moss.
Let me leave the world. Let me alight, like you,
On your western mountain with phœnixes and cranes.

CHANG CHIU-LING

齡九張

*Looking at the Moon and
Thinking of One Far Away*

The moon, grown full now over the sea,
Brightening the whole of heaven,
Brings to separated hearts
The long thoughtfulness of night. . . .
It is no darker though I blow out my candle.
It is no warmer though I put on my coat.
So I leave my message with the moon
And turn to my bed, hoping for dreams.

Orchid and Orange

(*A Plea for Official Preferment*)

I

Tender orchid-leaves in spring
And cinnamon-blossoms bright in autumn
Are as self-contained as life is,
Which conforms them to the seasons.
Yet why will you think that a forest-hermit,
Allured by sweet winds and contented with beauty,
Would no more ask to be transplanted
Than would any other natural flower?

II

Here, south of the Yang-tsze, grows a red orange-tree.
All winter long its leaves are green,
Not because of a warmer soil,

But because its nature is used to the cold.
Though it might serve your honourable guests,
You leave it here, far below mountain and river.
Circumstance governs destiny.
Cause and effect are an infinite cycle.
You plant your peach-trees and your plums,
You forget the shade from this other tree.

CHANG HSÜ

旭 張

Peach-Blossom River

A bridge flies away through a wild mist,
Yet here are the rocks and the fisherman's boat.
Oh, if only this river of floating peach-petals
Might lead me at last to the mythical cave!

(2)

CHANG HU

祜　張

She Sings an Old Song

A lady of the palace these twenty years,
She has lived here a thousand miles from her home—
Yet ask her for this song and, with the first few words of it,
See how she tries to hold back her tears.

(3)

On the Terrace of Assembled Angels

I

The sun has gone slanting over a lordly roof
And red-blossoming branches have leaned toward the dew
Since the Emperor last night summoned a new favourite
And Lady Yang's bright smile came through the curtains.

II

The Emperor has sent for Lady Kuo Kuo.
In the morning, riding toward the palace-gate,
Disdainful of the paint that might have marred her beauty,
To meet him she smooths her two moth-tiny eyebrows.

(4)

Of One in the Forbidden City

When the moonlight, reaching a tree by the gate,
Shows her a quiet bird on its nest,
She removes her jade hairpins and sits in the shadow
And puts out a flame where a moth was flying.

At Nan-king Ferry

This one-story inn at Nan-king ferry
Is a miserable lodging-place for the night—
But across the dead moon's ebbing tide,
Lights from Kua-chou beckon on the river.

CHANG PI

泌 張

A Message

I go in a dream to the house of Hsieh—
Through a zigzag porch with arching rails
To a court where the spring moon lights for ever
Phantom flowers and a single figure.

CH'ÊN T'AO

畎 鄭

Turkestan

Thinking only of their vow that they would crush the Tartars—
On the desert, clad in sable and silk, five thousand of them
   fell. . . .
But arisen from their crumbling bones on the banks of the river
   at the border,
Dreams of them enter, like men alive, into rooms where their
   loves lie sleeping.

CH'ÊN TZǓ-ANG

昂子陳

On a Gate-Tower at Yu-chou

Where, before me, are the ages that have gone?
And where, behind me, are the coming generations?
I think of heaven and earth, without limit, without end,
And I am all alone and my tears fall down.

CHÊNG T'IEN

陶　陳

On Ma-wêi Slope

When the Emperor came back from his ride, they had murdered
　　Lady Yang—
That passion unforgettable through all the suns and moons.
They had led him to forsake her by reminding him
Of an emperor slain with his lady once, in a well at Ching-yang
　　Palace.

(4, 4a)

CHIA TAO

島 賈

A Note Left for an Absent Recluse

When I questioned your pupil, under a pine-tree,
"My teacher," he answered, "went for herbs,
But toward which corner of the mountain,
How can I tell, through all these clouds?"

CH'IEN CH'I

起 錢

*Farewell to a Japanese Buddhist
Priest Bound Homeward*

You were foreordained to find the source.
Now, tracing your way as in a dream
There where the sea floats up the sky,
You wane from the world in your fragile boat. . . .
The water and the moon are as calm as your faith,
Fishes and dragons follow your chanting,
And the eye still watches beyond the horizon
The holy light of your single lantern.

(5, 5a)

*From My Study at
the Mouth of the Valley*

A Message to Censor Yang

At a little grass-hut in the valley of the river,
Where a cloud seems born from a viney wall,
You will love the bamboos new with rain,
And mountains tender in the sunset.
Cranes drift early here to rest
And autumn flowers are slow to fade. . . .
I have bidden my pupil to sweep the grassy path
For the coming of my friend.

To My Friend at the Capital

Secretary P'ai

Finches flash yellow through the Imperial Grove
Of the Forbidden City, pale with spring dawn;
Flowers muffle a bell in the Palace of Bliss
And rain has deepened the Dragon Lake willows;
But spring is no help to a man bewildered,
Who would be like a cloud upholding the Light of Heaven,
Yet whose poems, ten years refused, are shaming
These white hairs held by the petalled pin.

(6, 7)

CHIN CH'ANG-HSÜ

緒昌金

A Spring Sigh

Drive the orioles away,
All their music from the trees. . . .
When she dreamed that she went to Liao-hsi Camp
To join him there, they wakened her.

CH'IN T'AO-YÜ

玉韜秦

A Poor Girl

Living under a thatch roof, never wearing fragrant silk,
She longs to arrange a marriage, but how could she dare?
Who would know her simple face the loveliest of them all
When we choose for worldliness, not for worth?
Her fingers embroider beyond compare,
But she cannot vie with painted brows;
And year after year she has sewn gold thread
On bridal robes for other girls.

CH'IU WÊI

爲 邱

After Missing the Recluse
on the Western Mountain

To your hermitage here on the top of the mountain
I have climbed, without stopping, these ten miles.
I have knocked at your door, and no one answered;
I have peeped into your room, at your seat beside the table.
Perhaps you are out riding in your canopied chair,
Or fishing, more likely, in some autumn pool.
Sorry though I am to be missing you,
You have become my meditation—
The beauty of your grasses, fresh with rain,
And close beside your window the music of your pines,
I take into my being all that I see and hear,
Soothing my senses, quieting my heart;
And though there be neither host nor guest,
Have I not reasoned a visit complete?
. . . After enough, I have gone down the mountain.
Why should I wait for you any longer?

CH'I-WU CH'IEN

潛毋綦

A Boat in Spring on Jo-ya Lake

Thoughtful elation has no end:
Onward I bear it to whatever come.
And my boat and I, before the evening breeze
Passing flowers, entering the lake,
Turn at nightfall toward the western valley,
Where I watch the south star over the mountain
And a mist that rises, hovering soft,
And the low moon slanting through the trees;
And I choose to put away from me every worldly matter
And only to be an old man with a fishing-pole.

CHU CH'ING-YÜ

餘 慶 朱

A Song of the Palace

Now that the palace-gate has softly closed on its flowers,
Ladies file out to their pavilion of jade,
Abrim to the lips with imperial gossip
But not daring to breathe it with a parrot among them.

On the Eve of Government Examinations

To Secretary Chang

Out go the great red wedding-chamber candles.
Tomorrow in state the bride faces your parents.
She has finished preparing; she asks of you meekly
Whether her eyebrows are painted in fashion.

(7a)

CH'ÜAN TÊ-YÜ

輿德權

The Jade Dressing-Table

Last night my girdle came undone,
And this morning a luck-beetle flew over my bed.
So here are my paints and here are my powders—
And a welcome for my yoke again.

(8)

HAN HUNG

翃　韓

After the Day of No Fire

Petals of spring fly all through the city
From the wind in the willows of the Imperial River.
And at dusk, from the palace, candles are given out
To light first the mansions of the Five Great Lords.
(1)

An Autumn Evening

Harmonizing Ch'êng Chin's Poem

While a cold wind is creeping under my mat,
And the city's naked wall grows pale with the autumn moon,
I see a lone wildgoose crossing the River of Stars,
And I hear, on stone in the night, thousands of washing-
mallets. . . .
But, instead of wishing the season, as it goes,
To bear me also far away,
I have found your poem so beautiful
That I forget the homing birds.
(9, 10)

Inscribed in the Temple of
the Wandering Genie

I face, high over this enchanted lodge, the Court of the Five
Cities of Heaven,
And I see a countryside blue and still, after the long rain.
The distant peaks and trees of Ch'in merge into twilight,

And Han Palace washing-stones make their autumnal echoes.
Thin pine-shadows brush the outdoor pulpit,
And grasses blow their fragrance into my little cave.
. . . Who need be craving a world beyond this one?
Here, among men, are the Purple Hills!

(10, 11)

HAN WU

偓 韓

Cooler Weather

Her jade-green alcove curtained thick with silk,
Her vermilion screen with its pattern of flowers,
Her eight-foot dragon-beard mat and her quilt brocaded in
   squares
Are ready now for nights that are neither warm nor cold.

(12)

HAN YÜ

愈 韓

Mountain-Stones

Rough were the mountain-stones, and the path very narrow;
And when I reached the temple, bats were in the dusk.
I climbed to the hall, sat on the steps, and drank the rain-washed
    air
Among the round gardenia-pods and huge banana-leaves.
On the old wall, said the priest, were Buddhas finely painted,
And he brought a light and showed me, and I called them won-
    derful.
He spread the bed, dusted the mats, and made my supper ready,
And, though the food was coarse, it satisfied my hunger.
At midnight, while I lay there not hearing even an insect,
The mountain moon with her pure light entered my door. . . .
At dawn I left the mountain and, alone, lost my way:
In and out, up and down, while a heavy mist
Made brook and mountain green and purple, brightening every-
    thing.
I am passing sometimes pines and oaks, which ten men could
    not girdle,
I am treading pebbles barefoot in swift-running water—
Its ripples purify my ear, while a soft wind blows my gar-
    ments. . . .
These are the things which, in themselves, make life happy.
Why should we be hemmed about and hampered with people?
O chosen pupils, far behind me in my own country,
What if I spent my old age here and never went back home?

On the Festival of the Moon

To Sub-Official Chang

The fine clouds have opened and the River of Stars is gone,
A clear wind blows across the sky, and the moon widens its
 wave,
The sand is smooth, the water still, no sound and no shadow,
As I offer you a cup of wine, asking you to sing.
But so sad is this song of yours and so bitter your voice
That before I finish listening my tears have become a rain:
"Where Lake Tung-t'ing is joined to the sky by the lofty Nine-
 Doubt Mountain,
Dragons, crocodiles, rise and sink, apes, flying foxes, whim-
 per. . . .
At a ten to one risk of death, I have reached my official post,
Where lonely I live and hushed, as though I were in hiding.
I leave my bed, afraid of snakes; I eat, fearing poisons;
The air of the lake is putrid, breathing its evil odours. . . .
Yesterday, by the district office, the great drum was announcing
The crowning of an emperor, a change in the realm.
The edict granting pardons runs three hundred miles a day,
All those who were to die have had their sentences commuted,
The unseated are promoted and exiles are recalled,
Corruptions are abolished, clean officers appointed.
My superior sent my name in, but the governor would not listen
And has only transferred me to this barbaric place.
My rank is very low and useless to refer to;
They might punish me with lashes in the dust of the street.
Most of my fellow exiles are now returning home—
A journey which, to me, is a heaven beyond climbing."
 . . . Stop your song, I beg you, and listen to mine,
A song that is utterly different from yours:
"Tonight is the loveliest moon of the year.
All else is with fate, not ours to control;
But, refusing this wine, may we choose more tomorrow?"

Stopping at a Temple on Hêng Mountain
I Inscribe This Poem in the Gate-Tower

The five Holy Mountains have the rank of the Three Dukes.
The other four make a ring, with the Sung Mountain midmost.
To this one, in the fire-ruled south, where evil signs are rife,
Heaven gave divine power, ordaining it a peer.
All the clouds and hazes are hidden in its girdle;
And its forehead is beholden only by a few.
. . . I came here in autumn, during the rainy season,
When the sky was overcast and the clear wind gone.
I quieted my mind and prayed, hoping for an answer;
For assuredly righteous thinking reaches to high heaven.
And soon all the mountain-peaks were showing me their faces;
I looked up at a pinnacle that held the clean blue sky:
The wide Purple Canopy joined the Celestial Column;
The Stone Granary leapt, while the Fire God stood still.
Moved by this token, I dismounted to offer thanks.
A long path of pine and cypress led to the temple.
Its white walls and purple pillars shone, and the vivid colour
Of gods and devils filled the place with patterns of red and blue.
I climbed the steps and, bending down to sacrifice, besought
That my pure heart might be welcome, in spite of my humble
    offering.
The old priest professed to know the judgment of the God:
He was polite and reverent, making many bows.
He handed me divinity-cups, he showed me how to use them
And told me that my fortune was the very best of all.
Though exiled to a barbarous land, mine is a happy life.
Plain food and plain clothes are all I ever wanted.
To be prince, duke, premier, general, was never my desire;
And if the God would bless me, what better could he grant than
    this?—
At night I lie down to sleep in the top of a high tower;
While moon and stars glimmer through the darkness of the
    clouds. . . .

Apes call, a bell sounds. And ready for dawn,
I see arise, far in the east, the cold bright sun.

(13, 13a, 14, 14a)

A Poem on the Stone Drums

Chang handed me this tracing, from the stone drums,
Beseeching me to write a poem on the stone drums.
Tu Fu has gone. Li Po is dead.
What can my poor talent do for the stone drums?
. . . When the Chou power waned and China was bubbling,
Emperor Hsüan, up in wrath, waved his holy spear
And opened his Great Audience, receiving all the tributes
Of kings and lords who came to him with a tune of clanging
     weapons.
They held a hunt in Ch'i-yang and proved their marksmanship:
Fallen birds and animals were strewn three thousand miles.
And the exploit was recorded, to inform new generations. . . .
Cut out of jutting cliffs, these drums made of stone—
On which poets and artisans, all of the first order,
Had indited and chiselled—were set in the deep mountains
To be washed by rain, baked by sun, burned by wildfire,
Eyed by evil spirits, and protected by the gods.
. . . Where can he have found the tracing on this paper?—
True to the original, not altered by a hair,
The meaning deep, the phrases cryptic, difficult to read,
And the style of the characters neither square nor tadpole.
Time has not yet vanquished the beauty of these letters—
Looking like sharp daggers that pierce live crocodiles,
Like phœnix-mates dancing, like angels hovering down,
Like trees of jade and coral with interlocking branches,
Like golden cord and iron chain tied together tight,
Like incense-tripods flung in the sea, like dragons mounting
     heaven.
Historians, gathering ancient poems, forgot to gather these,

To make the two Books of Musical Song more colourful and
    striking;
Confucius journeyed in the west, but not to the Ch'in Kingdom,
He chose our planet and our stars but missed the sun and
    moon. . . .
I who am fond of antiquity, was born too late
And, thinking of these wonderful things, cannot hold back my
    tears . . .
I remember, when I was awarded my highest degree,
During the first year of Yüan-ho,
How a friend of mine, then at the western camp,
Offered to assist me in removing these old relics.
I bathed and changed, then made my plea to the college president
And urged on him the rareness of these most precious things.
They could be wrapped in rugs, be packed and sent in boxes
And carried on only a few camels: ten stone drums
To grace the Imperial Temple like the Incense-Pot of Kao—
Or their lustre and their value would increase a hundredfold,
If the monarch would present them to the university,
Where students could study them and doubtless decipher them,
And multitudes, attracted to the capital of culture
From all corners of the Empire, would be quick to gather.
We could scour the moss, pick out the dirt, restore the original
    surface,
And lodge them in a fitting and secure place for ever,
Covered by a massive building with wide eaves
Where nothing more might happen to them as it had before.
. . . But government officials grow fixed in their ways
And never will initiate beyond old precedent;
So herd-boys strike the drums for fire, cows polish horns on
    them,
With no one to handle them reverentially.
Still ageing and decaying, soon they may be effaced.
Six years I have sighed for them, chanting toward the west. . . .
The familiar script of Wang Hsi-chih, beautiful though it was,
Could be had, several pages, just for a few white geese!

But now, eight dynasties after the Chou, and all the wars over,
Why should there be nobody caring for these drums?
The Empire is at peace, the government free.
Poets again are honoured and Confucians and Mencians. . . .
Oh, how may this petition be carried to the throne?
It needs indeed an eloquent flow, like a cataract—
But, alas, my voice has broken, in my song of the stone drums,
To a sound of supplication choked with its own tears.

(15, 16)

HÊ CHIH-CHANG

章知賀

Coming Home

I left home young. I return old,
Speaking as then, but with hair grown thin;
And my children, meeting me, do not know me.
They smile and say: "Stranger, where do you come from?"

(17)

HSÜ HUN

渾　許

Inscribed in the Inn at T'ung Gate on an Autumn Trip to the Capital

Red leaves are fluttering down the twilight
Past this arbour where I take my wine;
Cloud-rifts are blowing toward Great Flower Mountain,
And a shower is crossing the Middle Ridge.
I can see trees colouring a distant wall.
I can hear the river seeking the sea,
As I the Imperial City tomorrow—
But I dream of woodsmen and fishermen.

(14)

Early Autumn

There's a harp in the midnight playing clear,
While the west wind rustles a green vine;
There's a low cloud touching the jade-white dew
And an early wildgoose in the River of Stars. . . .
Night in the tall trees clings to dawn;
Light makes folds in the distant hills;
And here on the Huai, by one falling leaf,
I can feel a storm on Lake Tung-t'ing.

(18)

EMPEROR HSÜAN-TSUNG
(*Ming Huang*)

宗 玄

I Pass Through the Lu Dukedom with a Sigh and a Sacrifice for Confucius

O Master, how did the world repay
Your life of long solicitude?—
The Lords of Tsou have misprized your land,
And your home has been used as the palace of Lu. . . .
You foretold that when phœnixes vanished, your fortunes too
    would end,
You knew that the captured unicorn would be a sign of the close
    of your teaching. . . .
Can this sacrifice I watch, here between two temple-pillars,
Be the selfsame omen of death you dreamed of long ago?

(4a, 4c, 4d, 19, 19a)

HSÜEH FÊNG

逢 薛

A Palace Poem

In twelve chambers the ladies, decked for the day,
Peer afar for their lord from their Fairy-View Lodge;
The golden toad guards the lock on the door-chain,
And the bronze-dragon water-clock drips through the morning—
Till one of them, tilting a mirror, combs her cloud of hair
And chooses new scent and a change of silk raiment;
For she sees, between screen-panels, deep in the palace,
Eunuchs in court-dress preparing a bed.

HUANG-FU JAN

冉甫皇

Spring Thoughts

Finch-notes and swallow-notes tell the new year . . .
But so far are the Town of the Horse and the Dragon Mound
From this our house, from these walls and Han Gardens,
That the moon takes my heart to the Tartar sky.
I have woven in the frame endless words of my grieving . . .
Yet this petal-bough is smiling now on my lonely sleep.
. . . Oh, ask General Tou when his flags will come home
And his triumph be carved on the rock of Yen-jan Mountain!
(20)

KAO SHIH

適 高

To Vice-Prefects Li and Wang Degraded and Transferred to Hsia-chung and Ch'ang-sha

What are you thinking as we part from one another,
Pulling in our horses for the stirrup-cups?
Do these tear-streaks mean Wu Valley monkeys all weeping,
Or wildgeese returning with news from Hêng Mountain? . . .
On the river between green maples an autumn sail grows dim,
There are only a few old trees by the wall of the White God
    City . . .
But the year is bound to freshen us with a dew of heavenly
    favour—
Take heart, we shall soon be together again!
(21, 14)

A Song of the Yen Country

(*Written to Music*)

(*In the sixth year of K'ai-yüan, a friend returned from the border and showed me the Yen Song. Moved by what he told me of the expedition, I have written this poem to the same rhymes.*)

The northeastern border of China was dark with smoke and dust.
To repel the savage invaders, our generals, leaving their families,
Strode forth together, looking as heroes should look;
And having received from the Emperor his most gracious favour,
They marched to the beat of gong and drum through the Elm
    Pass.

They circled the Stone Tablet with a line of waving flags,
Till their captains over the Sea of Sand were twanging feathered
orders.
The Tartar chieftain's hunting-fires glimmered along Wolf
Mountain,
And heights and rivers were cold and bleak there at the outer
border;
But soon the barbarians' horses were plunging through wind and
rain.
Half of our men at the front were killed, but the other half are
living,
And still at the camp beautiful girls dance for them and sing.
. . . As autumn ends in the grey sand, with the grasses all
withered,
The few surviving watchers by the lonely wall at sunset,
Serving in a good cause, hold life and the foeman lightly.
And yet, for all that they have done, Elm Pass is still unsafe.
Still at the front, iron armour is worn and battered thin,
And here at home food-sticks are made of jade tears.
Still in this southern city young wives' hearts are breaking,
While soldiers at the northern border vainly look toward home.
The fury of the wind cuts our men's advance
In a place of death and blue void, with nothingness ahead.
Three times a day a cloud of slaughter rises over the camp;
And all night long the hour-drums shake their chilly booming,
Until white swords can be seen again, spattered with red blood.
. . . When death becomes a duty, who stops to think of fame?
Yet in speaking of the rigours of warfare on the desert
We name to this day Li, the great General, who lived long ago.
(22)

KU K'UANG

況　顧

A Palace Poem

High above, from a jade chamber, songs float half-way to
　heaven,
The palace-girls' gay voices are mingled with the wind—
But now they are still, and you hear a water-clock drip in the
　Court of the Moon. . . .
They have opened the curtain wide, they are facing the River of
　Stars.

LI CH'I

頎 李

*A Farewell to Wêi Wan
Bound for the Capital*

The travellers' parting-song sounds in the dawn.
Last night a first frost came over the river;
And the crying of the wildgeese grieves my sad heart
Bounded by a gloom of cloudy mountains. . . .
Here in the Gate City, day will flush cold
And washing-flails quicken by the gardens at twilight—
How long shall the capital content you,
Where the months and the years so vainly go by?

An Old Air

There once was a man, sent on military missions,
A wanderer, from youth, on the Yu and Yen frontiers.
Under the horses' hoofs he would meet his foes
And, recklessly risking his seven-foot body,
Would slay whoever dared confront
Those moustaches that bristled like porcupine-quills.
. . . There were dark clouds below the hills, there were white
        clouds above them,
But before a man has served full time, how can he go back?
In eastern Liao a girl was waiting, a girl of fifteen years,
Deft with a guitar, expert in dance and song.
. . . She seems to be fluting, even now, a reed-song of home,
Filling every soldier's eyes with homesick tears.

A Farewell to My Friend Ch'ên Chang-fu

In the Fourth-month the south wind blows plains of yellow
barley,
Date-flowers have not faded yet and lakka-leaves are long.
The green peak that we left at dawn we still can see at evening,
While our horses whinny on the road, eager to turn homeward.
. . . Ch'ên, my friend, you have always been a great and good
man,
With your dragon's moustache, tiger's eyebrows and your mas-
sive forehead.
In your bosom you have shelved away ten thousand volumes.
You have held your head high, never bowed it in the dust.
. . . After buying us wine and pledging us, here at the eastern
gate,
And taking things as lightly as a wildgoose feather,
Flat you lie, tipsy, forgetting the white sun;
But now and then you open your eyes and gaze at a high lone
cloud.
. . . The tide-head of the long river joins the darkening sky.
The ferryman beaches his boat. It has grown too late to sail.
And people on their way from Chêng cannot go home,
And people from Lo-yang sigh with disappointment.
. . . I have heard about the many friends around your woodland
dwelling.
Yesterday you were dismissed. Are they your friends today?

A Lute Song

Our host, providing abundant wine to make the night mellow,
Asks his guest from Yang-chou to play for us on the lute.
Toward the moon that whitens the city-wall, black crows are
flying,
Frost is on ten thousand trees, and the wind blows through our
clothes;

But a copper stove has added its light to that of flowery candles,
And the lute plays *The Green Water*, and then *The Queen of Ch'u*.
Once it has begun to play, there is no other sound:
A spell is on the banquet, while the stars grow thin. . . .
But three hundred miles from here, in Huai, official duties await him,
And so it's farewell, and the road again, under cloudy mountains.

On Hearing Tung Play the Flageolet

A Poem to Palace-Attendant Fang

When this melody for the flageolet was made by Lady Ts'ai,
When long ago one by one she sang its eighteen stanzas,
Even the Tartars were shedding tears into the border-grasses,
And the envoy of China was heart-broken, turning back home with his escort.
. . . Cold fires now of old battles are grey on ancient forts,
And the wilderness is shadowed with white new-flying snow.
. . . When the player first brushes the Shang string and the Chüeh and then the Yü,
Autumn-leaves in all four quarters are shaken with a murmur.
Tung, the master,
Must have been taught in heaven.
Demons come from the deep pine-wood and stealthily listen
To music slow, then quick, following his hand,
Now far away, now near again, according to his heart.
A hundred birds from an empty mountain scatter and return;
Three thousand miles of floating clouds darken and lighten;
A wildgoose fledgling, left behind, cries for its flock,
And a Tartar child for the mother he loves.
Then river waves are calmed
And birds are mute that were singing,
And Wu-chu tribes are homesick for their distant land,
And out of the dust of Siberian steppes rises a plaintive sorrow.

. . . Suddenly the low sound leaps to a freer tune,
Like a long wind swaying a forest, a downpour breaking tiles,
A cascade through the air, flying over tree-tops.
. . . A wild deer calls to his fellows. He is running among the
   mansions
In the corner of the capital by the Eastern Palace wall . . .
Phœnix Lake lies opposite the Gate of Green Jade;
But how can fame and profit concern a man of genius?
Day and night I long for him to bring his lute again.

(23)

On Hearing An Wan-shan
Play the Reed-Pipe

Bamboo from the southern hills was used to make this pipe.
And its music, that was introduced from Persia first of all,
Has taken on new magic through later use in China.
And now the Tartar from Liang-chou, blowing it for me,
Drawing a sigh from whosoever hears it,
Is bringing to a wanderer's eyes homesick tears. . . .
Many like to listen; but few understand.
To and fro at will there's a long wind flying,
Dry mulberry-trees, old cypresses, trembling in its chill.
There are nine baby phœnixes, outcrying one another;
A dragon and a tiger spring up at the same moment;
Then in a hundred waterfalls ten thousand songs of autumn
Are suddenly changing to *The Yü-yang Lament*;
And when yellow clouds grow thin and the white sun darkens,
They are changing still again to *Spring in the Willow-Trees*.
Like Imperial Garden flowers, brightening the eye with beauty,
Are the high-hall candles we have lighted this cold night,
And with every cup of wine goes another round of music.

An Old War-Song

(Written to Music)

Through the bright day up the mountain, we scan the sky for a
    war-torch;
At yellow dusk we water our horses in the boundary-river;
And when the throb of watch-drums hangs in the sandy wind,
We hear the guitar of the Chinese Princess telling her endless
    woe. . . .
Three thousand miles without a town, nothing but camps,
Till the heavy sky joins the wide desert in snow.
With their plaintive calls, barbarian wildgeese fly from night to
    night.
And children of the Tartars have many tears to shed;
But we hear that the Jade Pass is still under siege,
And soon we stake our lives upon our light war-chariots.
Each year we bury in the desert bones unnumbered,
Yet we only watch for grape-vines coming into China.

(24, 25)

LI P'IN

頻 李

Crossing the Han River

Away from home, I was longing for news
Winter after winter, spring after spring.
Now, nearing my village, meeting people,
I dare not ask a single question.

LI PO

白 李

In the Quiet Night

So bright a gleam on the foot of my bed—
Could there have been a frost already?
Lifting myself to look, I found that it was moonlight.
Sinking back again, I thought suddenly of home.

A Bitter Love

How beautiful she looks, opening the pearly casement,
And how quiet she leans, and how troubled her brow is!
You may see the tears now, bright on her cheek,
But not the man she so bitterly loves.

A Sigh from a Staircase of Jade

(Written to Music)

Her jade-white staircase is cold with dew;
Her silk soles are wet, she lingered there so long . . .
Behind her closed casement, why is she still waiting,
Watching through its crystal pane the glow of the autumn moon?
(27)

A Farewell to Mêng Hao-jan
on His Way to Yang-chou

You have left me behind, old friend, at the Yellow Crane Terrace,
On your way to visit Yang-chou in the misty month of flowers;

Your sail, a single shadow, becomes one with the blue sky,
Till now I see only the river, on its way to heaven.
(*28, 28a*)

Through the Yang-tsze Gorges

From the walls of Po-ti high in the coloured dawn
To Kiang-ling by night-fall is three hundred miles,
Yet monkeys are still calling on both banks behind me
To my boat these ten thousand mountains away.
(*29*)

A Song of Pure Happiness

(*Written to Music for Lady Yang*)

I

Her robe is a cloud, her face a flower;
Her balcony, glimmering with the bright spring dew,
Is either the tip of earth's Jade Mountain
Or a moon-edged roof of paradise.

II

There's a perfume stealing moist from a shaft of red blossom,
And a mist, through the heart, from the magical Hill of Wu—
The palaces of China have never known such beauty—
Not even Flying Swallow with all her glittering garments.

III

Lovely now together, his lady and his flowers
Lighten for ever the Emperor's eye,
As he listens to the sighing of the far spring wind
Where she leans on a railing in the Aloe Pavilion.
(*4, 4b, 26, 26a*)

A Message to Mêng Hao-jan

Master, I hail you from my heart,
And your fame arisen to the skies. . . .
Renouncing in ruddy youth the importance of hat and chariot,
You chose pine-trees and clouds; and now, white-haired,
Drunk with the moon, a sage of dreams,
Flower-bewitched, you are deaf to the Emperor . . .
High mountain, how I long to reach you,
Breathing your sweetness even here!

(32a)

Bidding a Friend Farewell at Ching-mên Ferry

Sailing far off from Ching-mên Ferry,
Soon you will be with people in the south,
Where the mountains end and the plains begin
And the river winds through wilderness. . . .
The moon is lifted like a mirror,
Sea-clouds gleam like palaces,
And the water has brought you a touch of home
To draw your boat three hundred miles.

A Farewell to a Friend

With a blue line of mountains north of the wall,
And east of the city a white curve of water,
Here you must leave me and drift away
Like a loosened water-plant hundreds of miles. . . .
I shall think of you in a floating cloud;
So in the sunset think of me.
. . . We wave our hands to say good-bye,
And my horse is neighing again and again.

On Hearing Chün the Buddhist Monk from Shu Play His Lute

The monk from Shu with his green silk lute-case,
Walking west down O-mêi Mountain,
Has brought me by one touch of the strings
The breath of pines in a thousand valleys.
I hear him in the cleansing brook,
I hear him in the icy bells;
And I feel no change though the mountain darkens
And cloudy autumn heaps the sky.

Thoughts of Old Time from a Night-Mooring Under Mount Niu-chu

This night to the west of the river-brim
There is not one cloud in the whole blue sky,
As I watch from my deck the autumn moon,
Vainly remembering old General Hsieh. . . .
I have poems; I can read;
He heard others, but not mine.
. . . Tomorrow I shall hoist my sail,
With fallen maple-leaves behind me.
(30)

On Climbing in Nan-king to the Terrace of Phœnixes

Phœnixes that played here once, so that the place was named for
      them,
Have abandoned it now to this desolate river;
The paths of Wu Palace are crooked with weeds;
The garments of Chin are ancient dust.
. . . Like this green horizon halving the Three Peaks,
Like this Island of White Egrets dividing the river,

A cloud has arisen between the Light of Heaven and me,
To hide his city from my melancholy heart.
(6, 31)

Down Chung-nan Mountain to the Kind Pillow and Bowl of Hu Ssü

Down the blue mountain in the evening,
Moonlight was my homeward escort.
Looking back, I saw my path
Lie in levels of deep shadow . . .
I was passing the farm-house of a friend,
When his children called from a gate of thorn
And led me twining through jade bamboos
Where green vines caught and held my clothes.
And I was glad of a chance to rest
And glad of a chance to drink with my friend. . . .
We sang to the tune of the wind in the pines;
And we finished our songs as the stars went down,
When, I being drunk and my friend more than happy,
Between us we forgot the world.
(32)

Drinking Alone with the Moon

From a pot of wine among the flowers
I drank alone. There was no one with me—
Till, raising my cup, I asked the bright moon
To bring me my shadow and make us three.
Alas, the moon was unable to drink
And my shadow tagged me vacantly;
But still for a while I had these friends
To cheer me through the end of spring. . . .
I sang. The moon encouraged me.
I danced. My shadow tumbled after.

As long as I knew, we were boon companions.
And then I was drunk, and we lost one another.
. . . . Shall goodwill ever be secure?
I watched the long road of the River of Stars.

In Spring

Your grasses up north are as blue as jade,
Our mulberries here curve green-threaded branches;
And at last you think of returning home,
Now when my heart is almost broken. . . .
O breeze of the spring, since I dare not know you,
Why part the silk curtains by my bed?

The Moon at the Fortified Pass

(*Written to Music*)

The bright moon lifts from the Mountain of Heaven
In an infinite haze of cloud and sea,
And the wind, that has come a thousand miles,
Beats at the Jade Pass battlements. . . .
China marches its men down Po-têng Road
While Tartar troops peer across blue waters of the bay . . .
And since not one battle famous in history
Sent all its fighters back again,
The soldiers turn round, looking toward the border,
And think of home, with wistful eyes,
And of those tonight in the upper chambers
Who toss and sigh and cannot rest.

A Song of an Autumn Midnight

(*Written to a Su-chou Melody*)

A slip of the moon hangs over the capital;
Ten thousand washing-mallets are pounding;

And the autumn wind is blowing my heart
For ever and ever toward the Jade Pass. . . .
Oh, when will the Tartar troops be conquered,
And my husband come back from the long campaign!

A Song of Ch'ang-kan

(Written to Music)

My hair had hardly covered my forehead.
I was picking flowers, playing by my door,
When you, my lover, on a bamboo horse,
Came trotting in circles and throwing green plums.
We lived near together on a lane in Ch'ang-kan,
Both of us young and happy-hearted.
. . . At fourteen I became your wife,
So bashful that I dared not smile,
And I lowered my head toward a dark corner
And would not turn to your thousand calls;
But at fifteen I straightened my brows and laughed,
Learning that no dust could ever seal our love,
That even unto death I would await you by my post
And would never lose heart in the tower of silent watching.
. . . Then when I was sixteen, you left on a long journey
Through the Gorges of Ch'ü-t'ang, of rock and whirling water.
And then came the Fifth-month, more than I could bear,
And I tried to hear the monkeys in your lofty far-off sky.
Your footprints by our door, where I had watched you go,
Were hidden, every one of them, under green moss,
Hidden under moss too deep to sweep away.
And the first autumn wind added fallen leaves.
And now, in the Eighth-month, yellowing butterflies
Hover, two by two, in our west-garden grasses. . . .
And, because of all this, my heart is breaking
And I fear for my bright cheeks, lest they fade.
. . . Oh, at last, when you return through the three Pa districts,
Send me a message home ahead!

And I will come and meet you and will never mind the distance,
All the way to Chang-fêng-sha.

(33)

A Song of Lu Mountain

To Censor Lu Hsü-chou

I am the madman of the Ch'u country
Who sang a mad song disputing Confucius.
. . . Holding in my hand a staff of green jade,
I have crossed, since morning at the Yellow Crane Terrace,
All five Holy Mountains, without a thought of distance,
According to the one constant habit of my life.
. . . Lu Mountain stands beside the Southern Dipper
In clouds reaching silken like a nine-panelled screen,
With its shadows in a crystal lake deepening the green water.
The Golden Gate opens into two mountain-ranges.
A silver stream is hanging down to three stone bridges
Within sight of the mighty Tripod Falls.
Ledges of cliff and winding trails lead to blue sky
And a flush of cloud in the morning sun,
Whence no flight of birds could be blown into Wu.´
. . . I climb to the top. I survey the whole world.
I see the long river that runs beyond return,
Yellow clouds that winds have driven hundreds of miles
And a snow-peak whitely circled by the swirl of a ninefold
    stream.
And so I am singing a song of Lu Mountain,
A song that is born of the breath of Lu Mountain.
. . . Where the Stone Mirror makes the heart's purity purer
And green moss has buried the footsteps of Hsieh,
I have eaten the immortal pellet and, rid of the world's troubles,
Before the lute's third playing have achieved my element.
Far away I watch the angels riding coloured clouds
Toward heaven's Jade City, with hibiscus in their hands.

And so, when I have traversed the nine sections of the world,
I will follow Saint Lu-ao up the Great Purity.
(14, 34, 34a)

T'ien-mu Mountain Ascended in a Dream

A seafaring visitor will talk about Japan,
Which waters and mists conceal beyond approach;
But Yüeh people talk about Heavenly Mother Mountain,
Still seen through its varying deepnesses of cloud.
In a straight line to heaven, its summit enters heaven,
Tops the five Holy Peaks, and casts a shadow through China
With the hundred-mile length of the Heavenly Terrace Range,
Which, just at this point, begins turning southeast.
. . . My heart and my dreams are in Wu and Yüeh
And they cross Mirror Lake all night in the moon.
And the moon lights my shadow
And me to Yien River—
With the hermitage of Hsieh still there
And the monkeys calling clearly over ripples of green water.
I wear his pegged boots
Up a ladder of blue cloud,
Sunny ocean half-way,
Holy cock-crow in space,
Myriad peaks and more valleys and nowhere a road.
Flowers lure me, rocks ease me. Day suddenly ends.
Bears, dragons, tempestuous on mountain and river,
Startle the forest and make the heights tremble.
Clouds darken with darkness of rain,
Streams pale with pallor of mist.
The Gods of Thunder and Lightning
Shatter the whole range.
The stone gate breaks asunder
Venting in the pit of heaven,
An impenetrable shadow.

. . . But now the sun and moon illumine a gold and silver
    terrace,
And, clad in rainbow garments, riding on the wind,
Come the queens of all the clouds, descending one by one,
With tigers for their lute-players and phœnixes for dancers.
Row upon row, like fields of hemp, range the fairy figures. . . .
I move, my soul goes flying,
I wake with a long sigh,
My pillow and my matting
Are the lost clouds I was in.
. . . And this is the way it always is with human joy:
Ten thousand things run for ever like water toward the east.
And so I take my leave of you, not knowing for how long.
. . . But let me, on my green slope, raise a white deer
And ride to you, great mountain, when I have need of you.
Oh, how can I gravely bow and scrape to men of high rank and
    men of high office
Who never will suffer being shown an honest-hearted face!
(34a)

Parting at a Wine-Shop in Nan-king

A wind, bringing willow-cotton, sweetens the shop,
And a girl from Wu, pouring wine, urges me to share it
With my comrades of the city who are here to see me off;
And as each of them drains his cup, I say to him in parting,
Oh, go and ask this river running to the east
If it can travel farther than a friend's love!

A Farewell to Secretary Shu-yün
at the Hsieh T'iao Villa in Hsüan-chou

Since yesterday had to throw me and bolt,
Today has hurt my heart even more.
The autumn wildgeese have a long wind for escort

As I face them from this villa, drinking my wine.
The bones of great writers are your brushes, in the School of
    Heaven,
And I am a Lesser Hsieh growing up by your side.
We both are exalted to distant thought,
Aspiring to the sky and the bright moon.
But since water still flows, though we cut it with our swords,
And sorrows return, though we drown them with wine,
Since the world can in no way answer our craving,
I will loosen my hair tomorrow and take to a fishing-boat.
(35)

Hard Roads in Shu

(Written to Music)

Oh, but it is high and very dangerous!
Such travelling is harder than scaling the blue sky.
. . . Until two rulers of this region
Pushed their way through in the misty ages,
Forty-eight thousand years had passed
With nobody arriving across the Ch'in border.
And the Great White Mountain, westward, still has only a bird's
    path
Up to the summit of O-mêi Peak—
Which was broken once by an earthquake and there were brave
    men lost,
Just finishing the stone rungs of their ladder toward heaven.
. . . High, as on a tall flag, six dragons drive the sun,
While the river, far below, lashes its twisted course.
Such height would be hard going for even a yellow crane,
So pity the poor monkeys who have only paws to use.
The Mountain of Green Clay is formed of many circles—
Each hundred steps, we have to turn nine turns among its
    mounds.
Panting, we brush Orion and pass the Well Star,

Then, holding our chests with our hands and sinking to the
    ground with a groan,
We wonder if this westward trail will never have an end.
The formidable path ahead grows darker, darker still,
With nothing heard but the call of birds hemmed in by the
    ancient forest,
Male birds smoothly wheeling, following the females;
And there come to us the melancholy voices of the cuckoos
Out on the empty mountain, under the lonely moon . . .
Such travelling is harder than scaling the blue sky.
Even to hear of it turns the cheek pale,
With the highest crag barely a foot below heaven.
Dry pines hang, head down, from the face of the cliffs,
And a thousand plunging cataracts outroar one another
And send through ten thousand valleys a thunder of spinning
    stones.
With all this danger upon danger,
Why do people come here who live at a safe distance?
. . . Though Dagger-Tower Pass be firm and grim,
And while one man guards it
Ten thousand cannot force it,
What if he be not loyal,
But a wolf toward his fellows?
. . . There are ravenous tigers to fear in the day
And venomous reptiles in the night
With their teeth and their fangs ready
To cut people down like hemp.
. . . Though the City of Silk be delectable, I would rather turn
    home quickly.
Such travelling is harder than scaling the blue sky . . .
But I still face westward with a dreary moan.

(36)

Endless Yearning
(Written to Music)

I

"I am endlessly yearning
To be in Ch'ang-an.
. . . Insects hum of autumn by the gold brim of the well;
A thin frost glistens like little mirrors on my cold mat;
The high lantern flickers; and deeper grows my longing.
I lift the shade and, with many a sigh, gaze upon the moon,
Single as a flower, centred from the clouds.
Above, I see the blueness and deepness of sky.
Below, I see the greenness and the restlessness of water . . .
Heaven is high, earth wide; bitter between them flies my sorrow.
Can I dream through the gateway, over the mountain?
Endless longing
Breaks my heart."

II

"The sun has set, and a mist is in the flowers;
And the moon grows very white and people sad and sleepless.
A Chao harp has just been laid mute on its phœnix-holder,
And a Shu lute begins to sound its mandarin-duck strings . . .
Since nobody can bear to you the burden of my song,
Would that it might follow the spring wind to Yen-jan Mountain.
I think of you far away, beyond the blue sky,
And my eyes that once were sparkling
Are now a well of tears.
. . . Oh, if ever you should doubt this aching of my heart,
Here in my bright mirror come back and look at me!"
(37)

The Hard Road

(Written to Music)

Pure wine costs, for the golden cup, ten thousand coppers a
flagon,
And a jade plate of dainty food calls for a million coins.
I fling aside my food-sticks and cup, I cannot eat nor drink . . .
I pull out my dagger, I peer four ways in vain.
I would cross the Yellow River, but ice chokes the ferry;
I would climb the T'ai-hang Mountains, but the sky is blind with
snow . . .
I would sit and poise a fishing-pole, lazy by a brook—
But I suddenly dream of riding a boat, sailing for the sun . . .
Journeying is hard,
Journeying is hard.
There are many turnings—
Which am I to follow? . . .
I will mount a long wind some day and break the heavy waves
And set my cloudy sail straight and bridge the deep, deep sea.

Bringing in the Wine

(Written to Music)

See how the Yellow River's waters move out of heaven.
Entering the ocean, never to return.
See how lovely locks in bright mirrors in high chambers,
Though silken-black at morning, have changed by night to snow.
. . . Oh, let a man of spirit venture where he pleases
And never tip his golden cup empty toward the moon!
Since heaven gave the talent, let it be employed!
Spin a thousand pieces of silver, all of them come back!
Cook a sheep, kill a cow, whet the appetite,
And make me, of three hundred bowls, one long drink!
. . . To the old master, Ts'ên,
And the young scholar, Tan-ch'iu,

Bring in the wine!
Let your cups never rest!
Let me sing you a song!
Let your ears attend!
What are bell and drum, rare dishes and treasure?
Let me be forever drunk and never come to reason!
Sober men of olden days and sages are forgotten,
And only the great drinkers are famous for all time.
. . . Prince Ch'ên paid at a banquet in the Palace of Perfection
Ten thousand coins for a cask of wine, with many a laugh and
    quip.
Why say, my host, that your money is gone?
Go and buy wine and we'll drink it together!
My flower-dappled horse,
My furs worth a thousand,
Hand them to the boy to exchange for good wine,
And we'll drown away the woes of ten thousand generations!

(38)

LI SHANG-YIN

隱商李

The Lo-yu Tombs

With twilight shadows in my heart
I have driven up among the Lo-yu Tombs
To see the sun, for all his glory,
Buried by the coming night.

A Note on a Rainy Night to a Friend in the North

You ask me when I am coming. I do not know.
I dream of your mountains and autumn pools brimming all night
  with the rain.
Oh, when shall we be trimming wicks again, together in your
  western window?
When shall I be hearing your voice again, all night in the rain?

A Message to Secretary Ling-hu

I am far from the clouds of Sung Mountain, a long way from
  trees in Ch'in;
And I send to you a message carried by two carp:
—Absent this autumn from the Prince's garden,
There's a poet at Mao-ling sick in the rain.

(39, 39a)

There Is Only One

There is only one Carved-Cloud, exquisite always—
Yet she dreads the spring, blowing cold in the palace,

When her husband, a Knight of the Golden Tortoise,
Will leave her sweet bed, to be early at court.

(40)

The Suêi Palace

When gaily the Emperor toured the south
Contrary to every warning,
His whole empire cut brocades,
Half for wheel-guards, half for sails.

(4a)

The Jade Pool

The Mother of Heaven, in her window by the Jade Pool,
Hears *The Yellow Bamboo Song* shaking the whole earth . . .
Where is Emperor Mu, with his eight horses running
Ten thousand miles a day? Why has he never come back?

(41)

To the Moon Goddess

Now that a candle-shadow stands on the screen of carven marble
And the River of Heaven slants and the morning stars are low,
Are you sorry for having stolen the potion that has set you
Over purple seas and blue skies, to brood through the long
     nights?

(42, 4b)

Chia Yi

When the Emperor sought guidance from wise men, from exiles,
He found no calmer wisdom than that of young Chia

And assigned him the foremost council-seat at midnight,
Yet asked him about gods, instead of about people.

(43)

A Cicada

Pure of heart and therefore hungry,
All night long you have sung in vain—
Oh, this final broken indrawn breath
Among the green indifferent trees!
Yes, I have gone like a piece of driftwood,
I have let my garden fill with weeds. . . .
I bless you for your true advice
To live as pure a life as yours.

(44)

Wind and Rain

I ponder on the poem of *The Precious Dagger*.
My road has wound through many years.
. . . Now yellow leaves are shaken with a gale;
Yet piping and fiddling keep the Blue Houses merry.
On the surface, I seem to be glad of new people;
But doomed to leave old friends behind me,
I cry out from my heart for Shin-fêng wine
To melt away my thousand woes.

(45, 45a)

Falling Petals

Gone is the guest from the Chamber of Rank,
And petals, confused in my little garden,
Zigzagging down my crooked path,
Escort like dancers the setting sun.

Oh, how can I bear to sweep them away?
To a sad-eyed watcher they never return.
Heart's fragrance is spent with the ending of spring
And nothing left but a tear-stained robe.

Thoughts in the Cold

You are gone. The river is high at my door.
Cicadas are mute on dew-laden boughs.
This is a moment when thoughts enter deep.
I stand alone for a long while.
. . . The North Star is nearer to me now than spring,
And couriers from your southland never arrive—
Yet I doubt my dream on the far horizon
That you have found another friend.

North Among Green Vines

Where the sun has entered the western hills,
I look for a monk in his little straw hut;
But only the fallen leaves are at home,
And I turn through chilling levels of cloud.
I hear a stone gong in the dusk,
I lean full-weight on my slender staff . . .
How within this world, within this grain of dust,
Can there be any room for the passions of men?

The Inlaid Harp

I wonder why my inlaid harp has fifty strings,
Each with its flower-like fret an interval of youth.
. . . The sage Chuang-tzǔ is day-dreaming, bewitched by but-
terflies,
The spring-heart of Emperor Wang is crying in a cuckoo,

Mermen weep their pearly tears down a moon-green sea,
Blue fields are breathing their jade to the sun . . .
And a moment that ought to have lasted for ever
Has come and gone before I knew.

(46, 1a)

To One Unnamed

The stars of last night and the wind of last night
Are west of the Painted Chamber and east of Cinnamon Hall.
. . . Though I have for my body no wings like those of the
bright-coloured phœnix,
Yet I feel the harmonious heart-beat of the Sacred Unicorn.
Across the spring-wine, while it warms me, I prompt you how to
bet
Where, group by group, we are throwing dice in the light of a
crimson lamp;
Till the rolling of a drum, alas, calls me to my duties
And I mount my horse and ride away, like a water-plant cut
adrift.

(47)

The Palace of the Suêi Emperor

His Palace of Purple Spring has been taken by mist and cloud,
As he would have taken all Yang-chou to be his private domain.
But for the seal of imperial jade being seized by the first T'ang
Emperor,
He would have bounded with his silken sails the limits of the
world.
Fire-flies are gone now, have left the weathered grasses,
But still among the weeping-willows crows perch at twilight.
. . . If he meets, there underground, the Later Ch'ên Emperor,
Do you think that they will mention *A Song of Courtyard
Flowers?*

(4a)

To One Unnamed

I

You said you would come, but you did not, and you left me with
    no other trace
Than the moonlight on your tower at the fifth-watch bell.
I cry for you forever gone, I cannot waken yet,
I try to read your hurried note, I find the ink too pale.
. . . Blue burns your candle in its kingfisher-feather lantern
And a sweet breath steals from your hibiscus-broidered curtain.
But far beyond my reach is the Enchanted Mountain,
And you are on the other side, ten thousand peaks away.

II

A misty rain comes blowing with a wind from the east,
And wheels faintly thunder beyond Hibiscus Pool.
. . . Round the golden-toad lock, incense is creeping;
The jade tiger tells, on its cord, of water being drawn. . . .
A great lady once, from behind a screen, favoured a poor youth;
A fairy queen brought a bridal mat once for the ease of a prince
    and then vanished.
. . . Must human hearts blossom in spring, like all other flowers?
And of even this bright flame of love, shall there be only ashes?
(48)

In the Camp of the Sketching Brush

Monkeys and birds are still alert for your orders
And winds and clouds eager to shield your fortress.
. . . You were master of the brush, and a sagacious general,
But your Emperor, defeated, rode the prison-cart.
You were abler than even the greatest Chou statesmen,
Yet less fortunate than the two Shu generals who were killed in
    action.

And, though at your birth-place a temple has been built to you,
You never finished singing your *Song of the Holy Mountain.*
(49, 49c, 50)

To One Unnamed

Time was long before I met her, but is longer since we parted,
And the east wind has arisen and a hundred flowers are gone;
And the silk-worms of spring will weave until they die
And every night the candles will weep their wicks away.
Mornings in her mirror she sees her hair-cloud changing,
Yet she dares the chill of moonlight with her evening song.
. . . It is not so very far to her Enchanted Mountain—
O blue-birds, be listening!—Bring me what she says!
(39a)

Spring Rain

I am lying in a white-lined coat while the spring approaches,
But am thinking only of the White Gate City where I cannot be.
. . . There are two red chambers fronting the cold, hidden by the
    rain,
And a lantern on a pearl screen swaying my lone heart home-
    ward.
. . . The long road ahead will be full of new hardship,
With, late in the nights, brief intervals of dream.
Oh, to send you this message, this pair of jade ear-rings!—
I watch a lonely wildgoose in three thousand miles of cloud.
(39a)

To One Unnamed

I

A faint phœnix-tail gauze, fragrant and doubled,
Lines your green canopy, closed for the night. . . .

Will your shy face peer round a moon-shaped fan,
And your voice be heard hushing the rattle of my carriage?
It is quiet and quiet where your gold lamp dies,
How far can a pomegranate-blossom whisper?
. . . I will tether my horse to a river willow
And wait for the will of the southwest wind.

II

There are many curtains in your care-free house,
Where rapture lasts the whole night long.
. . . What are the lives of angels but dreams
If they take no lovers into their rooms?
. . . Storms are ravishing the nut-horns,
Moon-dew sweetening cinnamon-leaves—
I know well enough naught can come of this union,
Yet how it serves to ease my heart!

The Han Monument

The Son of Heaven in Yüan-ho times was martial as a god
And might be likened only to the Emperors Hsüan and Hsi.
He took an oath to reassert the glory of the empire,
And tribute was brought to his palace from all four quarters.
Western Huai for fifty years had been a bandit country,
Wolves becoming lynxes, lynxes becoming bears.
They assailed the mountains and rivers, rising from the plains,
With their long spears and sharp lances aimed at the Sun.
But the Emperor had a wise premier, by the name of Tu,
Who, guarded by spirits against assassination,
Hung at his girdle the seal of state, and accepted chief command,
While these savage winds were harrying the flags of the Ruler of
   Heaven.
Generals Suo, Wu, Ku, and T'ung became his paws and claws;
Civil and military experts brought their writing-brushes,
And his recording adviser was wise and resolute.

A hundred and forty thousand soldiers, fighting like lions and
    tigers,
Captured the bandit chieftains for the Imperial Temple.
So complete a victory was a supreme event;
And the Emperor said: "To you, Tu, should go the highest
    honour,
And your secretary, Yü, should write a record of it."
When Yü had bowed his head, he leapt and danced, saying:
"Historical writings on stone and metal are my especial art;
And, since I know the finest brush-work of the old masters,
My duty in this instance is more than merely official,
And I should be at fault if I modestly declined."
The Emperor, on hearing this, nodded many times.
And Yü retired and fasted and, in a narrow work-room,
His great brush thick with ink as with drops of rain,
Chose characters like those in the *Canons of Yao and Hsun*,
And a style as in the ancient poems *Ch'ing-miao* and *Shêng-min*.
And soon the description was ready, on a sheet of paper.
In the morning he laid it, with a bow, on the purple stairs.
He memorialized the throne: "I, unworthy,
Have dared to record this exploit, for a monument."
The tablet was thirty feet high, the characters large as dippers;
It was set on a sacred tortoise, its columns flanked with drag-
    ons . . .
The phrases were strange with deep words that few could under-
    stand;
And jealousy entered and malice and reached the Emperor—
So that a rope a hundred feet long pulled the tablet down
And coarse sand and small stones ground away its face.
But literature endures, like the universal spirit,
And its breath becomes a part of the vitals of all men.
The T'ang plate, the Confucian tripod, are eternal things,
Not because of their forms, but because of their inscriptions. . . .
Sagacious is our sovereign and wise his minister,
And high their successes and prosperous their reign;
But unless it be recorded by a writing such as this,

How may they hope to rival the three and five good rulers?
I wish I could write ten thousand copies to read ten thousand
     times,
Till spittle ran from my lips and calluses hardened my fingers,
And still could hand them down, through seventy-two genera-
     tions,
As corner-stones for Rooms of Great Deeds on the Sacred Moun-
     tains.

(13, 51, 6)

LI TÜAN

端 李

On Hearing Her Play the Harp

Her hands of white jade by a window of snow
Are glimmering on a golden-fretted harp—
And to draw the quick eye of Chou Yü,
She touches a wrong note now and then.

(52)

LI YI

益 李

A Song of the Southern River
(Written to Music)

Since I married the merchant of Ch'ü-t'ang
He has failed each day to keep his word. . . .
Had I thought how regular the tide is,
I might rather have chosen a river-boy.

On Hearing a Flute at Night
from the Wall of Shou-hsiang

The sand below the border-mountain lies like snow,
And the moon like frost beyond the city-wall,
And someone somewhere, playing a flute,
Has made the soldiers homesick all night long.

A Brief but Happy Meeting
with My Brother-in-Law

"Meeting by accident, only to part"

After these ten torn wearisome years
We have met again. We were both so changed
That hearing first your surname, I thought you a stranger—
Then hearing your given name, I remembered your young
    face. . . .
All that has happened with the tides
We have told and told till the evening bell. . . .
Tomorrow you journey to Yo-chou,
Leaving autumn between us, peak after peak.

LIU CHANG-CH'ING

卿長劉

On Parting with the
Buddhist Pilgrim Ling-ch'ê

From the temple, deep in its tender bamboos,
Comes the low sound of an evening bell,
While the hat of a pilgrim carries the sunset
Farther and farther down the green mountain.

On Hearing a Lute-Player

Your seven strings are like the voice
Of a cold wind in the pines,
Singing old beloved songs
Which no one cares for any more.

A Farewell to a Buddhist Monk

Can drifting clouds and white storks
Be tenants in this world of ours?—
Or you still live on Wu-chou Mountain,
Now that people are coming here?

Climbing in Autumn
for a View from the Temple
on the Terrace of General Wu

As the seasons have dealt with this ancient terrace,
So autumn breaks my homesick heart. . . .
Few pilgrims venture climbing to a temple so wild,

Up from the lake, in the mountain clouds.
. . . Sunset clings in the old defences,
A stone gong shivers through the empty woods.
. . . Of the Southern Dynasty, what remains?
Nothing but the great River.
(53)

A Farewell to Governor Li
on His Way Home to Han-yang

Sad wanderer, once you conquered the South,
Commanding a hundred thousand men;
Today, dismissed and dispossessed,
In your old age you remember glory.
Once, when you stood, three borders were still;
Your dagger was the scale of life.
Now, watching the great rivers, the Kiang and the Han,
On their ways in the evening, where do you go?

On Seeing Wang Leave for the South

Toward a mist upon the water
Still I wave my hand and sob,
For the flying bird is lost in space
Beyond a desolate green mountain . . .
But now the long river, the far lone sail,
The five lakes, gleam like spring in the sunset;
And down an island white with duckweed
Comes the quiet of communion.

While Visiting on the South Stream
the Taoist Priest Ch'ang

Walking along a little path,
I find a footprint on the moss,

A white cloud low on the quiet lake,
Grasses that sweeten an idle door,
A pine grown greener with the rain,
A brook that comes from a mountain source—
And, mingling with Truth among the flowers,
I have forgotten what to say.

(75, 75a)

New Year's at Ch'ang-sha

New Year's only deepens my longing,
Adds to the lonely tears of an exile
Who, growing old and still in harness,
Is left here by the homing spring . . .
Monkeys come down from the mountains to haunt me.
I bend like a willow, when it rains on the river.
I think of Chia Yi, who taught here and died here—
And I wonder what my term shall be.

(43)

On Leaving Kiu-kiang Again

To Hsuëh and Liu

Dare I, at my age, accept my summons,
Knowing of the world's ways only wine and song? . . .
Over the moon-edged river come wildgeese from the Tartars;
And the thinner the leaves along the Huai, the wider the southern
    mountains . . .
I ought to be glad to take my old bones back to the capital,
But what am I good for in that world, with my few white
    hairs? . . .
As bent and decrepit as you are, I am ashamed to thank you,
When you caution me that I may encounter thunderbolts.

(54)

On Passing Chia Yi's House in Ch'ang-sha

Here, where you spent your three years' exile,
To be mourned in Ch'u ten thousand years,
Can I trace your footprint in the autumn grass—
Or only slanting sunlight through the bleak woods?
If even good Emperor Wên was cold-hearted,
Could you hope that the dull river Hsiang would understand you,
These desolate waters, these taciturn mountains,
When you came, like me, so far away?

(43)

An Evening View of the City of Yo-chou After Coming from Han-k'ou to Parrot Island

A Poem Sent to My Friend Governor Yüan

No ripples in the river, no mist on the islands,
Yet the landscape is blurred toward my friend in Ch'u . . .
Birds in the slanting sun cross Han-k'ou,
And the autumn sky mingles with Lake Tung-t'ing.
. . . From a bleak mountain wall the cold tone of a bugle
Reminds me, moored by a ruined fort,
That Chia Yi's loyal plea to the House of Han
Banned him to Ch'ang-sha, to be an exile.

(43)

LIU CHUNG-YUNG

庸中柳

A Trooper's Burden

For years, to guard the Jade Pass and the River of Gold,
With our hands on our horse-whips and our sword-hilts,
We have watched the green graves change to snow
And the Yellow Stream ring the Black Mountain forever.

LIU FANG-P'ING

平方劉

A Moonlight Night

When the moon has coloured half the house,
With the North Star at its height and the South Star setting,
I can feel the first motions of the warm air of spring
In the singing of an insect at my green-silk window.

Spring Heart-Break

With twilight passing her silken window,
She weeps alone in her chamber of gold;
For spring is departing from a desolate garden,
And a drift of pear-petals is closing a door.

LIU SHÊN-HSÜ

劉春虛

A Poem

(*Its Title Lost*)

On a road outreaching the white clouds,
By a spring outrunning the bluest river,
Petals come drifting on the wind
And the brook is sweet with them all the way.
My quiet gate is a mountain-trail,
And the willow-trees about my cottage
Sift on my sleeve, through the shadowy noon,
Distillations of the sun.

LIU TSUNG-YÜAN

元宗柳

River-Snow

A hundred mountains and no bird,
A thousand paths without a footprint;
A little boat, a bamboo cloak,
An old man fishing in the cold river-snow.

From the City-Tower of Liu-chou

To My Four Fellow-Officials at
Chang, Ting, Fêng, and Lien Districts

At this lofty tower where the town ends, wilderness begins;
And our longing has as far to go as the ocean or the sky . . .
Hibiscus-flowers by the moat heave in a sudden wind,
And vines along the wall are whipped with slanting rain.
Nothing to see for three hundred miles but a blur of woods and
    mountain—
And the river's nine loops, twisting in our bowels. . . .
This is where they have sent us, this land of tattooed people—
And not even letters, to keep us in touch with home.
(55)

Reading Buddhist Classics with Ch'ao
at His Temple in the Early Morning

I clean my teeth in water drawn from a cold well;
And while I brush my clothes, I purify my mind;
Then, slowly turning pages in the Tree-Leaf Book,
I recite, along the path to the eastern shelter.

. . . The world has forgotten the true fountain of this teaching
And people enslave themselves to miracles and fables.
Under the given words I want the essential meaning,
I look for the simplest way to sow and reap my nature.
Here in the quiet of the priest's temple-courtyard,
Mosses add their climbing colour to the thick bamboo;
And now comes the sun, out of mist and fog,
And pines that seem to be new-bathed;
And everything is gone from me, speech goes, and reading,
Leaving the single unison.

Dwelling by a Stream

I had so long been troubled by official hat and robe
That I am glad to be an exile here in this wild southland.
I am a neighbour now of planters and reapers.
I am a guest of the mountains and woods.
I plough in the morning, turning dewy grasses,
And at evening tie my fisher-boat, breaking the quiet stream.
Back and forth I go, scarcely meeting anyone,
And sing a long poem and gaze at the blue sky.

An Old Fisherman

An old fisherman spent the night here, under the western cliff;
He dipped up water from the pure Hsiang and made a bamboo
     fire;
And then, at sunrise, he went his way through the cloven mist,
With only the creak of his paddle left, in the greenness of moun-
     tain and river.
. . . I turn and see the waves moving as from heaven,
And clouds above the cliffs coming idly, one by one.

LIU YÜ-HSI

錫禹劉

Blacktail Row

Grass has run wild now by the Bridge of Red-Birds;
And swallows' wings, at sunset, in Blacktail Row
Where once they visited great homes,
Dip among doorways of the poor.

(56)

A Spring Song

In gala robes she comes down from her chamber
Into her courtyard, enclosure of spring . . .
When she tries from the centre to count the flowers,
On her hairpin of jade a dragon-fly poises.

In the Temple of the First King of Shu

Even in this world the spirit of a hero
Lives and reigns for thousands of years.
You were the firmest of the pot's three legs;
It was you who maintained the honour of the currency;
You chose a great premier to magnify your kingdom . . .
And yet you had a son so little like his father
That girls of your country were taken captive
To dance in the palace of the King of Wêi.

(49b,. 49c)

Thoughts of Old Time at West Fort Mountain

Since Wang Chün brought his towering ships down from Yi-
   chou,
The royal ghost has pined in the city of Nan-king.
Ten thousand feet of iron chain were sunk here to the bottom—
And then came the flag of surrender on the Wall of Stone. . . .
Cycles of change have moved into the past,
While still this mountain dignity has commanded the cold river;
And now comes the day of the Chinese world united,
And the old forts fill with ruin and with autumn reeds.

(57)

LO PIN-WANG

王賓駱

A Political Prisoner Listening to a Cicada

While the year sinks westward, I hear a cicada
Bid me to be resolute here in my cell,
Yet it needed the song of those black wings
To break a white-haired prisoner's heart. . . .
His flight is heavy through the fog,
His pure voice drowns in the windy world.
Who knows if he be singing still?—
Who listens any more to me?

(58, 44)

LU LUN

Border-Songs

(Written to Music)

I

His golden arrow is tipped with hawk's feathers,
His embroidered silk flag has a tail like a swallow.
One man, arising, gives a new order
To the answering shout of a thousand tents.

II

The woods are black and a wind assails the grasses,
Yet the general tries night archery—
And next morning he finds his white-plumed arrow
Pointed deep in the hard rock.

III

High in the faint moonlight, wildgeese are soaring.
Tartar chieftains are fleeing through the dark—
And we chase them, with horses lightly burdened
And a burden of snow on our bows and our swords.

IV

Let feasting begin in the wild camp!
Let bugles cry our victory!
Let us drink, let us dance in our golden armour!
Let us thunder on rivers and hills with our drums!

(59)

A Farewell to Li Tuan

By my old gate, among yellow grasses,
Still we linger, sick at heart.
The way you must follow through cold clouds
Will lead you this evening into snow.
Your father died; you left home young;
Nobody knew of your misfortunes.
We cry, we say nothing. What can I wish you,
In this blowing wintry world?

A Night-Mooring at Wu-ch'ang

Far off in the clouds stand the walls of Han-yang,
Another day's journey for my lone sail. . . .
Though a river-merchant ought to sleep in this calm weather,
I listen to the tide at night and voices of the boatmen.
. . . My thin hair grows wintry, like the triple Hsiang streams,
Three thousand miles my heart goes, homesick with the moon;
But the war has left me nothing of my heritage—
And oh, the pang of hearing these drums along the river!

MA TAI

戴　馬

An Autumn Cottage at Pa-shang

After the shower at Pa-shang,
I see an evening line of wildgeese,
The limp-hanging leaves of a foreign tree,
A lantern's cold gleam, lonely in the night,
An empty garden, white with dew,
The ruined wall of a neighbouring monastery.
. . . I have taken my ease here long enough.
What am I waiting for, I wonder.

Thoughts of Old Time on the Ch'u River

A cold light shines on the gathering dew,
As sunset fades beyond the southern mountains;
Trees echo with monkeys on the banks of Lake Tung-t'ing,
Where somebody is moving in an orchid-wood boat.
Marsh-lands are swollen wide with the moon,
While torrents are bent to the mountains' will;
And the vanished Queens of the Clouds leave me
Sad with autumn all night long.

(60)

MÊNG CHIAO

郊 孟

A Song of a Pure-Hearted Girl

(*Written to Music*)

Lakka-trees ripen two by two
And mandarin-ducks die side by side.
If a true-hearted girl will love only her husband,
In a life as faithfully lived as theirs,
What troubling wave can arrive to vex
A spirit like water in a timeless well?

A Traveller's Song

(*Written to Music*)

The thread in the hands of a fond-hearted mother
Makes clothes for the body of her wayward boy;
Carefully she sews and thoroughly she mends,
Dreading the delays that will keep him late from home.
But how much love has the inch-long grass
For three spring months of the light of the sun?

MÊNG HAO-JAN

然浩孟

A Night-Mooring on the Chien-tê River

While my little boat moves on its mooring of mist,
And daylight wanes, old memories begin. . . .
How wide the world was, how close the trees to heaven,
And how clear in the water the nearness of the moon!

A Spring Morning

I awake light-hearted this morning of spring,
Everywhere round me the singing of birds—
But now I remember the night, the storm,
And I wonder how many blossoms were broken.

A Message from Lake Tung-t'ing

To Premier Chang

Here in the Eighth-month the waters of the lake
Are of a single air with heaven,
And a mist from the Yun and Mêng valleys
Has beleaguered the city of Yo-chou.
I should like to cross, but I can find no boat.
. . . How ashamed I am to be idler than you statesmen,
As I sit here and watch a fisherman casting
And emptily envy him his catch.

On Climbing Yen Mountain with Friends

While worldly matters take their turn,
Ancient, modern, to and fro,
Rivers and mountains are changeless in their glory
And still to be witnessed from this trail.
. . . Where a fisher-boat dips by a waterfall,
Where the air grows colder, deep in the valley,
The monument of Yang remains;
And we have wept, reading the words.
(61)

At a Banquet in the House of the Taoist Priest Mêi

In my bed among the woods, grieving that spring must end,
I lifted up the curtain on a pathway of flowers,
And a flashing bluebird bade me come
To the dwelling-place of the Red Pine Genie.
. . . What a flame for his golden crucible—
Peach-trees magical with buds!—
And for holding boyhood in his face,
The rosy-flowing wine of clouds!
(62, 62a)

On Returning at the Year's End to Chung-nan Mountain

I petition no more at the north palace-gate.
. . . To this tumble-down hut on Chung-nan Mountain
I was banished for my blunders, by a wise ruler.
I have been sick so long I see none of my friends.
My white hairs hasten my decline,
Like pale beams ending the old year.

Therefore I lie awake and ponder
On the pine-shadowed moonlight in my empty window.

(32, 32a)

Stopping at a Friend's Farm-House

Preparing me chicken and rice, old friend,
You entertain me at your farm.
We watch the green trees that circle your village
And the pale blue of outlying mountains.
We open your window over garden and field,
To talk mulberry and hemp with our cups in our hands.
. . . Wait till the Mountain Holiday—
I am coming again in chrysanthemum time.

(64)

From Ch'in Country to
the Buddhist Priest Yuan

How gladly I would seek a mountain
If I had enough means to live as a recluse!
For I turn at last from serving the State
To the Eastern Woods Temple and to you, my master.
. . . Like ashes of gold in a cinnamon-flame,
My youthful desires have been burnt with the years—
And tonight in the chilling sunset-wind
A cicada, singing, weighs on my heart.

(63, 44)

From a Mooring on the T'ung-lu
to a Friend in Yang-chou

With monkeys whimpering on the shadowy mountain,
And the river rushing through the night,

And a wind in the leaves along both banks,
And the moon athwart my solitary sail,
I, a stranger in this inland district,
Homesick for my Yang-chou friends,
Send eastward two long streams of tears
To find the nearest touch of the sea.

Taking Leave of Wang Wêi

Slow and reluctant, I have waited
Day after day, till now I must go.
How sweet the road-side flowers might be
If they did not mean good-bye, old friend.
The Lords of the Realm are harsh to us
And men of affairs are not our kind.
I will turn back home, I will say no more,
I will close the gate of my old garden.

Memories in Early Winter

South go the wildgeese, for leaves are now falling,
And the water is cold with a wind from the north.
I remember my home; but the Hsiang River's curves
Are walled by the clouds of this southern country.
I go forward. I weep till my tears are spent.
I see a sail in the far sky.
Where is the ferry? Will somebody tell me?
It's growing rough. It's growing dark.

On Climbing Orchid Mountain
in the Autumn

To Chang

On a northern peak among white clouds
You have found your hermitage of peace;

And now, as I climb this mountain to see you,
High with the wildgeese flies my heart.
The quiet dusk might seem a little sad
If this autumn weather were not so brisk and clear;
I look down at the river bank, with homeward-bound villagers
Resting on the sand till the ferry returns;
There are trees at the horizon like a row of grasses
And against the river's rim an island like the moon. . . .
I hope that you will come and meet me, bringing a basket of
    wine—
And we'll celebrate together the Mountain Holiday.

(*64*)

In Summer at the South Pavilion

Thinking of Hsing

The mountain-light suddenly fails in the west,
In the east from the lake the slow moon rises.
I loosen my hair to enjoy the evening coolness
And open my window and lie down in peace.
The wind brings me odours of lotuses,
And bamboo-leaves drip with a music of dew. . . .
I would take up my lute and I would play,
But, alas, who here would understand?
And so I think of you, old friend,
O troubler of my midnight dreams!

At the Mountain-Lodge
of the Buddhist Priest Ye
Waiting in Vain for My Friend Ting

Now that the sun has set beyond the western range,
Valley after valley is shadowy and dim . . .
And now through pine-trees come the moon and the chill of eve-
    ning,

And my ears feel pure with the sound of wind and water. . . .
Nearly all the woodsmen have reached home,
Birds have settled on their perches in the quiet mist . . .
And still—because you promised—I am waiting for you, waiting,
Playing my lonely lute under a wayside vine.

Returning at Night to Lu-mên Mountain

A bell in the mountain-temple sounds the coming of night.
I hear people at the fishing-town stumble aboard the ferry,
While others follow the sand-bank to their homes along the river.
. . . I also take a boat and am bound for Lu-mên Mountain—
And soon the Lu-mên moonlight is piercing misty trees.
I have come, before I know it, upon an ancient hermitage,
The thatch door, the piney path, the solitude, the quiet,
Where a hermit lives and moves, never needing a companion.

(65)

ONE AT THE WESTERN FRONT

人鄙西

General Kê-shu

This constellation, with its seven high stars,
Is Kê-shu lifting his sword in the night:
And no more barbarians, nor their horses, nor cattle,
Dare ford the river boundary.

(66)

P'EI TI

迪 斐

A Farewell to Ts'uêi

Though you think to return to this maze of mountains,
Oh, let them brim your heart with wonder! . . .
Remember the fisherman from Wu-ling
Who had only a day in the Peach-Blossom Country.

(2)

PO CHÜ-YI

易居白

A Suggestion to My Friend Liu

There's a gleam of green in an old bottle,
There's a stir of red in the quiet stove,
There's a feeling of snow in the dusk outside—
What about a cup of wine inside?

A Song of the Palace

Her tears are spent, but no dreams come.
She can hear the others singing through the night.
She has lost his love. Alone with her beauty,
She leans till dawn on her incense-pillow.

(67)

Grasses

Boundless grasses over the plain
Come and go with every season;
Wildfire never quite consumes them—
They are tall once more in the spring wind.
Sweet they press on the old high-road
And reach the crumbling city-gate. . . .
O Prince of Friends, you are gone again. . . .
I hear them sighing after you.

(68)

To My Brothers and Sisters
Adrift in Troubled Times
This Poem of the Moon

(Since the disorders in Ho-nan and the famine in Kuan-nêi, my brothers and sisters have been scattered. Looking at the moon, I express my thoughts in this poem, which I send to my eldest brother at Fou-liang, my seventh brother at Yü-ch'ien, my fifteenth brother at Wu-chiang and my younger brothers and sisters at Fu-li and Hsia-kuêi.)

My heritage lost through disorder and famine,
My brothers and sisters flung eastward and westward,
My fields and gardens wrecked by the war,
My own flesh and blood become scum of the street,
I moan to my shadow like a lone-wandering wildgoose,
I am torn from my root like a water-plant in autumn:
I gaze at the moon, and my tears run down
For hearts, in five places, all sick with one wish.

(69)

A Song of Unending Sorrow

China's Emperor, craving beauty that might shake an empire,
Was on the throne for many years, searching, never finding,
Till a little child of the Yang clan, hardly even grown,
Bred in an inner chamber, with no one knowing her,
But with graces granted by heaven and not to be concealed,
At last one day was chosen for the imperial household.
If she but turned her head and smiled, there were cast a hundred
    spells,
And the powder and paint of the Six Palaces faded into nothing.
. . . It was early spring. They bathed her in the Flower-Pure
    Pool,

Which warmed and smoothed the creamy-tinted crystal of her
     skin,
And, because of her languor, a maid was lifting her
When first the Emperor noticed her and chose her for his bride.
The cloud of her hair, petal of her cheek, gold ripples of her
     crown when she moved,
Were sheltered on spring evenings by warm hibiscus-curtains;
But nights of spring were short and the sun arose too soon,
And the Emperor, from that time forth, forsook his early hear-
     ings
And lavished all his time on her with feasts and revelry,
His mistress of the spring, his despot of the night.
There were other ladies in his court, three thousand of rare
     beauty,
But his favours to three thousand were concentered in one body.
By the time she was dressed in her Golden Chamber, it would be
     almost evening;
And when tables were cleared in the Tower of Jade, she would
     loiter, slow with wine.
Her sisters and her brothers all were given titles;
And, because she so illumined and glorified her clan,
She brought to every father, every mother through the empire,
Happiness when a girl was born rather than a boy.
 . . . High rose Li Palace, entering blue clouds,
And far and wide the breezes carried magical notes
Of soft song and slow dance, of string and bamboo music.
The Emperor's eyes could never gaze on her enough—
Till war-drums, booming from Yü-yang, shocked the whole earth
And broke the tunes of *The Rainbow Skirt and the Feathered
     Coat.*
The Forbidden City, the nine-tiered palace, loomed in the dust
From thousands of horses and chariots headed southwest.
The imperial flag opened the way, now moving and now paus-
     ing—
But thirty miles from the capital, beyond the western gate,
The men of the army stopped, not one of them would stir

Till under their horses' hoofs they might trample those moth-
  eyebrows . . .
Flowery hairpins fell to the ground, no one picked them up,
And a green and white jade hair-tassel and a yellow-gold hair-
  bird.
The Emperor could not save her, he could only cover his face.
And later when he turned to look, the place of blood and tears
Was hidden in a yellow dust blown by a cold wind.
  . . . At the cleft of the Dagger-Tower Trail they criss-crossed
  through a cloud-line
Under O-mêi Mountain. The last few came.
Flags and banners lost their colour in the fading sunlight . . .
But as waters of Shu are always green and its mountains always
  blue,
So changeless was His Majesty's love and deeper than the days.
He stared at the desolate moon from his temporary palace.
He heard bell-notes in the evening rain, cutting at his breast.
And when heaven and earth resumed their round and the dragon-
  car faced home,
The Emperor clung to the spot and would not turn away
From the soil along the Ma-wêi Slope, under which was buried
That memory, that anguish. Where was her jade-white face?
Ruler and lords, when eyes would meet, wept upon their coats
As they rode, with loose rein, slowly eastward, back to the
  capital.
  . . . The pools, the gardens, the palace, all were just as before,
The Lake T'ai-yi hibiscus, the Wêi-yang Palace willows;
But a petal was like her face and a willow-leaf her eyebrow—
And what could he do but cry whenever he looked at them?
  . . . Peach-trees and plum-trees blossomed, in the winds of
  spring;
Lakka-foliage fell to the ground, after autumn rains;
The Western and Southern Palaces were littered with late grasses,
And the steps were mounded with red leaves that no one swept
  away.
Her Pear-Garden Players became white-haired

And the eunuchs thin-eyebrowed in her Court of Pepper-Trees;
Over the throne flew fire-flies, while he brooded in the twilight.
He would lengthen the lamp-wick to its end and still could never
sleep.
Bell and drum would slowly toll the dragging night-hours
And the River of Stars grow sharp in the sky, just before dawn,
And the porcelain mandarin-ducks on the roof grow thick with
morning frost
And his covers of kingfisher-blue feel lonelier and colder
With the distance between life and death year after year;
And yet no beloved spirit ever visited his dreams.
. . . At Lin-ch'iung lived a Taoist priest who was a guest of
heaven,
Able to summon spirits by his concentrated mind.
And people were so moved by the Emperor's constant brooding
That they besought the Taoist priest to see if he could find her.
He opened his way in space and clove the ether like lightning,
Up to heaven, under the earth, looking everywhere.
Above, he searched the Green Void, below, the Yellow Spring;
But he failed, in either place, to find the one he looked for.
And then he heard accounts of an enchanted isle at sea,
A part of the intangible and incorporeal world,
With pavilions and fine towers in the five-coloured air,
And of exquisite immortals moving to and fro,
And of one among them—whom they called The Ever True—
With a face of snow and flowers resembling hers he sought.
So he went to the West Hall's gate of gold and knocked at the
jasper door
And asked a girl, called Morsel-of-Jade, to tell The Doubly-
Perfect.
And the lady, at news of an envoy from the Emperor of China,
Was startled out of dreams in her nine-flowered canopy.
She pushed aside her pillow, dressed, shook away sleep,
And opened the pearly shade and then the silver screen.
Her cloudy hair-dress hung on one side because of her great
haste,

And her flower-cap was loose when she came along the terrace,
While a light wind filled her cloak and fluttered with her motion
As though she danced *The Rainbow Skirt and the Feathered Coat.*
And the tear-drops drifting down her sad white face
Were like a rain in spring on the blossom of the pear.
But love glowed deep within her eyes when she bade him thank her liege,
Whose form and voice had been strange to her ever since their parting—
Since happiness had ended at the Court of the Bright Sun,
And moons and dawns had become long in Fairy-Mountain Palace.
But when she turned her face and looked down toward the earth
And tried to see the capital, there were only fog and dust.
So she took out, with emotion, the pledges he had given
And, through his envoy, sent him back a shell box and gold hairpin,
But kept one branch of the hairpin and one side of the box,
Breaking the gold of the hairpin, breaking the shell of the box;
"Our souls belong together," she said, "like this gold and this shell—
Somewhere, sometime, on earth or in heaven, we shall surely meet."
And she sent him, by his messenger, a sentence reminding him
Of vows which had been known only to their two hearts:
"On the seventh day of the Seventh-month, in the Palace of Long Life,
We told each other secretly in the quiet midnight world
That we wished to fly in heaven, two birds with the wings of one,
And to grow together on the earth, two branches of one tree."
. . . Earth endures, heaven endures; some time both shall end,
While this unending sorrow goes on and on for ever.

(*4a, 4b, 70*)

The Song of a Guitar

*(In the tenth year of Yuan-ho I was banished and demoted to
be assistant official in Kiu-kiang. In the summer of the next year
I was seeing a friend leave P'ên-p'u and heard in the midnight
from a neighbouring boat a guitar played in the manner of the
capital. Upon inquiry, I found that the player had formerly been
a dancing-girl there and in her maturity had been married to a
merchant. I invited her to my boat to have her play for us. She
told me her story, heyday and then unhappiness. Since my
departure from the capital I had not felt sad; but that night, after
I left her, I began to realize my banishment. And I wrote this
long poem—six hundred and twelve characters.)*

I was bidding a guest farewell, at night on the Hsün-yang River,
Where maple-leaves and full-grown rushes rustled in the autumn.
I, the host, had dismounted, my guest had boarded his boat,
And we raised our cups and wished to drink—but, alas, there
    was no music.
For all we had drunk we felt no joy and were parting from each
    other,
When the river widened mysteriously toward the full moon—
We had heard a sudden sound, a guitar across the water.
Host forgot to turn back home, and guest to go his way.
We followed where the melody led and asked the player's name.
The sound broke off . . . then reluctantly she answered.
We moved our boat near hers, invited her to join us,
Summoned more wine and lanterns to recommence our banquet.
Yet we called and urged a thousand times before she started
    toward us,
Still hiding half her face from us behind her guitar.
. . . She turned the tuning-pegs and tested several strings;
We could feel what she was feeling, even before she played:
Each string a meditation, each note a deep thought,
As if she were telling us the ache of her whole life.
She knit her brows, flexed her fingers, then began her music,

Little by little letting her heart share everything with ours.
She brushed the strings, twisted them slow, swept them, plucked
    them—
First the air of *The Rainbow Skirt*, then *The Six Little Ones*.
The large strings hummed like rain,
The small strings whispered like a secret,
Hummed, whispered—and then were intermingled
Like a pouring of large and small pearls into a plate of jade.
We heard an oriole, liquid, hidden among flowers.
We heard a brook bitterly sob along a bank of sand. . . .
By the checking of its cold touch, the very string seemed broken
As though it could not pass; and the notes, dying away
Into a depth of sorrow and concealment of lament,
Told even more in silence than they had told in sound . . .
A silver vase abruptly broke with a gush of water,
And out leapt armoured horses and weapons that clashed and
    smote—
And, before she laid her pick down, she ended with one stroke,
And all four strings made one sound, as of rending silk. . . .
There was quiet in the east boat and quiet in the west,
And we saw the white autumnal moon enter the river's heart.
. . . When she had slowly placed the pick back among the
    strings,
She rose and smoothed her clothing and, formal, courteous,
Told us how she had spent her girlhood at the capital,
Living in her parents' house under the Mount of Toads,
And had mastered the guitar at the age of thirteen,
With her name recorded first in the class-roll of musicians,
Her art the admiration even of experts,
Her beauty the envy of all the leading dancers,
How noble youths of Wu-ling had lavishly competed
And numberless red rolls of silk been given for one song,
And silver combs with shell inlay been snapped by her rhythms,
And skirts the colour of blood been spoiled with stains of
    wine . . .
Season after season, joy had followed joy,

Autumn moons and spring winds had passed without her heeding,
Till first her brother left for the war, and then her aunt died,
And evenings went and evenings came, and her beauty faded—
With ever fewer chariots and horses at her door;
So that finally she gave herself as wife to a merchant
Who, prizing money first, careless how he left her,
Had gone, a month before, to Fou-liang to buy tea.
And she had been tending an empty boat at the river's mouth,
No company but the bright moon and the cold water.
And sometimes in the deep of night she would dream of her
    triumphs
And be wakened from her dreams by the scalding of her tears.
. . . Her very first guitar-note had started me sighing;
Now, having heard her story, I was sadder still.
"We are both unhappy—to the sky's end.
We meet. We understand. What does acquaintance matter?
I came, a year ago, away from the capital
And am now a sick exile here in Kiu-kiang—
And so remote is Kiu-kiang that I have heard no music,
Neither string nor bamboo, for a whole year.
My quarters, near the River Town, are low and damp,
With bitter reeds and yellowed rushes all about the house.
And what is to be heard here, morning and evening?—
The bleeding cry of cuckoos, the whimpering of apes.
On flowery spring mornings and moonlit autumn nights
I have often taken wine up and drunk it all alone,
Of course there are the mountain songs and the village pipes,
But they are crude and strident, and grate on my ears.
And tonight, when I heard you playing your guitar,
I felt as if my hearing were bright with fairy-music.
Do not leave us. Come, sit down. Play for us again.
And I will write you a ballad to the tune you have just sung."
. . . Moved by what I said, she stood there for a moment,
Then sat again to her strings—and they sounded even sadder,
Although the tunes were different from those she had played
    before . . .

The feasters, all listening, covered their faces.
But who of them all was crying the most?
This Kiu-kiang official. My blue sleeve was wet.

(71)

SÊNG CHIAO-JAN

然皎僧

Not Finding Lu Hung-chien at Home

To find you, moved beyond the city,
A wide path led me, by mulberry and hemp,
To a new-set hedge of chrysanthemums—
Not yet blooming although autumn had come.
. . . I knocked; no answer, not even a dog.
I waited to ask your western neighbour;
But he told me that daily you climb the mountain,
Never returning until sunset.

(72)

SHÊN CH'ÜAN-CH'I

期 佺 沈

Lines

Against the City of the Yellow Dragon
Our troops were sent long years ago,
And girls here watch the same melancholy moon
That lights our Chinese warriors—
And young wives dream a dream of spring,
That last night their heroic husbands,
In a great attack, with flags and drums,
Captured the City of the Yellow Dragon.

Beyond Seeing

(*Written to Music*)

A girl of the Lu clan who lives in Golden-Wood Hall,
Where swallows perch in pairs on beams of tortoise-shell,
Hears the washing-mallets' cold beat shake the leaves down.
. . . The Liao-yang expedition will be gone ten years,
And messages are lost in the White Wolf River.
. . . Here in the City of the Red Phœnix autumn nights are long,
Where one who is heart-sick to see beyond seeing,
Sees only moonlight on the yellow-silk wave of her loom.

(54)

SSŬ-K'UNG SHU

曙空司

A Farewell to Han Shen
at the Yun-yang Inn

Long divided by river and sea,
For years we two have failed to meet—
And suddenly to find you seems like a dream. . . .
With a catch in the throat, we ask how old we are.
. . . Our single lamp shines, through cold and wet,
On a bamboo-thicket sheathed in rain;
But forgetting the sadness that will come with tomorrow,
Let us share the comfort of this farewell wine.

When Lu Lun My Cousin
Comes for the Night

With no other neighbour but the quiet night,
Here I live in the same old cottage;
And as raindrops brighten yellow leaves,
The lamp illumines my white head. . . .
Out of the world these many years,
I am ashamed to receive you here.
But you cannot come too often,
More than brother, lifelong friend.

To a Friend Bound North
After the Rebellion

In dangerous times we two came south;
Now you go north in safety, without me.

But remember my head growing white among strangers,
When you look on the blue of the mountains of home.
. . . The moon goes down behind a ruined fort,
Leaving star-clusters above an old gate . . .
There are shivering birds and withering grasses,
Whichever way I turn my face.

SUNG CHIH-WÊN

問之宋

Inscribed on the Wall of an Inn
North of Ta-yü Mountain

They say that wildgeese, flying southward,
Here turn back, this very month . . .
Shall my own southward journey
Ever be retraced, I wonder.
. . . The river is pausing at ebb-tide,
And the woods are thick with clinging mist—
But tomorrow morning, over the mountain,
Dawn will be white with the plum-trees of home.
(73)

TAI SHU-LUN

倫叔戴

Chancing on Old Friends in a Village Inn

While the autumn moon is pouring full
On a thousand night-levels among towns and villages,
There meet by chance, south of the river,
Dreaming doubters of a dream . . .
In the trees a wind has startled the birds,
And insects cower from cold in the grass;
But wayfarers at least have wine
And nothing to fear—till the morning bell.

(74)

TS'ÊN TS'AN

On Meeting a Messenger to the Capital

It's a long way home, a long way east.
I am old and my sleeve is wet with tears.
We meet on horseback. I have no means of writing.
Tell them three words: "He is safe."

A Message to Censor Tu Fu
at His Office in the Left Court

Together we officials climbed vermilion steps,
To be parted by the purple walls . . .
Our procession, which entered the palace at dawn,
Leaves fragrant now at dusk with imperial incense.
. . . Grey heads may grieve for a fallen flower,
Or blue clouds envy a lilting bird;
But this reign is of heaven, nothing goes wrong,
There have been almost no petitions.

An Early Audience at the Palace of Light

Harmonizing Secretary Chia Chih's Poem

Cock-crow, the Purple Road cold in the dawn;
Linnet songs, court roofs tinted with April;
At the Golden Gate morning bell, countless doors open,
And up the jade steps float a thousand officials
With flowery scabbards. . . . Stars have gone down;
Willows are brushing the dew from the flags—

And, alone on the Lake of the Phœnix, a guest
Is chanting too well *The Song of Bright Spring*.
(9, 9a)

Ascending the Pagoda
at the Temple of Kind Favour

With Kao Shih and Hsüeh Ch'ü

The pagoda, rising abruptly from earth,
Reaches to the very Palace of Heaven . . .
Climbing, we seem to have left the world behind us,
With the steps we look down on hung from space.
It overtops a holy land
And can only have been built by toil of the spirit.
Its four sides darken the bright sun,
Its seven stories cut the grey clouds;
Birds fly down beyond our sight,
And the rapid wind below our hearing;
Mountain-ranges, toward the east,
Appear to be curving and flowing like rivers;
Far green locust-trees line broad roads
Toward clustered palaces and mansions;
Colours of autumn, out of the west,
Enter advancing through the city;
And northward there lie, in five graveyards,
Calm forever under dewy green grass,
Those who know life's final meaning
Which all humankind must learn.
. . . Henceforth I put my official hat aside.
To find the Eternal Way is the only happiness.
(75)

A Song of Running-Horse River

In Farewell to General Fêng of the Western Expedition

Look how swift to the snowy sea races Running-Horse River!—
And sand, up from the desert, flies yellow into heaven.
This Ninth-month night is blowing cold at Wheel Tower,
And valleys, like peck measures, fill with the broken boulders
That downward, headlong, follow the wind.
. . . In spite of grey grasses, Tartar horses are plump;
West of the Hill of Gold, smoke and dust gather.
O General of the Chinese troops, start your campaign!
Keep your iron armour on all night long,
Send your soldiers forward with a clattering of weapons!
. . . While the sharp wind's point cuts the face like a knife,
And snowy sweat steams on the horses' backs,
Freezing a pattern of five-flower coins,
Your challenge from camp, from an inkstand of ice,
Has chilled the barbarian chieftain's heart.
You will have no more need of an actual battle!—
We await the news of victory, here at the western pass!

A Song of Wheel Tower

In Farewell to General Fêng of the Western Expedition

On Wheel Tower parapets night-bugles are blowing,
Though the flag at the northern end hangs limp.
Scouts, in the darkness, are passing Ch'ü-li,
Where, west of the Hill of Gold, the Tartar chieftain has
    halted. . . .
We can see, from the look-out, the dust and black smoke
Where Chinese troops are camping, north of Wheel Tower.
. . . Our flags now beckon the General farther west—
With bugles in the dawn he rouses his Grand Army;
Drums like a tempest pound on four sides
And the Yin Mountains shake with the shouts of ten thousand;

Clouds and the war-wind whirl up in a point
Over fields where grass-roots will tighten around white bones;
In the Dagger River mist, through a biting wind,
Horseshoes, at the Sand Mouth line, break on icy boulders.
. . . Our General endures every pain, every hardship,
Commanded to settle the dust along the border.
We have read, in the Green Books, tales of old days—
But here we behold a living man, mightier than the dead.

(76)

A Song of White Snow

In Farewell to Field-Clerk Wu Going Home

The north wind rolls the white grasses and breaks them;
And the Eighth-month snow across the Tartar sky
Is like a spring gale, come up in the night,
Blowing open the petals of ten thousand pear-trees.
It enters the pearl blinds, it wets the silk curtains;
A fur coat feels cold, a cotton mat flimsy;
Bows become rigid, can hardly be drawn
And the metal of armour congeals on the men;
The sand-sea deepens with fathomless ice,
And darkness masses its endless clouds;
But we drink to our guest bound home from camp,
And play him barbarian lutes, guitars, harps;
Till at dusk, when the drifts are crushing our tents
And our frozen red flags cannot flutter in the wind,
We watch him through Wheel-Tower Gate going eastward
Into the snow-mounds of Heaven-Peak Road. . . .
And then he disappears at the turn of the pass,
Leaving behind him only hoof-prints.

TSU YUNG

詠 祖

On Seeing the Snow-Peak of Chung-nan

See how Chung-nan Mountain soars
With its white top over floating clouds—
And a warm sky opening at the snow-line
While the town in the valley grows colder and colder.

(32)

Looking Toward an Inner Gate
of the Great Wall

My heart sank when I headed north from Yen Country
To the camps of China echoing with bugle and drum.
. . . In an endless cold light of massive snow,
Tall flags on three borders rise up like a dawn.
War-torches invade the barbarian moonlight,
Mountain-clouds like chairmen bear the Great Wall from the sea.
. . . Though no youthful clerk meant to be a great general, I
    throw aside my writing-brush—
Like the student who tossed off cap for a lariat, I challenge what
    may come.

(77)

TS'UÊI HAO

灝 崔

A Song of Ch'ang-kan

(*Written to Music*)

I
"Tell me, where do you live?—
Near here, by the fishing-pool?
Let's hold our boats together, let's see
If we belong in the same town."

II
"Yes, I live here, by the river;
I have sailed on it many and many a time.
Both of us born in Ch'ang-kan, you and I!
Why haven't we always known each other?"

The Yellow Crane Terrace

Where long ago a yellow crane bore a sage to heaven,
Nothing is left now but the Yellow Crane Terrace.
The yellow crane never revisited earth,
And white clouds are flying without him for ever.
. . . Every tree in Han-yang becomes clear in the water,
And Parrot Island is a nest of sweet grasses;
But I look toward home, and twilight grows dark
With a mist of grief on the river waves.

(28a)

Passing Through Hua-yin

Lords of the capital, sharp, unearthly,
The Great Flower's three points pierce through heaven.
Clouds are parting above the Temple of the Warring Emperor,
Rain dries on the mountain, on the Giant's Palm.
Ranges and rivers are the strength of this western gate,
Whence roads and trails lead downward into China.
. . . O pilgrim of fame, O seeker of profit,
Why not remain here and lengthen your days?

(14)

TS'UÊI SHU

曙 崔

*A Climb on the Mountain Holiday
to the Terrace Whence One Sees
the Magician*

A Poem Sent to Vice-Prefect Liu

The Han Emperor Wên bequeathed us this terrace
Which I climb to watch the coming dawn.
Cloudy peaks run northward in the three Chin districts,
And rains are blowing westward through the two Ling valleys.
. . . Who knows but me about the Guard at the Gate,
Or where the Magician of the River Bank is,
Or how to find that magistrate, that poet,
Who was as fond as I am of chrysanthemums and winecups?

(64, 43, 75a, 78, 2a)

TS'UÊI T'U

塗 崔

On New Year's Eve

Farther and farther from the three Pa Roads,
I have come three thousand miles, anxious and watchful,
Through pale snow-patches in the jagged night-mountains—
A stranger with a lonely lantern shaken in the wind.
. . . Separation from my kin
Binds me closer to my servants—
Yet how I dread, so far adrift,
New Year's Day, tomorrow morning!

A Solitary Wildgoose

Line after line has flown back over the border.
Where are you headed all by yourself?
In the evening rain you call to them—
And slowly you alight on an icy pond.
The low wet clouds move faster than you
Along the wall toward the cold moon.
. . . If they caught you in a net or with a shot,
Would it be worse than flying alone?

TU CH'IU-NIANG

娘秋杜

The Gold-Threaded Robe

(Written to Music)

Covet not a gold-threaded robe,
Cherish only your young days!
If a bud open, gather it—
Lest you but wait for an empty bough.

(79)

TU FU

甫　杜

The Eight-Sided Fortress

The Three Kingdoms, divided, have been bound by his greatness.
The Eight-Sided Fortress is founded on his fame;
Beside the changing river, it stands stony as his grief
That he never conquered the Kingdom of Wu.
(49a, 52a)

On Meeting Li Kuêi-nien Down the River

I met you often when you were visiting princes
And when you were playing in noblemen's halls.
. . . Spring passes. . . . Far down the river now,
I find you alone under falling petals.
(80, 4b)

On a Moonlight Night

Far off in Fu-chou she is watching the moonlight,
Watching it alone from the window of her chamber—
For our boy and girl, poor little babes,
Are too young to know where the Capital is.
Her cloudy hair is sweet with mist,
Her jade-white shoulder is cold in the moon.
. . . When shall we lie again, with no more tears,
Watching this bright light on our screen?

A Spring View

Though a country be sundered, hills and rivers endure;
And spring comes green again to trees and grasses
Where petals have been shed like tears
And lonely birds have sung their grief.
. . . After the war-fires of three months,
One message from home is worth a ton of gold.
. . . I stroke my white hair. It has grown too thin
To hold the hairpins any more.

A Night-Vigil in the
Left Court of the Palace

Flowers are shadowed, the palace darkens,
Birds twitter by for a place to perch;
Heaven's ten thousand windows are twinkling,
And nine cloud-terraces are gleaming in the moonlight.
. . . While I wait for the golden lock to turn,
I hear jade pendants tinkling in the wind. . . .
I have a petition to present in the morning,
All night I ask what time it is.

Taking Leave of Friends
on My Way to Hua-chou

(*In the second year of Chih-tê, I escaped from the capital through
the Gate of Golden Light and went to Fêng-hsiang. In the first
year of Ch'ien-yuan, I was appointed as official to Hua-chou
from my former post of Censor. Friends and relatives gathered
and saw me leave by the same gate. And I wrote this poem.*)

This is the road by which I fled,
When the rebels had reached the west end of the city;
And terror, ever since, has clutched at my vitals

Lest some of my soul should never return.
. . . The court has come back now, filling the capital;
But the Emperor sends me away again.
Useless and old, I rein in my horse
For one last look at the thousand gates.

(4d)

Remembering My Brothers on a Moonlight Night

A wanderer hears drums portending battle.
By the first call of autumn from a wildgoose at the border,
He knows that the dews tonight will be frost.
. . . How much brighter the moonlight is at home!
O my brothers, lost and scattered,
What is life to me without you?
Yet if missives in time of peace go wrong—
What can I hope for during war?

To Li Po at the Sky's End

A cold wind blows from the far sky. . . . .
What are you thinking of, old friend?
The wildgeese never answer me.
Rivers and lakes are flooded with rain.
. . . A poet should beware of prosperity,
Yet demons can haunt a wanderer.
Ask an unhappy ghost, throw poems to him
Where he drowned himself in the Mi-lo River.

(81)

A Farewell at Fêng-chi Station

To General Yen

This is where your comrade must leave you,
Turning at the foot of these purple mountains. . . .
When shall we lift our cups again, I wonder,
As we did last night and walk in the moon?
The region is murmuring farewell
To one who was honoured through three reigns;
And back I go now to my river-village,
Into the final solitude.

On Leaving the Tomb of Premier Fang

Having to travel back now from this far place,
I dismount beside your lonely tomb.
The ground where I stand is wet with my tears;
The sky is dark with broken clouds. . . .
I who played chess with the great Premier
Am bringing to my lord the dagger he desired. . . .
But I find only petals falling down,
I hear only linnets answering.

(82)

A Night Abroad

A light wind is rippling at the grassy shore. . . .
Through the night, to my motionless tall mast,
The stars lean down from open space,
And the moon comes running up the river.
. . . If only my art might bring me fame
And free my sick old age from office!—
Flitting, flitting, what am I like
But a sand-snipe in the wide, wide world!

On the Gate-Tower at Yo-chou

I had always heard of Lake Tung-t'ing—
And now at last I have climbed to this tower.
With Wu country to the east of me and Ch'u to the south,
I can see heaven and earth endlessly floating.
. . . But no word has reached me from kin or friends.
I am old and sick and alone with my boat.
North of this wall there are wars and mountains—
And here by the rail how can I help crying?

The Temple of the Premier of Shu

Where is the temple of the famous Premier?—
In a deep pine grove near the City of Silk,
With the green grass of spring colouring the steps,
And birds chirping happily under the leaves.
. . . The third summons weighted him with affairs of state
And to two generations he gave his true heart,
But before he could conquer, he was dead;
And heroes have wept on their coats ever since.
(49b)

A Hearty Welcome

To Vice-Prefect Ts'uêi

North of me, south of me, spring is in flood,
Day after day I have seen only gulls . . .
My path is full of petals—I have swept it for no others.
My thatch gate has been closed—but opens now for you.
It's a long way to the market, I can offer you little—
Yet here in my cottage there is old wine for our cups.
Shall we summon my elderly neighbour to join us,
Call him through the fence, and pour the jar dry?

A View of the Wilderness

Snow is white on the westward mountains and on three fortified
    towns,
And waters in this southern lake flash on a long bridge.
But wind and dust from sea to sea bar me from my brothers;
And I cannot help crying, I am so far away.
I have nothing to expect now but the ills of old age.
I am of less use to my country than a grain of dust.
I ride out to the edge of town. I watch on the horizon,
Day after day, the chaos of the world.

Both Sides of the Yellow River
Recaptured by the Imperial Army

News at this far western station! The north has been recaptured!
At first I cannot check the tears from pouring on my coat—
Where is my wife? Where are my sons?
Yet crazily sure of finding them, I pack my books and poems—
And loud my song and deep my drink
On the green spring-day that starts me home,
Back from this mountain, past another mountain,
Up from the south, north again—to my own town!
(83)

A Long Climb

In a sharp gale from the wide sky apes are whimpering,
Birds are flying homeward over the clear lake and white sand,
Leaves are dropping down like the spray of a waterfall,
While I watch the long river always rolling on.
I have come three thousand miles away. Sad now with autumn
And with my hundred years of woe, I climb this height alone.
Ill fortune has laid a bitter frost on my temples,
Heart-ache and weariness are a thick dust in my wine.

From an Upper Story

Flowers, as high as my window, hurt the heart of a wanderer
For I see, from this high vantage, sadness everywhere.
The Silken River, bright with spring, floats between earth and
heaven
Like a line of cloud by the Jade Peak, between ancient days and
now.
. . . Though the State is established for a while as firm as the
North Star
And bandits dare not venture from the western hills,
Yet sorry in the twilight for the woes of a long-vanished Em-
peror,
I am singing the song his Premier sang when still unestranged
from the mountain.

(49c)

Staying at the General's Headquarters

The autumn night is clear and cold in the lakka-trees of this
courtyard.
I am lying forlorn in the river-town. I watch my guttering candle.
I hear the lonely notes of a bugle sounding through the dark.
The moon is in mid-heaven, but there's no one to share it with
me.
My messengers are scattered by whirls of rain and sand.
City-gates are closed to a traveller; mountains are walls in my
way—
Yet, I who have borne ten years of pitiable existence,
Find here a perch, a little branch, and am safe for this one night.

Night in the Watch-Tower

While winter daylight shortens in the elemental scale
And snow and frost whiten the cold-circling night,

Stark sounds the fifth-watch with a challenge of drum and bugle.
. . . The stars and the River of Heaven pulse over the three
    mountains;
I hear women in the distance, wailing after the battle;
I see barbarian fishermen and woodcutters in the dawn.
. . . Sleeping-Dragon, Plunging-Horse, are no generals now,
    they are dust—
Hush for a moment, O tumult of the world.

(84, 49d)

Thoughts of Old Time

I

Ten thousand ranges and valleys approach the Ching Gate
And the village in which the Lady of Light was born and bred.
She went out from the purple palace into the desert-land;
She has now become a green grave in the yellow dusk.
Her face!—Can you picture a wind of the spring?
Her spirit by moonlight returns with a tinkling
Song of the Tartars on her jade guitar,
Telling her eternal sorrow.

(25)

II

Chu-kê's prestige transcends the earth;
There is only reverence for his face;
Yet his will, among the Three Kingdoms at war,
Was only as one feather against a flaming sky.
He was brother of men like Yi and Lü
And in time would have surpassed the greatest of all statesmen.
Though he knew there was no hope for the House of Han,
Yet he wielded his mind for it, yielded his life.

(49, 49b, 49c, 85)

A View of T'ai-shan

What shall I say of the Great Peak?—
The ancient dukedoms are everywhere green,
Inspired and stirred by the breath of creation,
With the Twin Forces balancing day and night.
. . . I bare my breast toward opening clouds,
I strain my sight after birds flying home.
When shall I reach the top and hold
All mountains in a single glance?

(14, 19)

To My Retired Friend Wêi

It is almost as hard for friends to meet
As for the morning and evening stars.
Tonight then is a rare event,
Joining, in the candlelight,
Two men who were young not long ago
But now are turning grey at the temples.
. . . To find that half our friends are dead
Shocks us, burns our hearts with grief.
We little guessed it would be twenty years
Before I could visit you again.
When I went away, you were still unmarried;
But now these boys and girls in a row
Are very kind to their father's old friend.
They ask me where I have been on my journey;
And then, when we have talked awhile,
They bring and show me wines and dishes,
Spring chives cut in the night-rain
And brown rice cooked freshly a special way.
. . . My host proclaims it a festival,
He urges me to drink ten cups—
But what ten cups could make me as drunk
As I always am with your love in my heart?

. . . Tomorrow the mountains will separate us;
After tomorrow—who can say?

Alone in Her Beauty

Who is lovelier than she?
Yet she lives alone in an empty valley.
She tells me she came from a good family
Which is humbled now into the dust.
. . . When trouble arose in the Kuan district,
Her brothers and close kin were killed.
What use were their high offices,
Not even shielding their own lives?—
The world has but scorn for adversity;
Hope goes out, like the light of a candle.
Her husband, with a vagrant heart,
Seeks a new face like a new piece of jade;
And when morning-glories furl at night
And mandarin-ducks lie side by side,
All he can see is the smile of the new love,
While the old love weeps unheard.
The brook was pure in its mountain source,
But away from the mountain its waters darken.
. . . Waiting for her maid to come from selling pearls
For straw to cover the roof again,
She picks a few flowers, no longer for her hair,
And lets pine-needles fall through her fingers,
And, forgetting her thin silk sleeve and the cold,
She leans in the sunset by a tall bamboo.

Seeing Li Po in a Dream

I

There are sobs when death is the cause of parting;
But life has its partings again and again.

. . . From the poisonous damps of the southern river
You had sent me not one sign from your exile—
Till you came to me last night in a dream,
Because I am always thinking of you. . . .
I wondered if it were really you,
Venturing so long a journey.
You came to me through the green of a forest,
You disappeared by a shadowy fortress . . .
Yet out of the midmost mesh of your snare,
How could you lift your wings and use them?
. . . I woke, and the low moon's glimmer on a rafter
Seemed to be your face, still floating in the air.
. . . There were waters to cross, they were wild and tossing;
If you fell, there were dragons and river-monsters.

II

This cloud, that has drifted all day through the sky,
May, like a wanderer, never come back. . . .
Three nights now I have dreamed of you—
As tender, intimate and real as though I were awake.
And then, abruptly rising to go,
You told me the perils of adventure
By river and lake—the storms, the wrecks,
The fears that are borne on a little boat;
And, here in my doorway, you rubbed your white head
As if there were something puzzling you.
. . . Our capital teems with officious people,
While you are alone and helpless and poor.
Who says that the heavenly net never fails?
It has brought you ill fortune, old as you are.
. . . A thousand years' fame, ten thousand years' fame—
What good, when you are dead and gone?

(86)

A Drawing of a Horse by General Ts'ao at Secretary Wêi Fêng's House

Throughout this dynasty no one had painted horses
Like the master-spirit, Prince Chiang-tu—
And then to General Ts'ao through his thirty years of fame
The world's gaze turned, for royal steeds.
He painted the late Emperor's luminous white horse.
For ten days the thunder flew over Dragon Lake,
And a pink-agate plate was sent him from the palace—
The talk of the court-ladies, the marvel of all eyes.
The General danced, receiving it in his honoured home. . . .
After this rare gift, followed rapidly fine silks
From many of the nobles, requesting that his art
Lend a new lustre to their screens.
 . . . First came the curly-maned horse of Emperor T'ai-tsung,
Then, for the Kuos, a lion-spotted horse . . .
But now in this painting I see two horses,
A sobering sight for whosoever knew them.
They are war-horses. Either could face ten thousand.
They make the white silk stretch away into a vast desert.
And the seven others with them are almost as noble. . . .
Mist and snow are moving across a cold sky,
And hoofs are cleaving snow-drifts under great trees—
With here a group of officers and there a group of servants.
See how these nine horses all vie with one another—
The high clear glance, the deep firm breath.
 . . . Who understands distinction? Who really cares for art?
You, Wêi Fêng, have followed Ts'ao; Chih Tun preceded him.
 . . . I remember when the late Emperor came toward his Sum-
    mer Palace,
The procession, in green-feathered rows, swept from the eastern
    sky—
Thirty thousand horses, prancing, galloping,
Fashioned, every one of them, like the horses in this picture. . . .

But now the Imperial Ghost receives secret jade from the River-
   God,
For the Emperor hunts crocodiles no longer by the streams.
Where you see his Great Gold Tomb, you may hear among the
   pines
A bird grieving in the wind that the Emperor's horses are gone.
(87)

A Song of a Painting

To General Ts'ao

O General, descended from Wêi's Emperor Wu,
You are nobler now than when a noble. . . .
Conquerors and their valour perish,
But masters of beauty live forever.
   . . . With your brush-work learned from Lady Wêi
And second only to Wang Hsi-chih's,
Faithful to your art, you know no age,
Letting wealth and fame drift by like clouds.
   . . . In the years of K'ai-yüan you were much with the Emperor,
Accompanied him often to the Court of the South Wind.
When the spirit left great statesmen, on walls of the Hall of Fame
The point of your brush preserved their living faces.
You crowned all the premiers with coronets of office;
You fitted all commanders with arrows at their girdles;
You made the founders of this dynasty, with every hair alive,
Seem to be just back from the fierceness of a battle.
   . . . The late Emperor had a horse, known as Jade Flower,
Whom artists had copied in various poses.
They led him one day to the red marble stairs
With his eyes toward the palace in the deepening air.
Then, General, commanded to proceed with your work,
You centred all your being on a piece of silk.
And later, when your dragon-horse, born of the sky,
Had banished earthly horses for ten thousand generations,

There was one Jade Flower standing on the dais
And another by the steps, and they marvelled at each other. . . .
The Emperor rewarded you with smiles and with gifts,
While officers and men of the stud hung about and stared.
. . . Han Kan, your follower, has likewise grown proficient
At representing horses in all their attitudes;
But picturing the flesh, he fails to draw the bone—
So that even the finest are deprived of their spirit.
You, beyond the mere skill, used your art divinely—
And expressed, not only horses, but the life of a good man. . . .
Yet here you are, wandering in a world of disorder
And sketching from time to time some petty passer-by.
People note your case with the whites of their eyes.
There's nobody purer, there's nobody poorer.
. . . Read in the records, from earliest times,
How hard it is to be a great artist.

(88)

A Letter to Censor Han

I am sad. My thoughts are in Yo-chou.
I would hurry there—but I am sick in bed.
. . . Beauty would be facing me across the autumn waters.
Oh, to wash my feet in Lake Tung-t'ing and see at its eight
    corners
Wildgeese flying high, sun and moon both white,
Green maples changing to red in the frosty sky,
Angels bound for the Capital of Heaven, near the North Star,
Riding, some of them phœnixes, and others unicorns,
With banners of hibiscus and with melodies of mist,
Their shadows dancing upside-down in the southern rivers,
Till the Queen of the Stars, drowsy with her nectar,
Would forget the winged men on either side of her!
. . . From the Wizard of the Red Pine this word has come for
    me:

That after his earlier follower he has now a new disciple
Who, formerly at the capital as Emperor Liu's adviser,
In spite of great successes, never could be happy.
. . . What are a country's rise and fall?
Can flesh-pots be as fragrant as mountain fruit? . . .
I grieve that he is lost far away in the south.
May the star of long life accord him its blessing!
. . . O purity, to seize you from beyond the autumn waters
And to place you as an offering in the Court of Imperial Jade.
(89)

A Song of an Old Cypress

Beside the Temple of the Great Premier stands an ancient cypress
With a trunk of green bronze and a root of stone.
The girth of its white bark would be the reach of forty men
And its tip of kingfisher-blue is two thousand feet in heaven.
Dating from the days of a great ruler's great statesman,
Their very tree is loved now and honoured by the people.
Clouds come to it from far away, from the Wu cliffs,
And the cold moon glistens on its peak of snow.
. . . East of the Silk Pavilion yesterday I found
The ancient ruler and wise statesman both worshipped in one
    temple,
Whose tree, with curious branches, ages the whole landscape
In spite of the fresh colours of the windows and the doors.
And so firm is the deep root, so established underground,
That its lone lofty boughs can dare the weight of winds,
Its only protection the Heavenly Power,
Its only endurance the art of its Creator.
. . . When beams are required to restore a great house,
Though oxen sway ten thousand heads, they cannot move a
    mountain.
Though a tree writes no memorial, yet people understand
That not unless they fell it can use be made of it. . . .

Its bitter heart may be tenanted now by black and white ants,
But its odorous leaves were once the nest of phœnixes and
    pheasants.
. . . Let wise and hopeful men harbour no complaint.
The greater the timber, the tougher it is to use.

(90)

A Song of Dagger-Dancing

To a Girl-Pupil of Lady Kung-sun

*(On the 19th of the Tenth-month in the second year of Ta-li, I
saw, in the house of the K'uêi-fu official Yüan T'ê, a girl named
Li from Lin-ying dancing with a dagger. I admired her skill and
asked who was her teacher. She named Lady Kung-sun. I
remembered that in the third year of K'ai-yüan at Yen-ch'êng,
when I was a little boy, I saw Lady Kung-sun dance. She was the
only one in the Imperial Theatre who could dance with this
weapon. Now she is aged and unknown, and even her pupil has
passed the heyday of beauty. I wrote this poem to express my
wistfulness. The work of Chang Hsü of the Wu district, that
great master of grassy writing, was improved by his having
been present when Lady Kung-sun danced in the Yeh district.
From this may be judged the art of Kung-sun.)*

There lived years ago the beautiful Kung-sun,
Who, dancing with her dagger, drew from all four quarters
An audience like mountains lost among themselves.
Heaven and earth moved back and forth, following her motions,
Which were bright as when the Archer shot the nine suns down
    the sky
And rapid as angels before the wings of dragons.
She began like a thunderbolt, venting its anger,
And ended like the shining calm of rivers and the sea . . .
But vanished are those red lips and those pearly sleeves;
And none but this one pupil bears the perfume of her fame,

This beauty from Lin-ying, at the Town of the White God,
Dancing still and singing in the old blithe way.
And while we reply to each other's questions,
We sigh together, saddened by changes that have come.
There were eight thousand ladies in the late Emperor's court,
But none could dance the dagger-dance like Lady Kung-sun.
. . . Fifty years have passed, like the turning of a palm;
Wind and dust, filling the world, obscure the Imperial House.
Instead of the Pear-Garden Players, who have blown by like a
   mist,
There are one or two girl-musicians now—trying to charm the
   cold Sun.
There are man-size trees by the Emperor's Golden Tomb. . . .
I seem to hear dead grasses rattling on the cliffs of Ch'ü-t'ang.
. . . The song is done, the slow string and quick pipe have
   ceased.
At the height of joy, sorrow comes with the eastern moon rising.
And I, a poor old man, not knowing where to go,
Must harden my feet on the lone hills, toward sickness and
   despair.

(91)

A Song of War-Chariots

(*Written to Music*)

The war-chariots rattle,
The war-horses whinny.
Each man of you has a bow and a quiver at his belt.
Father, mother, son, wife, stare at you going,
Till dust shall have buried the bridge beyond Ch'ang-an.
They run with you, crying, they tug at your sleeves,
And the sound of their sorrow goes up to the clouds;
And every time a bystander asks you a question,
You can only say to him that you have to go.

. . . We remember others at fifteen sent north to guard the river
And at forty sent west to cultivate the camp-farms.
The mayor wound their turbans for them when they started out.
With their turbaned hair white now, they are still at the border,
At the border where the blood of men spills like the sea—
And still the heart of Emperor Wu is beating for war.
. . . Do you know that, east of China's mountains, in two hun-
    dred districts
And in thousands of villages, nothing grows but weeds,
And though strong women have bent to the ploughing,
East and west the furrows all are broken down?
. . . Men of China are able to face the stiffest battle,
But their officers drive them like chickens and dogs.
Whatever is asked of them,
Dare they complain?
For example, this winter
Held west of the gate,
Challenged for taxes,
How could they pay?
. . . We have learned that to have a son is bad luck—
It is very much better to have a daughter
Who can marry and live in the house of a neighbour,
While under the sod we bury our boys.
. . . Go to the Blue Sea, look along the shore
At all the old white bones forsaken—
New ghosts are wailing there now with the old,
Loudest in the dark sky of a stormy day.

A Song of Fair Women

(Written to Music)

On the third day of the Third-month in the freshening weather
Many beauties take the air by the Ch'ang-an water-front,
Receptive, aloof, sweet-mannered, sincere,
With soft fine skin and well-balanced bone.

Their embroidered silk robes in the spring sun are gleaming
With a mass of golden peacocks and silver unicorns.
And hanging far down from their temples
Are blue leaves of delicate kingfisher feathers.
And followng behind them
Is a pearl-laden train, rhythmic with bearers.
Some of them are kindred to the Royal House—
The titled Princesses Kuo and Ch'in.
Red camel-humps are brought them from jade broilers,
And sweet fish is offered them on crystal trays.
Though their food-sticks of unicorn-horn are lifted languidly
And the finely wrought phœnix carving-knife is very little used,
Fleet horses from the Yellow Gate, stirring no dust,
Bring precious dishes constantly from the imperial kitchen.
. . . While a solemn sound of flutes and drums invokes gods
    and spirits,
Guests and courtiers gather, all of high rank;
And finally, riding slow, a dignified horseman
Dismounts at the pavilion on an embroidered rug.
In a snow of flying willow-cotton whitening the duckweed,
Bluebirds find their way with vermilion handkerchiefs—
But power can be as hot as flame and burn people's fingers.
Be wary of the Premier, watch for his frown.

(4)

A Song of Sobbing by the River
(Written to Music)

I am only an old woodsman, whispering a sob,
As I steal like a spring-shadow down the Winding River.
. . . Since the palaces ashore are sealed by a thousand gates—
Fine willows, new rushes, for whom are you so green?
. . . I remember a cloud of flags that came from the South
    Garden,
And ten thousand colours, heightening one another,
And the Kingdom's first Lady, from the Palace of the Bright Sun,

Attendant on the Emperor in his royal chariot,
And the horsemen before them, each with bow and arrows,
And the snowy horses, champing at bits of yellow gold,
And an archer, breast skyward, shooting through the clouds
And felling with one dart a pair of flying birds.
. . . Where are those perfect eyes, where are those pearly teeth?
A blood-stained spirit has no home, has nowhere to return.
And clear Wêi waters running east, through the cleft on Dagger-
Tower Trail,
Carry neither there nor here any news of her.
People, compassionate, are wishing with tears
That she were as eternal as the river and the flowers.
. . . Mounted Tartars, in the yellow twilight, cloud the town
with dust.
I am fleeing south, but I linger—gazing northward toward the
throne.

(4a)

A Song of a Prince Deposed

(Written to Music)

Along the wall of the Capital a white-headed crow
Flies to the Gate where Autumn Enters and screams there in the
night,
Then turns again and pecks among the roofs of a tall mansion
Whose lord, a mighty mandarin, has fled before the Tartars,
With his golden whip now broken, his nine war-horses dead
And his own flesh and bone scattered to the winds. . . .
There's a rare ring of green coral underneath the vest
Of a Prince at a street-corner, bitterly sobbing,
Who has to give a false name to anyone who asks him—
Just a poor fellow, hoping for employment.
A hundred days' hiding in grasses and thorns
Show on his body from head to foot.
But, since their first Emperor, all with hook-noses,

These Dragons look different from ordinary men.
Wolves are in the palace now and Dragons are lost in the desert—
O Prince, be very careful of your most sacred person!
I dare not address you long, here by the open road,
Nor even to stand beside you for more than these few moments.
Last night with the spring-wind there came a smell of blood;
The old Capital is full of camels from the east.
Our northern warriors are sound enough of body and of hand—
Oh, why so brave in olden times and so craven now?
Our Emperor, we hear, has given his son the throne
And the southern border-chieftains are loyally inclined
And the Hua-mên and Li-mien tribes are gathering to avenge us.
But still be careful—keep yourself well hidden from the dagger.
Unhappy Prince, I beg you, be constantly on guard—
Till power blow to your aid from the Five Imperial Tombs.

(4d, 92)

TU HSÜN-HÊ

鵑 荀 杜

A Sigh in the Spring Palace

Knowing beauty my misfortune,
I face my mirror with a sigh.
To please a fastidious emperor,
How shall I array myself? . . .
Birds flock and sing when the wind is warm,
Flower-shadows climb when the sun is high—
And year after year girls in the south
Are picking hibiscus, dreaming of love!

(93)

TU MU

牧 杜

I Climb to the Lo-yu Tombs
Before Leaving for Wu-hsing

Even in this good reign, how can I serve?
The lone cloud rather, the Buddhist peace . . .
Once more, before crossing river and sea,
I face the great Emperor's mountain-tomb.

(94)

By the Purple Cliff

On a part of a spear still unrusted in the sand
I have burnished the symbol of an ancient kingdom. . . .
Except for a wind aiding General Chou Yü,
Spring would have sealed both Ch'iao girls in Copper-Bird
     Palace.

(52a)

A Mooring on the Ch'in-huai River

Mist veils the cold stream, and moonlight the sand,
As I moor in the shadow of a river-tavern,
Where girls, with no thought of a perished kingdom,
Gaily echo *A Song of Courtyard Flowers.*

(4a)

A Message to Han Cho
the Yang-chou Magistrate

There are faint green mountains and far green waters,
And grasses in this river region not yet faded by autumn;
And clear in the moon on the Twenty-Four Bridges,
Girls white as jade are teaching flute-music.

(95)

A Confession

With my wine-bottle, watching by river and lake
For a lady so tiny as to dance on my palm,
I awake, after dreaming ten years in Yang-chou,
Known as fickle, even in the Street of Blue Houses.

(26a, 45a)

In the Autumn Night

Her candle-light is silvery on her chill bright screen.
Her little silk fan is for fireflies. . . .
She lies watching her staircase cold in the moon,
And two stars parted by the River of Heaven.

(96)

Parting

I

She is slim and supple and not yet fourteen,
The young spring-tip of a cardamon-spray.
On the Yang-chou Road for three miles in the breeze
Every pearl-screen is open. But there's no one like her.

II

How can a deep love seem deep love,
How can it smile, at a farewell feast?
Even the candle, feeling our sadness,
Weeps, as we do, all night long.

The Garden of the Golden Valley

Stories of passion make sweet dust,
Calm water, grasses unconcerned.
At sunset, when birds cry in the wind,
Petals are falling like a girl's robe long ago.

(97)

A Night at a Tavern

Solitary at the tavern,
I am shut in with loneliness and grief.
Under the cold lamp, I brood on the past;
I am kept awake by a lost wildgoose.
. . . Roused at dawn from a misty dream,
I read, a year late, news from home—
And I remember the moon like smoke on the river
And a fisher-boat moored there, under my door.

(98)

TU SHÊN-YEN

言審杜

On a Walk in the Early Spring

Harmonizing a Poem by My Friend Lu
Stationed at Ch'ang-chou

Only to wanderers can come
Ever new the shock of beauty,
Of white cloud and red cloud dawning from the sea,
Of spring in the wild-plum and river-willow. . . .
I watch a yellow oriole dart in the warm air,
And a green water-plant reflected by the sun.
Suddenly an old song fills
My heart with home, my eyes with tears.

(99, 9)

WANG CH'ANG-LING

齡昌王

At Hibiscus Inn

Parting with Hsin Chien

With this cold night-rain hiding the river, you have come into
　　Wu.
In the level dawn, all alone, you will be starting for the
　　mountains of Ch'u.
Answer, if they ask of me at Lo-yang:
"One-hearted as ice in a crystal vase."

In Her Quiet Window

Too young to have learned what sorrow means,
Attired for spring, she climbs to her high chamber. . . .
The new green of the street-willows is wounding her heart—
Just for a title she sent him to war.

A Song of the Spring Palace

Last night, while a gust blew peach-petals open
And the moon shone high on the Palace Beyond Time,
The Emperor gave P'ing-yang, for her dancing,
Brocades against the cold spring-wind.

(93)

A Sigh in the Court of Perpetual Faith

(Written to Music)

She brings a broom at dawn to the Golden Palace doorway
And dusts the hall from end to end with her round fan,
And, for all her jade-whiteness, she envies a crow
Whose cold wings are kindled in the Court of the Bright Sun.

(100)

Over the Border

(Written to Music)

The moon goes back to the time of Ch'in, the wall to the time
    of Han,
And the road our troops are travelling goes back three hundred
    miles. . . .
Oh, for the Winged General at the Dragon City—
That never a Tartar horseman might cross the Yin Mountains!

(59)

With My Brother at the South Study

*Thinking in the Moonlight of Vice-Prefect
Ts'uêi in Shan-yin*

Lying on a high seat in the south study,
We have lifted the curtain—and we see the rising moon
Brighten with pure light the water and the grove
And flow like a wave on our window and our door.
It will move through the cycle, full moon and then crescent again,
Calmly, beyond our wisdom, altering new to old.
. . . Our chosen one, our friend, is now by a limpid river—
Singing, perhaps, a plaintive eastern song.
He is far, far away from us, three hundred miles away.
And yet a breath of orchids comes along the wind.

(101)

At a Border-Fortress

(Written to Music)

Cicadas complain of thin mulberry-trees
In the Eighth-month chill at the frontier pass.
Through the gate and back again, all along the road,
There is nothing anywhere but yellow reeds and grasses
And the bones of soldiers from Yu and from Ping
Who have buried their lives in the dusty sand.
. . . Let never a cavalier stir you to envy
With boasts of his horse and his horsemanship.

Under a Border-Fortress

(Written to Music)

Drink, my horse, while we cross the autumn water!—
The stream is cold and the wind like a sword,
As we watch against the sunset on the sandy plain,
Far, far away, shadowy Lin-t'ao.
Old battles, waged by those long walls,
Once were proud on all men's tongues.
But antiquity now is a yellow dust,
Confusing in the grasses its ruins and white bones.

WANG CHIEN

建 王

A Bride

On the third day, taking my place to cook,
Washing my hands to make the bridal soup,
I decide that not my mother-in-law
But my husband's young sister shall have the first taste.

WANG CHIH-HUAN

渙之王

At Heron Lodge

Mountains cover the white sun,
And oceans drain the golden river;
But you widen your view three hundred miles
By going up one flight of stairs.

Beyond the Border

A Song of Liang-chou

Where a yellow river climbs to the white clouds,
Near the one city-wall among ten-thousand-foot mountains,
A Tartar under the willows is lamenting on his flute
That spring never blows to him through the Jade Pass.

(102)

WANG HAN

A Song of Liang-chou

They sing, they drain their cups of jade,
They strum on horseback their guitars.
. . . Why laugh when they fall asleep drunk on the sand?—
How many soldiers ever come home?

WANG PO

勃 王

Farewell to Vice-Prefect Tu
Setting Out for His Official Post in Shu

By this wall that surrounds the three Ch'in districts,
Through a mist that makes five rivers one,
We bid each other a sad farewell,
We two officials going opposite ways. . . .
And yet, while China holds our friendship,
And heaven remains our neighbourhood,
Why should you linger at the fork of the road,
Wiping your eyes like a heart-broken child?

WANG WAN

A Mooring Under North Fort Hill

Under blue mountains we wound our way,
My boat and I, along green water;
Until the banks at low tide widened,
With no wind stirring my lone sail.
. . . Night now yields to a sea of sun,
And the old year melts in freshets.
At last I can send my messengers—
Wildgeese, homing to Lo-yang.

WANG WÊI

維 王

Deer-Park Hermitage

There seems to be no one on the empty mountain . . .
And yet I think I hear a voice,
Where sunlight, entering a grove,
Shines back to me from the green moss.
(103)

In a Retreat Among Bamboos

Leaning alone in the close bamboos,
I am playing my lute and humming a song
Too softly for anyone to hear—
Except my comrade, the bright moon.

A Parting

Friend, I have watched you down the mountain
Till now in the dark I close my thatch door. . . .
Grasses return again green in the spring,
But O my Prince of Friends, do you?
(68)

One-Hearted

When those red berries come in springtime,
Flushing on your southland branches,
Take home an armful, for my sake,
As a symbol of our love.

Lines

You who have come from my old country,
Tell me what has happened there!—
Was the plum, when you passed my silken window,
Opening its first cold blossom?

On the Mountain Holiday

Thinking of My Brothers in Shan-tung

All alone in a foreign land,
I am twice as homesick on this day
When brothers carry dogwood up the mountain,
Each of them a branch—and my branch missing.
(64)

A Song at Wêi-ch'êng

(Written to Music)

A morning-rain has settled the dust in Wêi-ch'êng;
Willows are green again in the tavern dooryard. . . .
Wait till we empty one more cup—
West of Yang Gate there'll be no old friends.
(104)

A Song of an Autumn Night

(Written to Music)

Under the crescent moon a light autumn dew
Has chilled the robe she will not change—
And she touches a silver lute all night,
Afraid to go back to her empty room.

A Message from My Lodge at Wang-ch'üan

To P'ei Ti

The mountains are cold and blue now
And the autumn waters have run all day.
By my thatch door, leaning on my staff,
I listen to cicadas in the evening wind.
Sunset lingers at the ferry,
Supper-smoke floats up from the houses.
. . . Oh, when shall I pledge the great Hermit again
And sing a wild poem at Five Willows?

(34, 2a)

An Autumn Evening in the Mountains

After rain the empty mountain
Stands autumnal in the evening,
Moonlight in its groves of pine,
Stones of crystal in its brooks.
Bamboos whisper of washer-girls bound home,
Lotus-leaves yield before a fisher-boat—
And what does it matter that springtime has gone,
While you are here, O Prince of Friends?

(68)

Bound Home to Mount Sung

The limpid river, past its bushes
Running slowly as my chariot,
Becomes a fellow voyager
Returning home with the evening birds.
A ruined city-wall overtops an old ferry,
Autumn sunset floods the peaks.

. . . Far away, beside Mount Sung,
I shall close my door and be at peace.
(14)

Mount Chung-nan

Its massive height near the City of Heaven
Joins a thousand mountains to the corner of the sea.
Clouds, when I look back, close behind me,
Mists, when I enter them, are gone.
A central peak divides the wilds
And weather into many valleys.
. . . Needing a place to spend the night,
I call to a wood-cutter over the river.
(32)

Answering Vice-Prefect Chang

As the years go by, give me but peace,
Freedom from ten thousand matters.
I ask myself and always answer:
What can be better than coming home?
A wind from the pine-trees blows my sash,
And my lute is bright with the mountain moon.
You ask me about good and evil fortune? . . .
Hark, on the lake there's a fisherman singing!

Toward the Temple of Heaped Fragrance

Not knowing the way to the Temple of Heaped Fragrance,
Under miles of mountain-cloud I have wandered
Through ancient woods without a human track;
But now on the height I hear a bell.
A rillet sings over winding rocks,

The sun is tempered by green pines. . . .
And at twilight, close to an emptying pool,
Thought can conquer the Passion-Dragon.

A Message to Commissioner Li
at Tsŭ-chou

From ten thousand valleys the trees touch heaven;
On a thousand peaks cuckoos are calling;
And, after a night of mountain rain,
From each summit come hundreds of silken cascades.
 . . . If girls are asked in tribute the fibre they weave,
Or farmers quarrel over taro fields,
Preside as wisely as Wên-wêng did. . . .
Is fame to be only for the ancients?
(105)

A View of the Han River

With its three southern branches reaching the Ch'u border,
And its nine streams touching the gateway of Ching,
This river runs beyond heaven and earth,
Where the colour of mountains both is and is not.
The dwellings of men seem floating along
On ripples of the distant sky—
These beautiful days here in Hsiang-yang
Make drunken my old mountain heart!

My Retreat at Mount Chung-nan

My heart in middle age found the Way,
And I came to dwell at the foot of this mountain.
When the spirit moves, I wander alone
Amid beauty that is all for me. . . .

I will walk till the water checks my path,
Then sit and watch the rising clouds—
And some day meet an old wood-cutter
And talk and laugh and never return.

(32, 75)

An Early Audience at the
Palace of Light

Harmonizing Secretary Chia Chih's Poem

The red-capped Cock-Man has just announced morning;
The Keeper of the Robes brings Jade-Cloud Furs;
Heaven's nine doors reveal the palace and its courtyards;
And the coats of many countries bow to the Pearl Crown.
Sunshine has entered the giants' carven palms;
Incense wreathes the Dragon Robe:
The audience adjourns—and the five-coloured edict
Sets girdle-beads clinking toward the Lake of the Phœnix.

(9, 9a, 106)

Looking Down in a Spring-Rain
on the Course from Fairy-Mountain
Palace to the Pavilion of Increase

Harmonizing the Emperor's Poem

Round a turn of the Ch'in Fortress winds the Wêi River,
And Yellow Mountain foot-hills enclose the Court of China;
Past the South Gate willows comes the Car of Many Bells
On the upper Palace-Garden Road—a solid length of blossom;
A Forbidden City roof holds two phœnixes in cloud;
The foliage of spring shelters multitudes from rain;
And now, when the heavens are propitious for action,
Here is our Emperor ready—no wasteful wanderer.

(4a, 9)

In My Lodge at Wang-ch'üan
After a Long Rain

The woods have stored the rain, and slow comes the smoke
As rice is cooked on faggots and carried to the fields;
Over the quiet marsh-land flies a white egret,
And mango-birds are singing in the full summer trees. . . .
I have learned to watch in peace the mountain morning-glories,
To eat split dewy sunflower-seeds under a bough of pine,
To yield the post of honour to any boor at all . . .
Why should I frighten sea-gulls, even with a thought?
(107)

Harmonizing a Poem By
Palace-Attendant Kuo

High beyond the thick wall a tower shines with sunset
Where peach and plum are blooming and the willow-cotton flies.
You have heard in your office the court-bell of twilight;
Birds find perches, officials head for home.
Your morning-jade will tinkle as you thread the golden palace;
You will bring the word of Heaven from the closing gates at
    night.
And I should serve there with you; but being full of years,
I have taken off official robes and am resting from my troubles.
(9)

At Parting

I dismount from my horse and I offer you wine,
And I ask you where you are going and why.
And you answer: "I am discontent
And would rest at the foot of the southern mountain.
So give me leave and ask me no questions.
White clouds pass there without end."

To Ch'i-wu Ch'ien Bound Home
After Failing in an Examination

In a happy reign there should be no hermits;
The wise and able should consult together. . . .
So you, a man of the eastern mountains,
Gave up your life of picking herbs
And came all the way to the Gate of Gold—
But you found your devotion unavailing.
. . . To spend the Day of No Fire on one of the southern rivers,
You have mended your spring clothes here in these northern
    cities.
I pour you the farewell wine as you set out from the capital—
Soon I shall be left behind here by my bosom-friend.
In your sail-boat of sweet cinnamon-wood
You will float again toward your own thatch door,
Led along by distant trees
To a sunset shining on a far-away town.
. . . What though your purpose happened to fail,
Doubt not that some of us can hear high music.

(1, 54)

A Green Stream

I have sailed the River of Yellow Flowers,
Borne by the channel of a green stream,
Rounding ten thousand turns through the mountains
On a journey of less than thirty miles. . . .
Rapids hum over heaped rocks;
But where light grows dim in the thick pines,
The surface of an inlet sways with nut-horns
And weeds are lush along the banks.
. . . Down in my heart I have always been as pure
As this limpid water is. . . .
Oh, to remain on a broad flat rock
And to cast a fishing-line forever!

A Farm-House on the Wêi River

In the slant of the sun on the country-side,
Cattle and sheep trail home along the lane;
And a rugged old man in a thatch door
Leans on a staff and thinks of his son, the herd-boy.
There are whirring pheasants, full wheat-ears,
Silk-worms asleep, pared mulberry-leaves.
And the farmers, returning with hoes on their shoulders,
Hail one another familiarly.
. . . No wonder I long for the simple life
And am sighing the old song, *Oh, to Go Back Again!*
(108)

The Beautiful Hsi Shih

Since beauty is honoured all over the Empire,
How could Hsi Shih remain humbly at home?—
Washing clothes at dawn by a southern lake—
And that evening a great lady in a palace of the north:
Lowly one day, no different from the others,
The next day exalted, everyone praising her.
No more would her own hands powder her face
Or arrange on her shoulders a silken robe.
And the more the King loved her, the lovelier she looked,
Blinding him away from wisdom.
. . . Girls who had once washed silk beside her
Were kept at a distance from her chariot.
And none of the girls in her neighbours' houses
By pursing their brows could copy her beauty.
(109)

A Song of a Girl from Lo-yang

(*Written to Music*)

There's a girl from Lo-yang in the door across the street,
She looks fifteen, she may be a little older.
. . . While her master rides his rapid horse with jade bit and
    bridle,
Her handmaid brings her cod-fish in a golden plate.
On her painted pavilions, facing red towers,
Cornices are pink and green with peach-bloom and with willow.
Canopies of silk awn her seven-scented chair,
And rare fans shade her, home to her nine-flowered curtains.
Her lord, with rank and wealth and in the bud of life,
Exceeds in munificence the richest men of old.
He favours this girl of lowly birth, he has her taught to dance;
And he gives away his coral-trees to almost anyone.
The wind of dawn just stirs when his nine soft lights go out,
Those nine soft lights like petals in a flying chain of flowers.
Between dances she has barely time for singing over the songs;
No sooner is she dressed again than incense burns before her.
Those she knows in town are only the rich and the lavish,
And day and night she is visiting the hosts of the gayest
    mansions.
. . . Who notices the girl from Yüeh with a face of white jade,
Humble, poor, alone, by the river, washing silk?

(*110*)

A Song of an Old General

(*Written to Music*)

When he was a youth of fifteen or twenty,
He chased a wild horse, he caught him and rode him,
He shot the white-browed mountain tiger,
He defied the yellow-bristled Horseman of Yeh.
Fighting single-handed for a thousand miles,
With his naked dagger he could hold a multitude.

. . . Granted that the troops of China were as swift as heaven's thunder

And that Tartar soldiers perished in pitfalls fanged with iron,

General Wêi Ch'ing's victory was only a thing of chance.

And General Li Kuang's thwarted effort was his fate, not his fault.

Since this man's retirement he is looking old and worn:

Experience of the world has hastened his white hairs.

Though once his quick dart never missed the right eye of a bird,

Now knotted veins and tendons make his left arm like an osier.

He is sometimes at the road-side selling melons from his garden,

He is sometimes planting willows round his hermitage.

His lonely lane is shut away by a dense grove,

His vacant window looks upon the far cold mountains. . . .

But, if he prayed, the waters would come gushing for his men

And never would he wanton his cause away with wine.

. . . War-clouds are spreading, under the Ho-lan Range;

Back and forth, day and night, go feathered messages;

In the three River Provinces, the governors call young men—

And five imperial edicts have summoned the old general.

So he dusts his iron coat and shines it like snow—

Waves his dagger from its jade hilt to a dance of starry steel.

He is ready with his strong northern bow to smite the Tartar chieftain—

That never a foreign war-dress may affront the Emperor.

. . . There once was an aged Prefect, forgotten and far away,

Who still could manage triumph with a single stroke.

(111)

A Song of Peach-Blossom River
(Written to Music)

A fisherman is drifting, enjoying the spring mountains,

And the peach-trees on both banks lead him to an ancient source.

Watching the fresh-coloured trees, he never thinks of distance

Till he comes to the end of the blue stream and suddenly—strange men!

It's a cave—with a mouth so narrow that he has to crawl
   through;
But then it opens wide again on a broad and level path—
And far beyond he faces clouds crowning a reach of trees,
And thousands of houses shadowed round with flowers and
   bamboos. . . .
Woodsmen tell him their names in the ancient speech of Han;
And clothes of the Ch'in Dynasty are worn by all these people
Living on the uplands, above the Wu-ling River,
On farms and in gardens that are like a world apart,
Their dwellings at peace under pines in the clear moon,
Until sunrise fills the low sky with crowing and barking.
. . . At news of a stranger the people all assemble,
And each of them invites him home and asks him where he was
   born.
Alleys and paths are cleared for him of petals in the morning,
And fishermen and farmers bring him their loads at dusk. . . .
They had left the world long ago, they had come here seeking
   refuge;
They have lived like angels ever since, blessedly far away,
No one in the cave knowing anything outside,
Outsiders viewing only empty mountains and thick clouds.
. . . The fisherman, unaware of his great good fortune,
Begins to think of country, of home, of wordly ties,
Finds his way out of the cave again, past mountains and past
   rivers,
Intending some time to return, when he has told his kin.
He studies every step he takes, fixes it well in mind,
And forgets that cliffs and peaks may vary their appearance.
. . . It is certain that to enter through the deepness of the
   mountain,
A green river leads you, into a misty wood.
But now, with spring-floods everywhere and floating peach-
   petals—
Which is the way to go, to find that hidden source?

(2)

WÊI CHUANG

莊 韋

A Nan-king Landscape

Though a shower bends the river-grass, a bird is singing,
While ghosts of the Six Dynasties pass like a dream
Around the Forbidden City, under weeping willows
Which loom still for three miles along the misty moat.
(112)

A Night Thought on Terrace Tower

Far through the night a harp is sighing
With a sadness of wind and rain in the strings. . . .
There's a solitary lantern, a bugle-call—
And beyond Terrace Tower down goes the moon.
. . . Fragrant grasses have changed and faded
While still I have been hoping that my old friend would
    come. . . .
There are no more messengers I can send him,
Now that the wildgeese have turned south.
(39a)

WÊI YING-WU

韋應物

An Autumn Night Message
To Ch'iu

As I walk in the cool of the autumn night,
Thinking of you, singing my poem,
I hear a mountain pine-cone fall. . . .
You also seem to be awake.

At Ch'u-chou on the Western Stream

Where tender grasses rim the stream
And deep boughs trill with mango-birds,
On the spring flood of last night's rain
The ferry-boat moves as though someone were poling.
(113)

A Greeting on the Huai River
to My Old Friends from Liang-ch'üan

We used to be companions on the Kiang and the Han,
And as often as we met, we were likely to be tipsy.
Since we left one another, floating apart like clouds,
Ten years have run like water—till at last we join again.
And we talk again and laugh again just as in earlier days,
Except that the hair on our heads is tinged now with grey. . . .
Why not come along, then, all of us together,
And face the autumn mountains and sail along the Huai?

A Farewell in the Evening Rain
To Li Ts'ao

Is it raining on the river all the way to Ch'u?—
The evening bell comes to us from Nan-king.
Your wet sail drags and is loath to be going
And shadowy birds are flying slow.
We cannot see the deep ocean-gate—
Only the boughs at Pu-kou, newly dripping.
Likewise, because of our great love,
There are threads of water on our faces.

To My Friends Li Tan and Yüan Hsi

We met last among flowers, among flowers we parted,
And here, a year later, there are flowers again;
But, with ways of the world too strange to foretell,
Spring only brings me grief and fatigue.
I am sick, and I think of my home in the country—
Ashamed to take pay while so many are idle.
. . . In my western tower, because of your promise,
I have watched the full moons come and go.

Entertaining Literary Men
in My Official Residence
on a Rainy Day

Outside are insignia, shown in state;
But here are sweet incense-clouds, quietly ours.
Wind and rain, coming in from sea,
Have cooled this pavilion above the lake
And driven the feverish heat away
From where my eminent guests are gathered.
. . . Ashamed though I am of my high position
While people lead unhappy lives,

Let us reasonably banish care
And just be friends, enjoying nature.
Though we have to go without fish and meat,
There are fruits and vegetables aplenty.
. . . We bow, we take our cups of wine,
We give our attention to beautiful poems.
When the mind is exalted, the body is lightened
And feels as if it could float in the wind.
. . . Su-chou is famed as a centre of letters;
And all you writers, coming here,
Prove that the name of a great land
Is made by better things than wealth.

Setting Sail on the Yang-tsze

To Secretary Yüan

Wistful, away from my friends and kin,
Through mist and fog I float and float
With the sail that bears me toward Lo-yang.
In Yang-chou trees linger bell-notes of evening,
Marking the day and the place of our parting. . . .
When shall we meet again and where?
. . . Destiny is a boat on the waves,
Borne to and fro, beyond our will.

A Poem to a Taoist Hermit on Ch'üan-chiao Mountain

My office has grown cold today;
And I suddenly think of my mountain friend
Gathering firewood down in the valley
Or boiling white stones for potatoes in his hut . . .
I wish I might take him a cup of wine
To cheer him through the evening storm;

But in fallen leaves that have heaped the bare slopes,
How should I ever find his footprints!
(62a)

On Meeting My Friend Fêng Chu
in the Capital

Out of the east you visit me,
With the rain of Pa-ling still on your clothes,
I ask you what you have come here for;
You say: "To buy an ax for cutting wood in the mountains."
. . . Hidden deep in a haze of blossom,
Swallow fledglings chirp at ease
As they did when we parted, a year ago. . . .
How grey our temples have grown since then!

Mooring at Twilight in Yü-yi District

Furling my sail near the town of Huai,
I find for harbour a little cove
Where a sudden breeze whips up the waves.
. . . The sun is growing dim now and sinks in the dusk.
People are coming home. The bright mountain-peak darkens.
Wildgeese fly down to an island of white weeds.
. . . At midnight I think of a northern city-gate,
And I hear a bell tolling between me and sleep.

East of the Town

From office confinement all year long,
I have come out of town to be free this morning
Where willows harmonize the wind
And green hills lighten the cares of the world.
I lean by a tree and rest myself

Or wander up and down a stream.
. . . Mists have wet the fragrant meadows;
A spring dove calls from some hidden place.
. . . With quiet surroundings, the mind is at peace,
But beset with affairs, it grows restless again . . .
Here I shall finally build me a cabin,
As T'ao Ch'ien built one long ago.

(2a)

To My Daughter
on Her Marriage into the Yang Family

My heart has been heavy all day long
Because you have so far to go.
The marriage of a girl, away from her parents,
Is the launching of a little boat on a great river.
. . . You were very young when your mother died,
Which made me the more tender of you.
Your elder sister has looked out for you,
And now you are both crying and cannot part.
This makes my grief the harder to bear;
Yet it is right that you should go.
. . . Having had from childhood no mother to guide you,
How will you honour your mother-in-law?
It's an excellent family; they will be kind to you,
They will forgive you your mistakes—
Although ours has been so pure and poor
That you can take them no great dowry.
Be gentle and respectful, as a woman should be,
Careful of word and look, observant of good example.
. . . After this morning we separate,
There's no knowing for how long . . .
I always try to hide my feelings—
They are suddenly too much for me,
When I turn and see my younger daughter
With the tears running down her cheek.

WÊN T'ING-YÜN
筠庭溫

She Sighs on Her Jade Lute

A cool-matted silvery bed; but no dreams. . . .
An evening sky as green as water, shadowed with tender clouds;
But far off over the southern rivers the calling of a wildgoose,
And here a twelve-story building, lonely under the moon.

To a Friend Bound East

The old fort brims with yellow leaves. . . .
You insist upon forsaking this place where you have lived.
A high wind blows at Han-yang Ferry
And sunrise lights the summit of Ying-mên . . .
Who will be left for me along the upper Yang-tsze
After your solitary skiff has entered the end of the sky?
I ask you over and over when we shall meet again,
While we soften with winecups this ache of farewell.

Near the Li-chou Ferry

The sun has set in the water's clear void,
And little blue islands are one with the sky.
On the bank a horse neighs. A boat goes by.
People gather at a willow-clump and wait for the ferry.
Down by the sand-bushes sea-gulls are circling,
Over the wide river-lands flies an egret.
. . . Can you guess why I sail, like an ancient wise lover,
Through the misty Five Lakes, forgetting words?
(109)

The Temple of Su Wu

Though our envoy, Su Wu, is gone, body and soul,
This temple survives, these trees endure . . .
Wildgeese through the clouds are still calling to the moon there
And hill-sheep unshepherded graze along the border.
. . . Returning, he found his country changed
Since with youthful cap and sword he had left it.
His bitter adventures had won him no title . . .
Autumn-waves endlessly sob in the river.

(114)

YÜAN CHÊN

稹　元

The Summer Palace

In the faded old imperial palace,
Peonies are red, but no one comes to see them. . . .
The ladies-in-waiting have grown white-haired
Debating the pomps of Emperor Hsüan-tsung.
(4d)

An Elegy

I

O youngest, best-loved daughter of Hsieh,
Who unluckily married this penniless scholar,
You patched my clothes from your own wicker basket,
And I coaxed off your hairpins of gold, to buy wine with;
For dinner we had to pick wild herbs—
And to use dry locust-leaves for our kindling.
. . . Today they are paying me a hundred thousand—
And all that I can bring to you is a temple sacrifice.

II

We joked, long ago, about one of us dying,
But suddenly, before my eyes, you are gone.
Almost all your clothes have been given away;
Your needlework is sealed, I dare not look at it. . . .
I continue your bounty to our men and our maids—
Sometimes, in a dream, I bring you gifts.
. . . This is a sorrow that all mankind must know—
But not as those know it who have been poor together.

III

I sit here alone, mourning for us both.
How many years do I lack now of my threescore and ten?
There have been better men than I to whom heaven denied a son,
There was a poet better than I whose dead wife could not hear
    him.
What have I to hope for in the darkness of our tomb?
You and I had little faith in a meeting after death—
Yet my open eyes can see all night
That lifelong trouble of your brow.

(115)

YÜAN CHIEH

結　元

To the Tax-Collectors
After the Bandits' Retreat

(*In the year Kuêi-mao the bandits from Hsi-yüan entered Tao-chou, set fire, raided, killed, and looted. The whole district was almost ruined. The next year the bandits came again and, attacking the neighbouring prefecture, Yung, passed this one by. It was not because we were strong enough to defend ourselves, but, probably, because they pitied us. And how now can these commissioners bear to impose extra taxes? I have written this poem for the collectors' information.*)

I still remember those days of peace—
Twenty years among mountains and forests,
The pure stream running past my yard,
The caves and valleys at my door.
Taxes were light and regular then,
And I could sleep soundly and late in the morning—
Till suddenly came a sorry change.
. . . For years now I have been serving in the army.
When I began here as an official,
The mountain bandits were rising again;
But the town was so small it was spared by the thieves,
And the people so poor and so pitiable
That all the other districts were looted
And this one this time let alone.
. . . Do you imperial commissioners
Mean to be less kind than bandits?
The people you force to pay the poll
Are like creatures frying over a fire.

And how can you sacrifice human lives,
Just to be known as able collectors?—
. . . Oh, let me fling down my official seal,
Let me be a lone fisherman in a small boat
And support my family on fish and wheat
And content my old age with rivers and lakes!

A Drinking Song at Stone-Fish Lake

*(I have used grain from the public fields, for distilling wine. After
my office hours I have the wine loaded on a boat and then I seat
my friends on the bank of the lake. The little wine-boats come to
each of us and supply us with wine. We seem to be drinking on
Pa Islet in Lake Tung-t'ing. And I write this poem.)*

Stone-Fish Lake is like Lake Tung-t'ing—
When the top of Chün is green and the summer tide is rising.
. . . With the mountain for a table, and the lake a fount of wine,
The tipplers all are settled along the sandy shore.
Though a stiff wind for days has roughened the water,
Wine-boats constantly arrive. . . .
I have a long-necked gourd and, happy on Pa Island,
I am pouring a drink in every direction, doing away with care.

Appendices

HISTORICAL CHRONOLOGY

I

The Five Ti Periods, 2953–2206 B.C.
The Hsia Dynasty, 2205–1766 B.C.
The Shang Dynasty, 1765–1122 B.C.
The Chou Dynasty, 1121–256 B.C.
The Ch'in Dynasty, 255–207 B.C.
The Han Dynasty, 206 B.C.–219 A.D.
The Three Kingdoms Period, 220–264
The Chin Dynasty, 265–419
The Southern and Northern Dynasties, 420–588
The Suêi Dynasty, 589–617
The T'ang Dynasty, 618–906
The Five Dynasties, 907–959
The Sung Dynasty, 960–1279
The Liao and Chin Tartar Dynasties, 916–1234
The Yüan or Mongol Dynasty, 1280–1367
The Ming Dynasty, 1368–1643
The Ch'ing or Manchu Dynasty, 1644–1911

II

THE T'ANG DYNASTY

1. Emperor Kao-tsu, Wu-tê Period, 618–626
2. Emperor T'ai-tsung, Chêng-kuan Period, 627–649
3. Emperor Kao-tsung, Yung-huêi Period, 650–655
      Hsien-ch'ing Period, 656–660
      Lung-so Period, 661–663

Lin-tê Period, 664–665
Ch'ien-fêng Period, 666–667
Tsung-chang Period, 668–669
Hsien-hêng Period, 670–673
Shang-yuan Period, 674–675
Yi-fêng Period, 676–678
T'iao-lu Period, 679
Yung-lung Period, 680
K'ai-yao Period, 681
Yung-shun Period, 682
Hung-tao Period, 683

4. Emperor Chung-tsung, Ssŭ-shêng Period, 684
5. Emperor Juêi-tsung, Ch'uêi-kung Period, 685–688
6. The Woman-Emperor Wu-chao, T'ien-shou Period, 690–691
Ju-yi Period, 692
Ch'ang-shou Period, 693
Yen-tsai Period, 694
T'ien-ts'e-wan-suêi Period, 695
Wan-suêi-t'ung-t'ien Period, 696
Shên-kung Period, 697
Shêng-li Period, 698–699
Chiu-shih Period, 700
Ch'ang-an Period, 701–704
7. Emperor Chung-tsung restored, Shên-lung Period, 705–706
Chin-lung Period, 707–709
8. Emperor Juêi-tsung, Ching-yun Period, 710–711
Hsien-t'ien Period, 712
9. Emperor Hsüan-tsung, K'ai-yuan Period, 713–741
T'ien-pao Period, 742–755
10. Emperor Su-tsung, Chih Tê Period, 756–757
Ch'ien-yuan Period, 758–759
Shang-yuan Period, 760–761
Pao-yin Period, 762
11. Emperor Tai-tsung, Kuang-tê Period, 763–764
Yung-t'ai Period, 765
Ta-li Period, 766–779

12. Emperor Tê-tsung, Chien-chung Period, 780–783
    Hsing-yuan Period, 784
    Cheng-yuan Period, 785–804
13. Emperor Shun-tsung, Yung-cheng Period, 805
14. Emperor Hsien-tsung, Yuan-ho Period, 806–820
15. Emperor Mu-tsung, Ch'ang-ch'ing Period, 821–824
16. Emperor Ching-tsung, Pao-li Period, 825–826
17. Emperor Wên-tsung, T'ai-ho Period, 827–835
    K'ai-ch'eng Period, 836–840
18. Emperor Wu-tsung, Huêi-ch'ang Period, 841–846
19. Emperor Hsüan-tsung, Ta-chung Period, 847–859
20. Emperor Yi-tsung, Hsien-tung Period, 860–873
21. Emperor Hsi-tsung, Ch'ien-fu Period, 874–879
    Kuang-ming Period, 880
    Chung-ho Period, 881–884
    Kuang-ch'i Period, 885–887
    Wên Tê Period, 888
22. Emperor Chao-tsung, Lung-chi Period, 889
    Ta-shun Period, 890–891
    Ch'ing-fu Period, 892–893
    Ch'ien-ning Period, 894–897
    Kuang-hua Period, 898–900
    T'ien-fu Period, 901–903
    T'ien-yu Period, 904–906

CHRONOLOGY OF
THE POETS

Names		*Dates*
Anonymous	氏名無	
Chang Chi (1)	繼 張	Graduated* between 742 and 755, lived to 780
Chang Chi (2)	籍 張	Graduated 799

* The term "graduated" is used in the sense of receiving an official degree at the government examinations.

Names			Dates
Chang Ch'iao	喬	張	Graduated about 870
Ch'ang Chien	建	常	Graduated 727
Chang Chiu-ling	齡九	張	673–740
Chang Hsü	旭	張	Early 8th century
Chang Hu	祜	張	9th century
Chang Pi	泌	礬	10th century
Ch'ên T'ao	陶	陳	824–882
Ch'ên Tzǔ-ang	昂子	陳	656–698
Chêng T'ien	畋	鄭	656–698
Chia Tao	島	賈	788–843
Ch'ien Ch'i	起	錢	Graduated 751
Chin Ch'ang-hsü	緒昌	金	10th century
Ch'in T'ao-yü	玉韜	秦	Graduated 882
Ch'iu Wêi	爲	邱	8th century, died at age 96
Ch'i-wu Ch'ien	潛毋	綦	Graduated 726
Chu Ch'ing-yü	餘慶	朱	Graduated 825
Ch'üan Tê-yü	輿德	權	759–818
Han Hung	翃	韓	Graduated 754
Han Wu	偓	韓	Graduated 889, died 905
Han Yü	愈	韓	768–823
Hê Chih-chang	章知	賀	659–744
Hsü Hun	渾	許	Graduated 832
Hsüan-tsung, Emperor	宗	玄	685–761, reigned 713–755

Names			Dates
Hsüeh Fêng	逢	薛	Graduated about 845
Huang-fu Jan	冉甫皇		714–767
Kao Shih	適	高	Died 765
Ku K'uang	況	顧	Graduated either in 756 or in 757
Li Ch'i	頎	李	Graduated 725
Li P'in	頻	李	Graduated 854
Li Po	白	李	699–762
Li Shang-yin	隱商李		813–858
Li Tüan	端	李	Graduated 770
Li Yi	益	李	Graduated 769, died 827
Liu Chang-ch'ing	卿長劉		Graduated 733
Liu Chung-yung	庸中柳		8th and 9th centuries
Liu Fang-p'ing	平方劉		8th and 9th centuries
Liu Shên-hsü	虛眘劉		Flourished about 742–755
Liu Tsung-yüan	元宗柳		773–819
Liu Yü-hsi	錫禹劉		772–842
Lo Pin-wang	王賓駱		Flourished early 7th century
Lu Lun	綸	盧	Circa 766
Ma Tai	戴	馬	Graduated 844
Mêng Chiao	郊	孟	751–814
Mêng Hao-jan	然浩孟		699–740
One at the Western Front	人鄙西		Unknown
P'ei Ti	迪	斐	9th century

Names		Dates
Po Chü-yi	白居易	772–846
Sêng Chiao-jan	僧皎然	Died 785
Shên Ch'üan-ch'i	沈佺期	Graduated about 680, died about 713
Ssŭ-k'ung Shu	司空曙	Flourished 766–779
Sung Chih-wên	宋之問	Died 710
Tai Shu-lun	戴叔倫	732–789
Ts'ên Ts'an	岑　參	Graduated 744
Tsu Yung	祖　詠	Graduated 724
Ts'uêi Hao	崔　灝	Graduated 723, died 754
Ts'uêi Shu	崔　曙	Graduated 738
Ts'uêi T'u	崔　塗	Graduated 888
Tu Ch'iu-niang	杜秋娘	Early 9th century
Tu Fu	杜　甫	712–770
Tu Hsün-hê	杜荀鶴	Graduated 891, died about 904
Tu Mu	杜　牧	803–852
Tu Shên-yen	杜審言	Between 7th and 8th centuries
Wang Ch'ang-ling	王昌齡	Graduated 726
Wang Chien	王　建	Graduated 775
Wang Chih-huan	王之渙	8th century
Wang Han	王　翰	Graduated about 735
Wang Po	王　勃	648–675
Wang Wan	王　灣	Graduated 712
Wang Wêi	王　維	699–759

Names		Dates
Wêi Chuang	莊 韋	Graduated 902
Wêi Ying-wu	物應韋	773–828
Wên T'ing-yün	筠庭溫	9th century
Yüan Chên	稹 元	799–831
Yüan Chieh	結 元	719–772

TOPOGRAPHY

We have thought it best to substitute now and then in the text of the poems the modern names of places, with an attempt at consistent spelling, for the T'ang names used in the original; sometimes we have indulged in English translations of the names; but this index records the old names, for scholars who may be interested. It also locates in modern geography the towns, lakes, rivers, mountains, and, roughly, the larger regions, for the possible interest of students and travellers. We use, however, the suffix "ou" instead of "ow": Han-k'ou, Su-chou and Yang-chou, instead of Hankow, Soochow and Yang-chow. The T'ang capital, often mentioned in these poems, was Ch'ang-an, now Hsi-an-fu in Shen-si Province. Han was China, and Fan the outside world. The Three Kingdoms (220–264) were Shu, now Sze-chuan Province; Wu, now Kiang-su Province and other provinces in the Yang-tsze valley; and Wêi, now Ho-nan Province and other provinces in the Huang-ho valley.

The T'ang names of regional divisions most important for readers of the poems are, with approximate modern equivalents:

Chin (Shan-si Province)
Ch'in (Shen-si Province)
Chu (Hu-nan Province)
Ping (Shan-si Province)
Shu (Sze-chuan Province)

Wêi (Ho-nan Province)
Wu (Kiang-su Province)
Yen (Chih-li Province)
Yu (Chih-li Province)
Yüeh (Chê-kiang Province).

General List

Broken Mountain Temple (P'o-shan): in Ch'ang-shu district, Kiang-su Province

Ch'ang-an: the T'ang capital, now Hsi-an-fu, in Shen-si Province

Chang-chou: a district in Fu-kien Province

Ch'ang-chou: a district in Kiang-su Province

Chang-fêng-sha (Wind-swept Sands): in An-huêi Province

Ch'ang-kan: a small town near Nan-king

Ch'ang-sha: the capital of Hu-nan Province

Chao: a district in Chih-li Province

Chêng: a district in Ho-nan Province

Ch'êng-tu (Ching-ch'êng, called the City of Silk): the capital of Sze-chuan Province

Chien-tê: a town and a river in Chê-kiang Province

Chin: Shan-si Province

Ch'in: Shen-si Province

Ching Gate (Ching-mên): at Ching-chou, in Hu-pêi Province

Ch'in-huai River: at Nan-king

Ch'i-yang: in Shen-si Province

Ch'u: Hu-nan Province

Ch'u Mountains: in Hu-nan Province

Ch'u Rivers: the Han and Hsiang Rivers in Hu-pêi and Hu-nan Provinces

Chüan-chiao Mountain: in An-huêi Province

Ch'u-chou: a district in An-huêi Province

Ch'ü-li: in Manchuria

Chung-nan Mountain (Southernmost Mountain): fifteen miles south of Ch'ang-an, one of the Nan-shan Range, in Shen-si Province

Ch'ü-t'ang: the first of the three great gorges on the upper Yang-tsze; also a district in Sze-chuan Province

City of Silk: Ch'êng-tu, in Sze-chuan Province

Dagger River (Chien-ho): the upper part of the Yang-tsze, in Sin-kiang Province

Dagger-Tower Trail: in Sze-chuan Province

Dragon City (Lung-ch'êng): in Manchuria
Dragon Mound (Lung-tuêi): in Turkestan
Fêng-chi Station: in Sze-chuan Province
Fêng-chou: a district in Kuang-tung Province
Fêng-hsiang: a district in Shen-si Province
Fou-liang: a district in Kiang-si Province
Fu-chou: a district in Shen-si Province
Fu-li: a district in An-huêi Province
Giant's Palm (Hsien-jên-chang): one of the peaks of Great
    Flower Mountain
Great Flower Mountain (T'ai-hua or Hua-shan): in Shen-si
    Province
Great White Mountain (T'ai-po): in Sze-chuan Province
Green Clay Mountain (Ch'ing-ni): in Sze-chuan Province
Han: China
Han-k'ou (Hsia-k'ou): in Hu-pêi Province
Han River: joins the Yang-tsze in Hu-pêi Province
Han-yang: in Hu-pêi Province
Heavenly Mother Mountain (T'ien-mu): a peak of the T'ien-t'ai
    Mountains in Chê-kiang Province
Heavenly Terrace Range (T'ien-t'ai): in Chê-kiang Province
Heaven-Peak Road: on T'ien-shan, in Turkestan
Hêng Mountain: in Hu-nan Province, one of the Five Holy
    Mountains
Hill of Gold (Chin-shan): between Mongolia and Manchuria
Ho-lan Range: in Kan-su Province, near Turkestan
Hsia-kuêi: a district in Shen-si Province
Hsiang River: in Hu-nan Province
Hsiang-yang: a district in Hu-pêi Province
Hsiao River: in Hu-nan Province
Hsia-yung: a district in Sze-chuan Province
Hsi-yüan: a district in Shen-si Province
Hsüan-chou: a district in An-huêi Province
Hsün-yang River: at Kiu-kiang
Hua-chou: a district in Shen-si Province
Huai: a district in Kiang-su Province

Huai River: a tributary of the Yang-tsze, in Kiang-su Province

Hua-mên tribes: Turkestanese

Hua-yin: the district under T'ai-hua (Great Flower Mountain) and around Hsien-yang, a local T'ang capital, in Shen-si Province

Jade Pass (Yü-mên, Yü-kuan, or Yü-mên-kuan): a gateway or divide between China and Turkestan, now in the western part of Tun-huang district, Kan-su Province

Jo-ya Lake: in Chê-kiang Province

Kiang-ling: a district in Hu-pêi Province

Kiu-kiang (Chiang-chou or Hsün-yang): in Kiang-si Province

Kua-chou: a town in Kiang-su Province, across the Yang-tsze from Chin-kiang

Kuan-nêi: within the Great Wall, in Shen-si Province

Liang-chou: a district in Kan-su Province

Liang-ch'üan: unknown

Liao: near Mukden, Manchuria

Liao-hsi: a border-camp, in Manchuria

Li-chou Ferry: unknown

Liao-yang: a district in Feng-tien Province, Manchuria

Lien-chou: a district in Kuang-tung Province

Li-mien tribes: Manchus

Lin-ch'iung: a district in Sze-chuan Province

Lin-t'ao: a district in Kan-su Province

Lin-t'ao River: between China and Tibet

Ling Valleys: in Shen-si Province

Lin-ying: a district in Ho-nan Province

Liu-chou: in Kuang-si Province

Lo-yang: a district in Ho-nan Province, a principal city of the T'ang Dynasty, formerly a capital of China

Lo-yu Tombs: in Ch'ang-an (Hsi-an-fu) in Shen-si Province

Lu Dukedom: near T'ai-shan, in Shan-tung Province

Lu-mên: near Hsiang-yang in Hu-pêi Province

Lu Mountain: near Kiu-kiang in Kiang-si Province

Ma-wêi Slope: near Ch'ang-an (Hsi-an-fu) in Shen-si Province

Mao-ling: in Hu-nan Province

Maple Bridge (Fêng-ch'iao): in Su-chou, Kiang-su Province
Mêng Valley: in Hu-pêi Province
Mi-lo River: in Hu-nan Province
Mirror Lake (Ching-hu): in Chê-kiang Province
Nan-king (Chin-ling or Chien-yê): in Kiang-su Province
Nan-ling: a district in An-huêi Province
Nine Doubts Mountain (Chiu-ni): in Hu-nan Province
Niu-chu Mountain: on the Yang-tsze not far from An-king, in
    An-huêi Province
North Fort Hill (Pêi-ku): in Chin-kiang, Kiang-su Province
O-mêi Mountain: one hundred and seventy miles south-west of
    Ch'êng-tu, in Sze-chuan Province
Orchid Mountain (Lan-shan): in Kan-su Province
Pa: a district in Sze-chuan Province
Pa-ling: a district in Shen-si Province
Pa Island: in Hu-nan Province
Parrot Island (Ying-wu-chou): near Han-k'ou, Hu-pêi Prov-
    ince
Pa-shang: near Ch'ang-an (Hsi-an-fu), Shen-si Province
P'ên-p'u: in Kiu-kiang, Kiang-si Province
Persia: Chiu-tzŭ
Ping: Shan-si Province
Po-têng Road: in Manchuria
Po-ti (the City of the White God): in Sze-chuan Province
Pu-kou: in Kiang-su Province
Red Phœnix City: Ch'ang-an
Running Horse River (Tsou-ma-ch'uan): in Manchuria
Sand Mouth (Sha-k'ou): in Turkestan
San-yuan (Yün-yang): a district in Shen-si Province
Shan-yin: a district in Chê-kiang Province
Shin-fêng: a place in Ch'ang-kan; also a district in Kiang-su
    Province
Shou-hsiang: a border-city near Mount Hui-lo in Manchuria
Shu: Sze-chuan Province
Siberia: Lo-so
Stone-Fish Lake (Shih-yǔ-hu): in An-huêi Province

Su-chou (Ku-su): in Kiang-su Province

Sung Mountain: near Lo-yang, in Ho-nan Province, one of the Five Holy Mountains

T'ai-shan: the Holy Mountain, in Shan-tung Province

Tao-chou: a district in Hu-nan Province

Ta-yü Mountain: between Kiang-si and Kuang-tung Provinces

Terrace Tower: a part of the Nan-king city-wall

Tibet: Yüeh-chih

Ting-chou: a district in Fu-kien Province

Town of the Horse (Ma-yi): in Turkestan

Tripod Fall (Hsiang-lu): one of the peaks of Lu Mountain, in Kiang-si Province

Tsou Realm: near T'ai-shan, in Shan-tung Province

Tsŭ-chou: in Sze-chuan Province

T'ung Gate (T'ung-kuan): a gate or pass by the T'ung River, in Shen-si Province

T'ung-lu River: in An-huêi Province

Tung-t'ing Lake: between Hu-nan and Hu-pêi Provinces

Turkestan (T'u-chüeh): Sin-kiang Province

Wang-ch'uan: in Shen-si Province

Wêi: Ho-nan Province

Wêi-ch'êng: near Ch'ang-an (Hsi-an-fu), in Shen-si Province

Wêi River: in Shen-si Province

West Fort Mountain (Hsi-sai): near Wu-ch'ang, in Hu-pêi Province

Wheel Tower (Lun-t'ai): in Manchuria

White Gate City: Nan-king

White God City (Po-ti): in Sze-chuan Province

White Wolf River (Pai-lang-ho): in Manchuria

Wu: Kiang-su Province

Wu-ch'ang (O-chou): a district by the Han River, now the capital of Hu-pêi Province

Wu-chiang: a district in Kiang-su Province

Wu-chou Mountain: in Chê-kiang Province

Wu-chu Tribes: Manchus

Wu-hsing: a district in Chê-kiang Province

Wu-ling: a district and a river in Hu-nan Province

Wu Valley: in Hsia-chou District, Sze-chuan Province

Yang-chou (Kuang-ling or Wêi-yang or Wu-chêng or Kiang-
tu): a district and city in Kiang-su Province

Yang Gate (Yang-kuan): south of the Jade Pass, between China
and Turkestan, now in Kan-su Province

Yang-tsze-kiang: the great artery river between north and south
China

Yellow Dragon City (Huang-lung): in Manchuria

Yellow River (Huang-ho): the second largest river, in north
China

Yen: the part of Chih-li Province centering at Pe-king

Yen-ch'êng: in Ho-nan Province

Yen-jan: the boundary mountain between China and Manchuria

Yen Mountain: near Hsiang-yang, in Hu-pêi Province

Yi-chou: in Sze-chuan Province

Yeh: a district in Ho-nan Province

Yien River: in Chê-kiang Province

Yin Mountains: between Turkestan and Mongolia

Ying-mên Mountain: in Hu-pêi Province

Yo-chou (Yüeh-yang or Yüeh-chou or Pa-ling): a district in
Hu-nan Province

Yu: Chih-li Province

Yü-ch'ien: in Chê-kiang Province

Yu-chou: in Chih-li Province

Yüeh: Chê-kiang Province

Yun Valley: in Hu-pêi Province

Yung: a district in Hu-nan Province

Yun-yang (now San-yuan): a district in Shen-si Province

Yü-yang (now Chi-hsien): a district in Chih-li Province

Yü-yi: a district in An-huêi Province

NOTES ON THE POEMS

1. *The Day of No Fire.* (The Chinese title is *Lines.*) Chieh
Chih-t'uêi, a scholar and statesman of the Chin State toward the

end of the Chou Dynasty, was disliked by the Duke Wên and exiled to the mountains. Later, trying to find him, but failing, the Duke had the forest set on fire to force him out, and Chieh Chih-t'uêi was burned to death. The Duke, remorseful, ordered the people to mourn the dead man and always to commemorate him on this day, late in spring, by lighting no fires and eating only cold food. When the custom of the Day of No Fire had become fixed, fire of any sort was forbidden until night, and, as told in Han Hung's *After the Day of No Fire*, the Emperor would then send candles to his favourite officials, no others to be lighted before theirs.

1a. The ancient Emperor Wang, who had lost his kingdom, in what is now Sze-chuan, entered at his death into a cuckoo, and his imperial spirit has cried for ever: "Oh, to go back again!" The name "Emperor Wang," meaning "Emperor of Hope," came to be one of the names of the cuckoo. There is a direct allusion to this legend in Li Shang-yin's *The Inlaid Harp*.

2. In an old story by T'ao Ch'ien (A.D. 365–427), the Peach-Blossom River flows to the Utopian land, T'ao-yüan. It seems that long ago a fisherman from Wu-ling, fishing on the river, lost his way, and, leaving his boat and walking along the bank, found at its end a little cave. At first narrow and dark, the cave opened presently into a wide and beautiful place where there were many people in the streets, dressed in strange fashion. They asked the fisherman whence he came; but they knew nothing of his country and age; for their ancestors, so they told him, had fled from the disorders of the Ch'in Dynasty eight hundred years before and had never gone back again. They spoke an old tongue and read old books. They had no laws, they paid no taxes. Everyone worked his own land and was happy in his own home. Family after family welcomed the fisherman and invited him to remain among them; but he thought instead that he would come back later and so said good-bye to them. He passed through the cave, fixing the way well in his mind; he returned home and reported his experience. But when officials of the Government asked him to guide them to T'ao-yüan, he could never find it again. (See Wang Wêi's *A Song of Peach-Blossom River* for a poetic version of the narrative; see also P'ei Ti's *A Farewell to Ts'uêi*.)

2a. T'ao Ch'ien, the poet who first set down the story, had been a magistrate at Pêng-tsê and, like Vice-Prefect Liu, to whom Ts'uêi Shu addresses *A Climb on the Mountain Holiday*, an appreciator of wine and chrysanthemums. Wang Wêi, in *A Message from My Lodge*, compares P'ei Ti to him by a reference to T'ao Ch'ien's home, Five Willows.

3. *She Sings an Old Song.* (The Chinese title is *Ho-man-tzŭ*, the name of the old Song.) According to Po Chü-yi, there was a singer of Ts'ang-chou in the K'ai-yuan period who, condemned to die, asked at the last moment to be allowed to sing this song, vainly hoping that it might win him clemency. His name became attached to the song. And it is known that later, in the Emperor Wên-tsung's time, Shên A-ch'iao, a palace-girl, was famous for singing it and dancing to it.

4. Lady Yang Kuêi-fêi, called in the original text of Chang Hu's poem *On the Terrace of Assembled Angels* T'ai-chên (The Ever-True), was the T'ang Emperor Hsüan-tsung's famous favourite. The Ladies Kuo Kuo and Ch'in Kuo were her beautiful sisters. The Premier, mentioned with them in Tu Fu's *A Song of Fair Women*, was Yang Kuo-chung, avowedly their brother, but supposed to be even more tenderly interested in them, and likely, therefore, to resent their receiving bluebird messages (love-letters) from other admirers.

4a. As told in Po Chü-yi's *A Song of Unending Sorrow*, Emperor Hsüan-tsung, known also as Ming Huang (Magnificent Monarch), was so enamoured of Lady Yang that he neglected his empire. His vassals revolted, and his armies refused to take orders. Forced to flee the capital, he escaped toward Sze-chuan with his lady and his officials, but even then his own body-guard protested that unless he gave her up, they would desert him. Finally they seized and slew her and officially announced that it had been by his own orders, whereupon the soldiers once more pledged loyalty to the dynasty. In Chêng T'ien's *On Ma-wêi*

Slope it is told that they persuaded the Emperor to yield his lady by reminding him of the tragic fate of an earlier monarch, known as "The Later King of the Ch'ên Dynasty." This King also had become unpopular because of a favourite. He had refused to give her up, and when trouble followed, had tied her to himself and hidden in a dry well at Ching-yang Palace. The revolutionists had found them there and killed them. Further reference is made to this earlier Emperor, and to *A Song of Courtyard Flowers*, which he composed for his favourite, in Tu Mu's *A Mooring on the Ch'in-huai River* and Li Shang-yin's *The Palace of the Suêi Emperor*. Girls on the river at Nan-king are still singing the song in flower-boats and taverns.

This Emperor was overthrown by the Suêi Emperor, Yang-ti, who became the most luxurious and depraved of the Chinese emperors and exhausted the country for his indulgences. In winter, for the trees of his garden, he had leaves and flowers made of silk, and birds were slaughtered broadcast that the palace cushions might be soft with only the finest down. (See Li Shang-yin's *The Suêi Palace*.) The end of the Suêi Dynasty came with his overthrow by the founder of the T'ang Dynasty, called "Peak of the Sun" (Jih-chüeh). Wang Wêi, in the last line of *Looking Down in a Spring-Rain* contrasts a good emperor with Emperor Yang-ti.

4b. Among the incidents told of Emperor Hsüan-tsung is the famous occasion when Li Po was called upon by the Emperor to compose a poem for Lady Yang. It was at the Feast of Peonies, and the Emperor announced to the poet that he and his guests wished to hear, not the old poems, but a new one. Happily drunken, the poet thereupon wrote the three stanzas called *A Song of Pure Happiness*. They were sung at once, the Emperor himself playing the melody upon a jade lute. Another lyrical event is referred to in Po Chü-yi's *A Song of Unending Sorrow*. The Emperor Hsüan-tsung visited the moon in a dream and was taught there by Ch'ang-o, the Goddess of the Moon, a dance-play called *The Rainbow Skirt and the Feathered Coat*. When he awoke, he remembered it, and, summoning his musicians and actors, the Pear-Garden Players, instructed them in the music and the steps. His beloved Lady Yang performed in the dance. (See note 42.)

4c. There is in this collection one poem by the Emperor himself, *I Pass Through the Lu Dukedom with a Sigh and a Sacrifice for Confucius*, in which, remembering the dream that brought Confucius an omen of death, the Emperor wonders if he should feel a similar premonition as to his own fate.

4d. Tu Fu, in *A Song of Sobbing by the River*, laments the passing of the Emperor and of Lady Yang. The end of Hsüan-tsung's reign came about in the following manner: An Lu-shan, son of a defeated Hun chieftain, had been captured in his youth, favoured by Hsüan-tsung, and adopted by Lady Yang; but, exiled later because of sedition, he aroused his people and led his bandit troops to the capture of the capital, Ch'ang-an. This was what caused the Emperor's unhappy flight, during which Lady Yang was killed. After An Lu-shan had reigned for a few months, he was murdered by his own adopted son, a Chinese; whereupon Ch'ang-an was recaptured by Chinese troops, and Su-tsung, son of Hsüan-tsung, was made Emperor. That this prince too had his troubles is told in Tu Fu's *A Song of a Prince Deposed*. Tu Fu, although loyal to the dynasty, tells in his poems *A Song of Sobbing* and *Taking Leave of Friends* how, during the troubles, he had fled the capital and was subsequently transferred in punishment to a provincial post.

Yüan Chên, in his poem *The Summer Palace*, speaks of court-ladies, long after Hsüan-tsung's downfall, remembering the brilliant and prosperous thirty years of his reign, before the final ten years of infatuation with Lady Yang, which brought about his ruin.

5. It is believed that this Japanese priest may have been Kobo-daishi, who spent twenty years in China at Ch'ang-an University. Chinese was the only language in which was written the whole Buddhist teaching, the light of which was the "single lantern." Kobo-daishi, returning home, founded the great monastery on Koya-san and devised from Chinese characters the Japanese alphabet, Kana.

"The source" meant China, the super-land in relation to Japan.

5a. The chant is specified in the original as Fan, chanting in Sanskrit; the faith, as in the seventh line of Liu Chang-ch'ing's *While Visiting on the South Stream the Taoist Priest Ch'ang*, is the Ch'an doctrine. This Buddhistic doctrine of serenity brought by Ta-mo, or Buddhidharma, from India during the period of the Six Dynasties, and later blent with Taoism, was the Shingon Buddhism carried back by Kobo-daishi to Japan, where it persists today, blent with Zen Buddhism, its principal seat still being the Monastery of Koya-san.

6. The term "The Sun," or "The Light of Heaven," is often used to mean the Emperor, as well as "The Son of Heaven" and "The Ruler of Heaven."

7. The Woman-Emperor Wu-chao (690–704) had established verse-writing as one of the requirements in the Government Examinations, through which, as through western Civil Service, posts of state were conferred. This applicant, having failed to qualify with his verse, feels himself unworthy of the hairpin of his family rank.

7a. Commentators explain that on the eve of his final examination the subject of the poem by Chu Ch'ing-yü, possibly the poet, hopefully addresses a friend who has received the degree and is an expert in the subject. Elaborated metaphor of this kind, rare in the best poetry of the T'ang period, became popular with later poets.

8. The phrase "Jade Dressing-Table" indicates a certain style of poem dealing with women.

The characters for this particular beetle and for good fortune have the same pronunciation, just as have the characters for bat and prosperity or the characters for deer and official Emolument.

The English term, "yoke," is used here as an inadequate equivalent of the original term, "washing-stone," which, though a familiar Chinese word for husband, would not be clear to a Western reader.

9. In the Ch'u Kingdom of the Chou Dynasty there were many poets. One of them once wrote a poem and asked the others to "harmonize" it, which they did. Then he wrote another, to which the responses were fewer because it was more difficult. Then he followed with *The Song of Bright Spring*, which only two or three could harmonize. The title has come to mean a song of the highest order.

There are four ways of harmonizing a poem: to sing of the same subject with any rhymes; with the same rhyme-sound, but different words; with the same rhyme-words, but in a different order; or with the same rhyme-words and in the same order.

9a. Chia Chih had written a poem on the Palace of Light and asked his friends to "harmonize" it. (See the poems called *An Early Audience at the Palace of Light* by Ts'ên Ts'an and Wang Wêi.)

10. The sound of mallets on stone came from women washing goods to make winter clothes, according to the custom still followed in China.

11. "The Purple Hills" was a name for paradise.

12. "Dragon-beard" was a kind of finely woven bamboo matting.

13. Han Yü, for opposing Buddhism, was exiled by Emperor Hsien-tsung. The Emperor had sent envoys to India to import Buddhistic doctrines and was preparing a great ceremony to receive a relic, a bone of the Buddha, when Han Yü, protesting against the introduction of a religion unsuited to China, remarked that whatever virtue there had been in Buddha, there could be none in his bone; which, besides, might be really that of a dog or a sheep. The Emperor angrily exiled the protestant.

On another occasion Han Yü, secretary to the Emperor's Premier, P'ai Tu, wrote an account of the conquering of the Huai-hsi rebels (see Li Shang-yin's *The Han Monument*). This writing was inscribed on stone as a monument of the victory; but afterward, owing to personal jealousy, the monument was cast down and an inferior inscription set in its place. (See Tu Fu's *A Letter to Censor Han.*)

13a. Divinity-cups are still used at temples for telling fortunes. Two small cups, originally of jade, now of wood, are thrown on the ground. The inquirer, kneeling before the altar, is told his lot according to their position and aspect.

14. There are five sacred peaks in China. Hêng-shan, the Nan-yueh, near Hêng-chou in Hu-nan Province (see Han Yü's *Stopping at a Temple on Hêng Mountain*), is the southernmost of them. Hua-shan, or T'ai-hua (the Great Flower), the Hsi-yueh (see Hsü Hun's *Inscribed in the Inn at T'ung Gate* and Ts'uêi Hao's *Passing Through Hua-yin*), is in Shen-si Province and is the westernmost. To Westerners the best-known of these mountains is the easternmost, T'sai-shan (the Great Peak), the Tung-yueh near T'ai-an in Shan-tung Province (see Tu Fu's *A View of T'ai-shan*). The other two of the sacred peaks are Sung-shan, the Chung-yueh, the midmost of them, near Lo-yang in Ho-nan Province; and a second Hêng-shan, the Pei-yueh, the northernmost, near Hun-yuan in Shan-si Province.

On these five mountains (see Han Yü's *Stopping at a Temple*) were conferred titles ranking with those of the Three Dukes, the highest in the Empire.

14a. The Purple Canopy, Celestial Column, Stone Granary, and Fire God are four mountain peaks around Hêng-shan, the Holy Mountain in Hu-nan Province.

15. Among the oldest known stone-carvings of the Chinese, these ten stone drums were made and engraved with poems, under the Emperor Hsüan of the Chou Dynasty. Three of them still exist and are now in the Confucian Temple at Peking, together with replicas of the other seven.

16. The writings of Wang Hsi-chih, even in his own time, were very valuable; but he would not sell them, except in exchange for a few white geese, of which he was extremely fond.

17. There is a popular anonymous parody of this poem, made by changing only two or three characters, mocking a husband who on a trip to the city had abandoned his moustache:

I left home old. I return young,
Speaking as then, but with no hair on my lip;
And my good wife, meeting me, does not know me.
She smiles and says: "Little boy, where do you come from?"

18. The last two lines are reminiscent of a poem by Sung Yü of the Chou Dynasty (300 B.C.) which concludes:

A single leaf, blown from a lakka-tree,
Whispers autumn through the world.

19. Tsou was a dukedom within the Lu Realm, in what is now Shan-tung.

During the Han Dynasty the Lu Duke, breaking down the walls of his palace and finding ancient writings, recognized it as the former abode of Confucius and therefore transformed it into a temple.

19a. In the *Analects* Confucius said: "When the phœnix no longer comes, it will mean the end of my fortunes." When a dead *chi'i-lin*, akin to a unicorn, was brought to him by official hunters for identification, he recognized it as the creature which was wont to appear for greeting during a successful reign, but he grieved that this time its coming had meant its death. He wrote a poem to it:

Unicorn and phœnix came once to happy kings.
What made you come at the wrong time, only to die?
Unicorn, unicorn, my heart is full of pity.

A few days before he died, he told his disciples that he had fore-seen his end in a dream, in which he had found himself at a large temple, witness of a sacrificial ceremony being conducted between two pillars, and he wrote this poem about it:

Alas, is this the crumbling of T'ai-shan?
Alas, is this the rotting of the beam?
Alas, is this the wise man's withering?

20. She weaves like the Lady Su Huêi, who embroidered the famous eight-hundred-character anagram, from which have been discovered already, as told in Dr. Kiang's Introduction, several hundred rhyming poems.

21. Wu Valley in the Hsia-chou district, Sze-chuan Province, is the destination of one friend; and Hêng Mountain near Ch'ang-sha, in Hu-nan Province, is the destination of the other.

"Dew from Heaven," in the original text, refers to the Emperor's favour.

22. The Yen Song was a musical song of the northern border.

The Great Chief, Chan-yü, was the title of the King of the Tartars who invaded China.

Li Mu, of the Chao State in the Chou Dynasty, had killed more than ten thousand Tartars, so that for a decade after there had been no more invaders.

23. Ts'ai Yen, called also Ts'ai Wên-chi, daughter of a famous scholar of the later Han Dynasty, was captured by Tartars and made the wife of their chieftain. She expressed her grief in a melody of eighteen stanzas on a barbarian musical instrument, *hu-chia*.

Musical notes in China still have the old names. The *shang*, the *chüeh*, and the *yü* are the second, third, and fifth of the total five.

24. Emperor Wu of the Han Dynasty, for the purpose of introducing grape-vines into China, had tried to conquer central Asia.

25. The Chinese or Han Princess, Wang Ch'ao-chün, the Lady of Light, was a beautiful court-lady living at the palace of Emperor Ch'êng. Since there were too many girls there for the Emperor to select from except by portrait, Mao Yen-shou made all their likenesses, painting them favourably or unfavourably according to the size of their bribes. The Lady Wang, failing to bribe, was made to look unsightly. And, when a chieftain of the Huns sent envoys to the Emperor, offering to submit to the Han Dynasty if he might marry into the imperial family, the Emperor chose, among those whom he did not desire, Wang Ch'ao-chün and sent her word asking whether she would like to go. She agreed; preferring, say some, to be the wife of the Hun rather than obscure in the Han palace. At the farewell feast Emperor Ch'êng found her, unlike her portrait, very beautiful. But it was too late; he had given his word to the envoys. So she married the Hun chieftain. When she died, she was buried, as she had requested, alongside the Chinese boundary, close to the Great Wall. And where she lies, the grass, which everywhere else on the Hun side is yellow, is as green as it is on the Chinese side. Po Chü-yi has a poem on *The Exiled Lady Wang Ch'ao-chün:*

> Let the envoy, going back to China, say this:
> Her heart is timing the day of return,
> And yet, should the Emperor wish to be told,
> This foreign sunlight is good for her beauty.

A play about her by Wang Shih-fu has been translated into English by Sir John Davis under the title *The Sorrow of Han.*

Lady Wang wrote the words and music of an eighteen-stanza song and used to play it on her guitar (*p'i-p'a*). When in Chinese paintings a woman is seen playing a guitar on horseback, it is she.

See Tu Fu's *Thoughts of Old Time.* In this volume it consists of only two of five poems he wrote under the one title, which is, more literally, *Pondering on Old Ruins.*

26. Wu Mountain was the abode of nymphs and fairies. It is told that a supernally beautiful fairy appeared once in a dream to King Hsiang of Ch'u, and to his entreaties answered only that she was "morning-cloud and evening-rain upon the hills of Wu." "Cloud and rain" has come to be in Chinese a phrase indicating passionate love.

26a. Flying Swallow, Chao Fêi-yen, originally a singing-girl and a famous beauty, became a favourite of Emperor Ch'êng of the Han Dynasty, in the first century B.C. As remembered in Tu Mu's *Confession,* this lady was supposed to be so exquisitely slender that she could dance on the palm of the hand.

27. Mr. Ezra Pound in his *Cathay,* translating this and other poems by Li Po, misled readers for a period by using the Japanese name Rihaku. The reason for this would appear to be that Mr. Pound discovered the poems among the papers of Fenellosa and, finding the name as set down by some Japanese scholar, did not recognize the poet as the great Li Po. Other translators have used the name Li T'ai-po. Li was his family name, Po his given name, and T'ai-po his social name.

28. Yang-chou, called in Li Po's poem Kuang-ling, at the southern end of the Grand Canal, was in T'ang times a rich and luxurious city, of which it was said:

> Happy is he who has a million
> And can ride on the stork back to Yang-chou.

It was a gala resort for the wealthy and distinguished.

28a. The Yellow Crane Terrace was a famous building on a terrace by the Yang-tsze at Wu-chang, Hu-pêi Province. (The Chinese word for it means literally a building of more than one story, a word for which we do not find an equivalent in English.)

Wang Tzŭ-ch'iao, attaining immortality six hundred years before Christ, is said to have flown up to heaven at this spot on the back of a yellow crane. The building commemorated the event. Li Po once came to it and wished to inscribe a poem, but finding Ts'uêi Hao's poem on the wall, wrote the following lines:

> Let my fist break down the Yellow Crane Terrace
> And my foot kick over Parrot Isle,
> Whose loveliness but finds me dumb—
> With Ts'uêi Hao's poem above my head.

29. This poem is an example of what the Chinese call one-current-of-air poetry, *yi-ch'i-ho-ch'êng*.

30. General Hsieh Shang of the Chin Dynasty was Commander of the Guard in the region about Niu-chu. He was also a literary man and a poet. One moonlight evening he heard somebody reading poetry in a small boat. On inquiry, he found that it was Yüan Hung, a very young poet, reading from his own works. The general sent for him and praised him highly. Yüan Hung afterwards became well known. Near here, according to some of his friends, Li Po was drowned while trying to embrace a reflection of the moon; and it is possible that this was his last poem.

31. The poet had evidently been sent away from Ch'ang-an, the capital.

32. Li Po, as well as Wang Wêi, Mêng Hao-jan, Tsu Yung, and others of the T'ang poets, seems to have enjoyed the region around Chung-nan Mountain, fifteen miles south of the capital, Ch'ang-an, in Shen-si Province.

32a. The Emperor, upon reading Mêng's poem about Chung-nan, was indignant and declared that the famous poet had not been dismissed, but, as Li Po declares in *A Message to Mêng Hao-jan*, had left service of his own accord.

33. The post and the tower of silent watching refer to two stories. This is one of the stories. A young man once waited for a girl by a certain post under a bridge. She was delayed. Rather than leave the appointed spot, he clung to the post and was drowned by the rising tide. The girl, arriving late, and seeing the fate of her lover, killed herself. This is the other story. Two young people, deeply in love, were married. After much happiness, the husband felt impelled to become a recluse. Sadly, but resolutely, he went away to a mountain-side and established his retreat. His wife then built a high tower, in the top of which she lived for many long years, her gaze ever fixed towards the mountain and her hermit.

34. The "madman" was Chieh-yü, a Ch'u Kingdom recluse, famous for drinking, but more for stopping Confucius's chariot and warning him against politics with the song:

O phœnix, O phœnix,
Virtue is corrupted!
What is past is past all counsel,
What is future may be moulded,—
But come away, come away,
Politics are dangerous!

Wang Wêi, in the original of the next to the last line of *A Message from My Lodge*, refers to P'ei Ti as Chieh-yü.

The Stone Mirror: a peak near Lu Mountain.

34a. Hsieh Ling-yun: a famous scholar of the Chin Dynasty (see Li Po's *T'ien-mu Mountain*).

"The immortal pellet" was a drug made by Taoist alchemists and supposed to confer immortality. "The lute's third playing" refers to the fact that there were usually three stanzas in a song.

The Jade City: the capital of heaven.

Saint Lu-ao had been mentioned by Chuang-tzǔ as ascending into heaven.

35. This villa at Hsüan-chou, in what is now An-huêi Province, was named after Hsieh T'iao, a famous writer of the Chin Dynasty who was known as the Lesser Hsieh because he was the nephew of the still more famous writer of the same surname, Hsieh Ling-yun, known as the Great Hsieh. Li Po, in high compliment, compares himself to Secretary Shu-yün as the Lesser Hsieh to the Great Hsieh. (See Li Po's *A Song of Lu Mountain* and *T'ien Mu Mountain*.)

"The bones of great writers" carries in the original a specific reference to Chien-an, a celebrated period of letters during the Wêi Dynasty of the Three Kingdoms.

36. The road Li Po is describing runs from Shen-si Province (Ch'in) to Sze-chuan Province (Shu). In the original text the two early rulers are named: Ts'an-tsung and Yü-fu, both of the legendary ages.

"The City of Silk": Ch'êng-tu, the capital of Sze-chuan Province.

37. She was in Ch'ang-an, the T'ang capital, and he near Yen-jan, a boundary mountain. She has set down her harp from Chao (Chih-li Province) and significantly taken up her Sze-chuan lute, with its strings in attuned pairs.

38. The master, Ts'ên, refers to the poet, Ts'ên Ts'an, and the scholar, Tan-ch'iu, to a Taoist hermit of the early T'ang period, whose real name was unknown.

Prince Ch'ên was Ts'ao Chih of the Wêi Dynasty in the Three Kingdoms period.

The translation "flower-dappled horse" simplifies a comparison in the original to the five-flowered coin, a comparison which, though familiar and quick to the Chinese imagination, would for a Westerner impede the rush of the poem. (See Ts'ên Ts'an *A Song of Running-Horse River*.)

39. The poet, according to Chinese custom, means himself when in the original he names someone well known to whose lot or experience his own may be likened. Ssŭ-ma Hsiang-ju of the Han Dynasty, a famous scholar, was the guest of Prince Liang, but later retired and died in Mao-ling. The story is told that, invited to the house of a rich man, Cho Wang-sun, Hsiang-ju with a lute sang so beautifully his poem, *The Phœnix in Search of His Mate,* that Wên-chün, Cho Wang-sun's nineteen-year-old widowed daughter, fell in love with him. Rapt in wine, he sang with his lute another song, asking her to elope. She did. Having no money, they opened and conducted a small wine-house; and though the father, through family pride, bade them come home, the poet refused. The resort was so obscure that the Emperor Ch'êng, who liked his poetry, could not find him. But the Empress, unloved, discovered him and persuaded him with a bribe to write a poem with which she could regain imperial favour. This poem, which was read to the Emperor as hers, causing him to love her again, is a long one and still extant.

39a. Carp in the river and wildgeese or bluebirds in the sky were the classical messengers of love, or of friendship. In one of the Nineteen Ancient Poems, the poet tells how he was brought some carp by a boy and, cutting one of them open, found in its belly a letter from his beloved, declaring her love and wishing him happiness.

40. Only officials above the third rank in the T'ang Dynasty wore the decoration of the Golden Tortoise.

41. It was believed that paradise, with its Jade Pool, lay to the west of China and that there stood also the palace of Hsi-wang-mu, the Royal Mother of the West. Stories are frequent, in Chinese and Japanese literature and art, of emperors trying to communicate with her kingdom. Emperor Mu of the Chou Dynasty had eight horses, able to cover ten thousand miles in a day.

Driving them west, he reached the kingdom and found the goddess. But he never returned. And *The Yellow Bamboo Song* was composed as a mourning-song for him and his followers, all but a few of whom died on the way.

42. In ancient stories, King Yi was cruel to his wife, Ch'ang-o. Planning to escape him, she stole from heaven a miraculous potion by means of which she might flee away and be safe. When she had drunk the potion, she began to run very fast and could not stop. Finally she entered the moon and was unable to find her way out. So she remained there and became its goddess, her husband becoming, in his turn, God of the Sun. (See notes 4b and 91.)

43. When only twenty-four years old, Chia Yi, a statesman and man of letters, sent a ten-thousand-word memorial, offering his political views and plans for reform, to Emperor Wên of the Han Dynasty. The period was prosperous and the Emperor, though not warm-hearted, was a just ruler. But Chia Yi was sensitive and had fears for the future. Everyone thought him crazy. Even the Emperor considered him a visionary whose dreams were of no value, and sent him as a petty official to Ch'ang-sha, now capital of Hu-nan Province, but at that time an out-of-the-way place, where he died. After thirty or forty years his prophecies came true and he was remembered. While at Ch'ang-sha, he acted as tutor to a prince, as mentioned in Liu Chang-ch'ing's *New Year's*. Near the Hsiang River, Chia Yi had written a poem eulogizing Chü Yuan, the famous poet, who in exile had drowned himself there. In the same locality Liu Chang-ch'ing, also in exile, wrote *On Passing Chia Yi's House in Ch'ang-sha*. The same poet's *An Evening View of the City*, the poem he sent to Governor Yüan, intimates that Liu Chang-ch'ing in exile was as meritorious as Chia Yi.

44. It was a poetical belief that the cicada was the purest member of the insect world and lived only upon dew. Its advice to Li Shang-yin is rather to die nobly of hunger at home with his family than to lead an ignoble and uncertain official life.

45. *The Precious Dagger* was a long poem by Kuo Yüan-chên sent to the T'ang Woman-Emperor, Wu-Chao. (See note 7.) The theme of the poem was that a good scholar is like a precious dagger. The poet was summoned to become her attendant. During the fifteen years of her successful reign, akin in more ways than one to the reign of Queen Elizabeth in England, Tibet was conquered, and part of Turkestan.

45a. The Blue Houses are the quarters of the dancing-girls.

46. Chuang-tzǔ, dreaming once that he had been transformed into into a butterfly, awoke to find the butterfly gone and his own body on the bed. He said: "I do not know which is my real self, this or the butterfly." Another story is told of him. Walking with his friend Huêi-tzǔ, he saw some fish in the water and said: "How happy they are!" Huêi answered: "You are not a fish; how do you know they are happy?" And Chuang retorted: "You are not I. How do you know I do not know that they are happy?"

The tears of merfolk were supposed to become pearls. It was believed that in the fields of paradise grew only jewels and jade, which, under the sun's heat, would give off their colours in mist.

47. *Nameless Lines* are always love-poems, the designation having become a custom. We translate the title *To One Unnamed*.

48. In the original seventh line, Liu is named in the poet's place. Liu went once to a mountain, met a nymph there, and was entertained; but, coming away, lost his direction and never found it again; like the famous fisherman from Wu-ling, who lost his way to the Peach-Blossom Country.

It was supposed that a lock decorated with a golden toad was thereby made secure.

The jade tiger was a marker on a well-rope, gauging the water's depth.

Lady Chia, the daughter of a premier of the Chin Dynasty, and specified in the original text, fell in love with her father's young secretary, Han Shou, and finally married him, in spite of his low rank. Her father, recognizing on Han Shou's clothes a particular scent used by his daughter, could not withhold his approval of the marriage.

Prince Wêi, also specified in the original, met on the Lo River a fairy, Lady Mi, who gave him a bridal mat and disappeared. He wrote about the episode, a long and beautiful account in rhythmic prose.

49. General Chu-kê Liang, called also K'ung-ming, is a familiar figure in these poems. He was a celebrated general, scholar and statesman in the period of the Three Kingdoms, who as Premier advised and served the founder of the Shu Kingdom, Emperor Liu Pêi, restored rebellious lands, and in later times was honoured and worshipped by the people. (See Tu Fu's *A Song of an Old Cypress, The Temple of the Premier of Shu*, and *Thoughts of Old Time*, stanza II.)

49a. The Eight-Sided Fortress (*pa-chên-t'u*) was built on Chu-kê Liang's plan of the eight diagrams, beside the upper Yang-tsze in Sze-chuan. He advised his Emperor, campaigning against the other two kingdoms, to master the Wêi Kingdom first; but the Emperor, rejecting his advice, attacked first the Wu Kingdom and was defeated. (See note 52a.)

49b. Emperor Liu Pêi, before his accession, went twice to Chu-kê Liang's hut for counsel and was refused; but the third time, when the Emperor knelt by the bed and said: "Not for my sake, but for the sake of my people, assist me," Chu-kê Liang consented. He remained Premier into the reign of the succeeding Emperor. Finally, as general, he planned a victory which his death prevented.

Historians regard Emperor Liu Pêi, founder of the Shu Kingdom, as carrying on the Han Dynasty against two usurpers in the other two of the Three Kingdoms, Shu, Wu, and Wêi, which in Liu Yü-hsi's poem *In the Temple of the First King of Shu* are likened to a three-legged pot. The same poem refers to the fact that in the other kingdoms the five-pennyweight coin was given less than its proper weight. The "great premier" in this poem was the famous Chu-kê Liang.

49c. The Later Emperor of the Shu Kingdom, the second whom Chu-kê Liang served and advised, was defeated and captured after the Premier's death.

The Liang-fu Song (Song of the Holy Mountain) concerning one of the peaks of T'ai-shan, had been written by Chu-kê Liang while he was still a hermit, and before he yielded to the Emperor's third request for assistance.

49d. In Tu Fu's Night in the Watch-Tower, Chu-kê Liang is referred to as "Sleeping-Dragon," and Kung-sun Shu, another Han general, as "Plunging-Horse."

50. Kuan and Yüeh, specified in the original, were statesmen of the Chou Dynasty. Kuan and Chang, also specified, two great generals in the Shu Kingdom, were both killed in action; the first of them, Kuan Yü, has been made the Chinese god of war, called also Kuan Ti.

51. The Canons of Yao and Hsun were two volumes in the Confucian Book of History, Ch'ing-miao and Shêng-min two poems in the Confucian Book of Poetry, and the T'ang plate and Confucian tripod two art treasures.

The three Huang rulers and five Ti rulers were famous as good sovereigns of ancient China.

52. Chou Yü, a hero of the period of the Three Kingdoms, young, handsome, a statesman, a general, a scholar, a musician, was fond of listening to classical music and when a mistake would be made is said to have reminded the player with a glance. The listener here is of course not Chou Yü, but one whose eye the harpist likes to attract, and probably also a connoisseur of music.

52a. In Tu Mu's By the Purple Cliff (a cliff on the Yangtsze, east of Han-k'ou, Hu-pêi Province) allusion is made to a celebrated event occurring there, an exploit of Chou Yü's. A fleet from the Wêi Kingdom had come down the river to attack the Wu and Shu Kingdoms. The two generals, Chu-kê Liang of the Shu Kingdom, and Chou Yü of the Wu Kingdom, combined forces and destroyed the fleet by setting it afire. The King of Wêi, if he had won this battle, would have been able to bear captive to his Copper-Bird Palace the two famously beautiful girls of Ch'iao, one of them the wife of the King of Wu and the other the wife of General Chou Yü. These girls are celebrated in Chinese poetry, like Helen of Troy in European poetry, as a romantic source of war. In Tu Fu's poem *The Eight-Sided Fortress*, is sung Chu-kê Liang's grief that he had not conquered the Wu Kingdom; yet here are seen the Wu and Shu Kingdoms allied against the Wêi Kingdom. Changes in the military alignment of Chinese war-lords have always been rapid.

53. This temple, in Yang-chou, Kiang-su Province, was on a terrace erected by General Wu of the Ch'ên Dynasty and was named after him.

The river is the Yang-tsze.

54. In the original text of Liu Chang-ch'ing's *On Leaving Kiu-kiang* the familiar poetical term "Green-Wave Islands" is used for Ch'ang-an, the capital, from which he had been previously exiled because of a storm he had aroused by too freely expressing his own ideas.

In the original of Shên Ch'üan-ch'i's *Beyond Seeing*, the capital is called "The City of the Red Phœnix"; and in Wang Wêi's *To Chi-wu Ch'ien*, "The Gate of Gold."

55. The fellow-official sent to Lien-chou was Liu Yü-hsi, the poet.

56. The clans of Wang and Shieh, specified in the original, had been prominent in Nan-king. They had lived on Blacktail Row, which, decaying in the superseded capital, was now left to the swallows and the poor.

57. In the period of the Three Kingdoms, the Yang-tsze River was fortified with chains to defend Nan-king, capital of the Wu Kingdom. But Wang Chün, of the Chin Dynasty, building high-storied war-ships, brought them down from Sze-chuan, managed to cut to pieces the iron chains at the mouth of the river, and so captured the city.

58. The original text of the second line reads: "Sings me what I am thinking under my southern cap." A prisoner from the south would wear all of the northern prison-garb, but keep his own cap to remember his own land. And the phrase "southern cap" has come to symbolize a political prisoner, with the implication that he maintains his ideas. This prisoner, for instance, cannot make his pure thoughts heard by the Emperor through the noise of the confused world.

59. Li Kuang of the Han Dynasty, an eminent general against the Tartars, shot one night at a black tiger and next morning found that the point of his arrow was stuck in a solid piece of rock. There is brief reference to him in Wang Wêi's *Song of an Old General*. In Wang Ch'ang-ling's *Over the Border* he is called "The Winged General." (See note 111.)

60. There was a myth that when the two sisters, O-huang and Nü-yin, wives of the dead Emperor Shun, had finished their period of mourning, they became Queens of the Clouds. Lake Tung-t'ing is the only place from which comes a certain spotted bamboo popular with both Chinese and Japanese for its decorative effect. The spots were made by the Queens' tears.

61. Yang Hu of the Chin Dynasty, a governor stationed at Hsiang-yang, now in Hu-pêi Province, was famous as scholar, statesman and general and was much loved by the people. After his death a monument was erected on the Yen Mountain and inscribed with his deeds and was visited by so many mourners that it was called the Monument of Tears.

62. The bluebird, a messenger of the affections, summoned him to the house of his friend, whom he likens to the Han Dynasty Genie of the Red Pine. (See note 89.)

62a. Taoists were often alchemists, with crucibles and potions. Wêi Ying-wu in his *Poem to a Taoist Hermit* speaks of his friend "boiling white stones"—to be eaten thereafter like potatoes.

63. The original second line reads: "If I had enough for the Three Paths." The Three Paths indicated a hermit's hut, one to the front door, one to the back door, and one around the house.

In ancient alchemy it was believed that the flame of cinnamon-wood consumed gold.

64. In Mêng Hao-jan's poem the phrase used for the Mountain Holiday, a day on which everyone goes mountain-climbing for seeing the view, drinking wine, and writing poems, is the Feast of the Two Nines, the ninth day of the ninth month. In Wang Wêi's *On the Mountain Holiday* reference is made to the custom of each climber's carrying a spray of dogwood. Ts'uêi Shu also has a poem concerning this festival.

65. The ancient hermitage is specified as that of P'ang, a hermit who lived on Lu-mên Mountain during the Han Dynasty; but the hermitage meant is probably Mêng's own.

66. The Great Dipper is compared to Kê-shu, the famous T'ang general who conquered Tibet, between which and China ran the Lin-t'ao River.

67. One of the palace luxuries was a pillow under which charcoal and incense were arranged, for fragrant warmth.

68. Wang Sun, a name akin to the English "Prince Charming," but more serious, and translated here "Prince of Friends," means a noble-hearted young scholar or, sometimes, lover. (See Wang Wêi's *A Parting* and *An Autumn Evening in the Mountains.*)

There was an old song:

The wild grass loves Wang Sun
And he the grasses;
And when he rides away,
They call to him.

69. The places mentioned in Po Chü-yi's note were widely separate: in Shan-si, Ho-nan, An-huêi, and Kiang-si Provinces.

70. Li Yen-nien of the Han Dynasty had said of an earlier beauty than Yang Kuêi-fêi:

One glance, and she could shatter down a city;
A second, she could tip an empire over.

71. The instrument translated "guitar" was a *p'i-p'a*, like the Japanese *biwa*, as in Tu Fu's *Thoughts of Old Time*, stanza I. (See note 25.)

72. Sêng, the poet's name, is a variant of Sanka, given as a family name to Buddhist priests.

73. Between Kiang-si and Kuang-tung, even the wildgeese find the Ta-yü (Great Granary) Mountains too high to cross.

Plum-blossoms have not yet opened farther north; but there are plenty in the warm south beyond this mountain.

74. The morning bell, tokening here the separation of friends, was a popular subject among poets as a symbol of finality. For instance, the Chinese spring, beginning on the first day of the First-month, corresponding to early February, ends on the thirtieth day of the Third-month, in our May; and its definite close is sung by Chia Tao in the latter two lines of a four-line poem called *The Thirtieth Day of the Third Month:*

I shall lie and share with you, awake,
The last of spring, till the morning bell.

75. "The Way" (Tao) is the Way of the Universe, the Flow of Unison. It is the essence of Taoism.

At the age of thirty-one, when his wife died, Wang Wêi left his post as Assistant Secretary of State and, as told in his poem *My Retreat at Mount Chung-nan*, came to live by Mount Chung-nan, turning his heart to the teachings of Laotzu.

75a. Laotzu, the founder and teacher of Taoism, despairing of mankind's acceptance of the Way, rode westward on a dun-coloured cow and disappeared for ever in the desert wilderness. At the wall, however, the guard of the gate, of whom nothing is known but his name, Yin-hsi, stopped the aged saint and kept him overnight at the border to set down his principles. The result was the famous mystical book *Tao-tê-ching:* Tao being the "Way" and Tê the exemplification of the mystical philosophy. (See Ts'uêi Shu's *A Climb on the Mountain Holiday* and Liu Chang-ch'ing's *While Visiting the Taoist Priest.*)

76. The Green Books: Chinese official history.

77. The references in the last two lines are to two youths of the Han Dynasty. The first, Pan Ch'ao, in his boyhood a copyist, threw his writing-brush to the ground one day and exclaimed: "I will join the army and fight the Huns!" He became later a famous and successful general. The other, Chung Chün, going to the border to fight the Huns, took off his student cap at the gate and demanded in exchange a lariat, with which he captured Hun chieftains.

78. Emperor Wên of the Han Dynasty, having trouble with the meaning of Laotzu's book, sent for the Old Magician of the River Bank, of whose wisdom he had heard. The wizard answered: "If the Emperor asked something else, I would go to him. But if he asks the meaning of Tao and Tê, he should come to me." Whereupon the Emperor visited him and referred to the Confucian Book of Poems, in which it says that every being within the Empire is subject to the emperor. The old man raised himself to the middle of the sky and answered: "Above I do not touch heaven, nor in the centre man, nor below earth. To whom am I subject?" The Emperor bowed and asked him other questions; but the wizard, dropping him a volume, a commentary on the *Tao-tê-ching*, vanished. Later, to commemorate the event, the Emperor built on the spot this Terrace Whence One Sees the Magician (*Wang-Hsien-T'ai*).

79. Tu Ch'iu-niang was a singing-girl, the only woman poet in this anthology.

80. This famous performer, Li Kuêi-nien, was court-musician to Emperor Hsüan-tsung.

81. Ch'ü Yüan, author of *The Songs of Ch'u*, the first rhythmic prose in Chinese, had drowned himself in the Mi-lo River.

82. In the original text, Premier Fang Kuan is indirectly meant by a direct allusion to Premier Hsieh An of the Chin Dynasty, famously fond of chess. Fang is likened also to Lord Hsü, in reference to the following story. Prince Chi-cha of the Chou Dynasty had a very fine dagger, and he knew that Lord Hsü, through whose lands he was passing, coveted it and would not ask for it. The Prince was travelling and could not be without it. When he returned from his journey, Lord Hsü was dead; and Chi-cha, visiting the tomb, hung on a tree there the coveted dagger.

83. Hearing that the bandits have been dispersed in

Northern Chi (Chih-li Province), the poet sets out from Chien Station in Sze-chuan, and passing in that province the two mountains, Pa-hsia and Wu-hsia, he reaches Hsiang-yang, in Hu-pêi Province, on his way home to Lo-yang in Ho-nan Province. These names, in the original text, are used in effective succession.

84. For a literal translation of this poem, character by character, see Dr. Kiang's Introduction.

85. Yi and Lü were celebrated early statesmen; and in the following line of the original text, Hsiao and Ts'ao were also specified: the greatest statesmen of the Han Dynasty.

86. Lao-tzŭ had said in the *Tao-tê-ching:* "The heavenly net is broad. It is loose, but never loses."

87. "The late Emperor" was Hsüan-tsung, and the Kuos the family of the famous general Kuo Tzŭ-yi. (See notes 4 and 4a, b, c, d.) T'ai-tsung was the grandfather of Hsüan-tsung.

One of the lines from this poem, "The high clear glance, the deep firm breath," is a phrase frequently quoted as applying to superior literature and brushmanship.

Secretary Wêi Fêng was himself a painter, as of course was Prince Chiang-tu; and Chih Tun was a famous horse-painter of the Chin Dynasty.

88. Lady Wêi was tutor of Wang Hsi-chih, who was a sage of the brush. (See note 16.)

The emperor referred to was Hsüan-tsung.

The origin of the line in which we use the phrase "founders of this dynasty" contains the names of the Princes Pao and Ê, two great generals who helped found the T'ang Dynasty, and in the later line in which we use the phrase "even the finest are deprived of their spirit," the original text specified Hua and Liu, two celebrated horses.

Han Kan's horse-paintings are much admired to this day.

89. "Unicorn" is the best translation we can make of the sacred animal, *ch'i-lin.* (See note 19a.)

The southern rivers are specified in the original as the Hsiao and Hsiang, which are in Hu-nan Province.

Of the Wizard of the Red Pine we have said: "After his earlier follower he has now a new disciple." Tu Fu's text reads: "He has a new disciple, a very Chang Liang." Chang Liang was a great statesmen, especially known as a wise adviser to the founder of the Han Dynasty. After Emperor Kao-tsu succeeded in unifying China, Chang Liang retired and followed his Taoist tutor, the Wizard of the Red Pine, and disappeared. Using a common convention in Chinese poetry, Tu Fu names Chang Liang, but means Censor Han, whose merit and case are comparable.

90. This was the temple of Chu-kê Liang. (See notes 49 and 49a, b, c, d.) The temple stood outside the city of Ch'êng-tu, the capital of Sze-chuan.

The poem intimates that in the reconstruction of a country strong statesmen are needed, but that it is difficult to enlist and direct their strength.

91. "Grassy writing" is familiarly and improperly referred to as the running handwriting, the same Chinese character meaning grass and draught.

In Chinese mythology, Yi, the famous archer, shot down from the sky nine of the ten suns and became afterward king of the one sun left; his wife, Ch'ang-o, becoming Queen of the Moon. (See Li Shang-yin's *To the Moon Goddess*, also notes 4b and 42.)

The Pear-Garden Players were the imperial troupe of actors at the court of Emperor Hsüan-tsung. (See note 4b.)

92. The deposed Prince may have been Su-tsung. (See note 4d.)

The crow, especially the white-headed, is a bird of ill omen.

The final line means that the spirits of the five emperors of the T'ang Dynasty are befriending the deposed Prince.

93. The term Spring Palace is still used in China to connote venery.

94. The Chao Tomb, specified in the original, was the tomb of Emperor T'ai-tsung, the second ruler of the T'ang Dynasty, and the most illustrious.

95. In the original, the river region is specified as Chiang-nan, the region along the lower Yang-tsze.

There is still a place in Yang-chou called Twenty-Four Bridges. It probably meant arches.

96. In the original, the two stars are named—the Cowherd and the Spinning-girl (Ch'ien-niu and Chih-nü): the reference being to a well-known story, the conclusion of which is that two sweethearts, having been changed into stars, are able to see each other across the Milky Way, but are allowed to meet only once a year, on the seventh night of the Seventh-month. Lafcadio Hearn has translated from the Japanese a long poem on this subject.

97. The man who owned this garden, Shih Ch'ung of the Chin Dynasty, was the richest man of his time. The last line of this poem alludes to one of many stories about him. A certain general coveted a favourite of his, a girl named Lu-chu, whom Shih Ch'ung refused to surrender. Presently the general, charging him with treason, sent troops to seize Lu-chu. She shut herself in her high chamber; and when they took Shih Ch'ung, she threw herself from the window to her death.

98. It was a poetical belief that the call of the wildgoose came never from pairs, but only from the solitary.

99. Tu Shên-yen was Tu Fu's grandfather.

100. The Court of Perpetual Faith meant the Ladies' Palace, and the Court of the Bright Sun the Emperor's Palace—where apparently some darker lady was in favour.

101. We have translated as "eastern song" the definite phrase of the original, "Yüeh song," meaning a song of Chê-kiang Province.

The orchid is known in China as the Flower of the Scholar.

102. The last line probably means that Chinese civilization had not crossed the boundary.

103. Wang Wêi is not only one of China's great poets, but one of her great painters. Su Tung-po of the Sung Dynasty said of him: "In his poems we find his paintings, in his paintings his poems."

104. This song is still popular as a song of farewell, and to this day the expression is often used, "Since we picked willow branches," meaning: "Since we parted."

105. In the original the girls who paid tribute were specified as the Han girls, and the quarrelling farmers as Pa people.

Wên-wêng was a Han Dynasty official, famous as being the first to civilize what is now Sze-chuan Province.

106. From the time of the Han Dynasty, palace guards wore red caps before dawn. The guard of the inner gate would announce dawn, and the others would echo his call till all the gates were opened.

The Jade-Cloud Furs, the Pearl Crown, and the Dragon Robe were accoutrements of the Emperor.

During the Han Dynasty there stood in the palace courtyard great bronze giants, holding up their hollowed palms to catch the dew of heaven.

The last line refers to the promulgation of the imperial edict from a five-coloured silken scroll by a procession of officials, one of whom was Chia Chih.

107. It is told by Chuang-tzŭ, that Yang-tzŭ, the scholar, before he became a student of Lao-tzŭ, was highly respected and honoured by his fellow men. Later, through the many years of his discipleship, he lost his prestige, and even a boor would take precedence over him; but he was glad, because he had got rid of pretensions.

There once was a hermit who was fond of sea-gulls; and they followed him wherever he went. His father, asking why they were not frightened, bade the son bring him some. But next day, when the hermit went out intending to take them to his father, they all flew away.

108. *Oh, to Go Back Again!* is a song from the Confucian Book of Poems.

109. When the Yüeh Kingdom (now Chê-kiang) was conquered by the Wu Kingdom (now Kiang-su), the Yüeh King still held his throne and plotted to throw off the tributary yoke. Aided by his able minister Fan Li, he planned to distract the King of Wu with women. Fan Li searched through the Yüeh Kingdom for beautiful girls and came upon Hsi Shih washing clothes beside a lake. Controlling his own love for her, he fiercely persuaded her to his plan. She remained at court for some time, and the Wu King, in his infatuation, forgot affairs of state. Weakened by this means, the Wu Kingdom was eventually overcome by the Yüeh Kingdom. Fan Li afterwards refused all reward except Hsi Shih, whom he then took travelling through the Five Lakes, the famous sacred lakes corresponding to the Five Sacred Mountains. There is an allusion to this in Wên T'ing-yun's *Near the Li-chou Ferry.*

Hsi Shih suffered from heart-trouble; and men said that her drawn brows, her look of gentleness in suffering, which the girls of her time tried unsuccessfully to imitate, increased her beauty.

110. In the original text where we have used the phrase "the richest men of old," Chi-lun and Shih Ch'ung are specified, celebrated rich men of the Chin Dynasty; and toward the end, where we have used the phrase "hosts of the gayest mansions," the original specifies Chao and Li, well-known rich men of the Han Dynasty who maintained in their homes many dancing-girls.

111. The Horseman of Yeh was Ts'ao Chang, a son of the founder of the Wêi Dynasty in the period of the Three Kingdoms.

General Wêi Ch'ing and General Li Kuang were contemporary generals of the Han Dynasty. The first of them was successful but not able. The second was an able man who happened to fail and is named here to indicate the general about whom the poem is written. Lu Lun's *Border-Songs* concern Li Kuang, also Wang Ch'ang-ling's *Over the Border.*

The original reference to the gushing water specifies "in Su-lê" and concerns Kên Kung, a general of the Han Dynasty who, surrounded by the Tartars in Su-lê City, was without water, but who prayed and was answered by the gushing of a spring which saved his men.

In the next line the original text names Ying-chüan, the native place of Kuan Fu, who is thereby indicated and who was a general of the Han Dynasty, a wine-drinking mischief-maker. In the original the last two lines refer definitely to "the Prefect of Yün-chung." This was Wêi Shang of the Han Dynasty. He was a venerable official at Yüng-chung near the Tartar border and was removed on account of his age. But when the Tartars began to advance, he was restored to his post by the Emperor and gave distinguished service.

112. Nan-king, called formerly and in the original of this poem Chin-ling, was the capital of the Six Dynasties (317–589).

113. In Giles's *History of Chinese Literature* the latter two lines of this poem are mistakenly ascribed to Tu Fu.

114. Sent by the Emperor Wu Ti of Han (140–87 B.C.) as envoy to the Huns, Su Wu was held captive by them near the Gobi Desert and lived there for nineteen years as a shepherd. When he returned, in 86 B.C., the first year of the reign of Chao Ti, he was rewarded with "two paltry millions and the chancellorship of the Tributary States . . . not a foot of soil . . . while some cringing courtier gets the marquisate of ten thousand families." Poems of great beauty and interest were interchanged between Su Wu and the renegade general Li Ling.

115. In the original text of the second line the poet, indicating himself, names Ch'ien-lou, a well-known but indigent scholar who finally starved to death; and in the later lines which we translate

> There have been better men than I to whom heaven denied
> a son,
> There was a poet better than I whose dead wife could not
> hear him,

the original text specifies Têng Yu, a man of good character and conduct, to whom Heaven was deaf and unjust, granting him no sons, and P'an Yüeh, a writer famous for his elegies to his wife.

The unknown Chinese editor entitled this volume "three hundred poems"; the number, as in the Confucian collection, being slightly inexact.

ACKNOWLEDGMENTS

For carefully recording and helpfully shaping Dr. Kiang's dictation of the literal texts of one of the two Chinese volumes comprising this work—the volume containing the longer poems—I am indebted to a well-chosen pupil and friend of his and mine, Mr. Will Garrett. For pertinent and wise suggestions I am grateful to Mr. Arthur Davison Ficke, Mr. Porter Garnett, Mr. Haniel Long, Mrs. Julia Ellsworth Ford, Mr. Cliff McCarthy, Dr. Hu Suh, Mr. Nieh Shih-chang, and Princess Der Ling.

Two hundred and seventy-eight of the poems have been printed in the following magazines and journals:

The Freeman, Asia, The Nation, Poetry, Orient, The International Interpreter, Palms, The New York Evening Post, The New Republic, The Dial, The Bookman, The China Review, The Christian Century, Contemporary Verse, The Double Dealer, The Forum, The Fugitive, The Harvard Advocate, Hearst's, Holland's, The Independent, The Little Review, The Measure, The Lyric, The Midland, The Modern Review, The New Orient, The North-China Herald, The Outlook, Parnassus, Pegasus, Phantasmus, The Review, Rhythmus, Shadowland, The Smart Set, The Poetry Folio, The Southwest Review, Voices, The Wave, The World Tomorrow, The Virginia Quarterly Review, Tambour, Beau, Caprice, The Santa Fe New Mexican, Pearson's Magazine and The London Mercury.

The introduction, *Poetry and Culture,* appeared in The Dial, and an expanded form of it under the title *The Persistence of Poetry* is being privately printed as a book by The Book Club of California.

W.B.

Indices

·❧❦❧·

INDEX OF TITLES

After Missing the Recluse on the Western Mountain 80
After the Day of Fire 84
Alone in Her Beauty 193
Autumn Cottage at Pa-Shang, An 148
Autumn Evening, An 84
Autumn Evening in the Mountains, An 220
Autumn Night Message, An 231
Answering Vice-Prefect Chang 221
Ascending the Pagoda at the Temple of Kind Favour 175
At a Banquet in the House of the Taoist Priest Mêi 151
At a Border-Fortress 212
At Ch'u-chou on the Western Stream 231
At Heron Lodge 214
At Hibiscus Inn 210
At Nan-king Ferry 70
At Parting 224
At the Mountain-Lodge of the Buddhist Priest Ye Waiting in Vain for My
    Friend Ting 154
At Wang Ch'ang-ling's Retreat 65

Beautiful Hsi Shih, The 226
Beyond Seeing 169
Beyond the Border 214
Bidding a Friend Farewell at Ching-mên Ferry 109
Bitter Love, A 107
Blacktail Row 143
Boat in Spring on Jo-ya Lake, A 81
Border-Songs 146
Both Sides of the Yellow River Recaptured by the Imperial Army 189
Bound Home to Mount Sung 220
Bride, A 213
Brief but Happy Meeting with My Brother-in-Law, A 133
Bringing in the Wine 120

Buddhist Retreat Behind Broken-Mountain Temple, A 65
By the Purple Cliff 206

Chancing on Old Friends in a Village Inn 173
Chia Yi 123
Cicada, A 124
Climb on the Mountain Holiday to the Terrace Whence One Sees the Magician, A 181
Climbing in Autumn for a View from the Temple on the Terrace of General Wu 134
Coming Home 93
Confession, A 207
Cooler Weather 86
Crossing the Han River 106

Day of No Fire, The 61
Deer-Park Hermitage 218
Down Chung-nan Mountain to the Kind Pillow and Bowl of Hu Ssü 111
Drawing of a Horse by General Ts'ao at Secretary Wêi Fêng's House, A 195
Drinking Alone with the Moon 111
Drinking Song at Stone-Fish Lake, A 241
Dwelling by a Stream 142

Early Audience at the Palace of Light, An 174
Early Audience at the Palace of Light, An 223
Early Autumn 94
East of the Town 234
Eight-Sided Fortress, The 184
Elegy, An 238
Endless Yearning 119
Entertaining Literary Men in My Official Residence on a Rainy Day 232
Evening View of the City of Yo-chou After Coming from Han-kou to Parrot Island, An 137

Falling Petals 124
Farewell at Fêng-chi Station, A 187
Farewell in the Evening Rain, A 232
Farewell to a Buddhist Monk, A 134
Farewell to a Friend, A 109
Farewell to a Japanese Buddhist Priest Bound Homeward 76
Farewell to Governor Li on His Way Home to Han-yang, A 135
Farewell to Han Shen at the Yun-yang Inn, A 170
Farewell to Li Tuan, A 147
Farewell to Mêng Hao-jan on His Way to Yang-chou, A 107

Farewell to My Friend Ch'ên Chang-fu, A *102*
Farewell to Secretary Shu-yün at the Hsieh T'iao Villa in Hsüan-chou, A *116*
Farewell to Ts'uêi, A *157*
Farewell to Vice-Prefect Tu Setting Out for His Official Post in Shu *216*
Farewell to Wêi Wan Bound for the Capital, A *101*
Farm-House on the Wêi River, A *226*
From a Mooring on the Tung-lu to a Friend in Yang-chou *152*
From an Upper Story *190*
From Ch'in Country to the Buddhist Priest Yuan *152*
From My Study at the Mouth of the Valley *76*
From the City-Tower of Liu-chou *141*

Garden of the Golden Valley, The *208*
General Kê-shu *156*
Gold-Threaded Robe, The *183*
Grasses *158*
Green Stream, A *225*
Greeting on the Huai River to My Old Friends from Liang-ch'üan, A *231*

Han Monument, The *129*
Hard Road, The *120*
Hard Roads in Shu *117*
Harmonizing a Poem by Palace-Attendant Kuo *224*
Hearty Welcome, A *188*

I Climb to the Lo-yu Tombs Before Leaving for Wu-hsing *206*
I Pass Through the Lu Dukedom with a Sigh and a Sacrifice for Confucius *95*
In a Retreat Among Bamboos *218*
In Her Quiet Window *210*
In My Lodge at Wang-ch'üan After a Long Rain *224*
In the Quiet Night *107*
In Spring *112*
In Summer at the South Pavilion *154*
In the Autumn Night *207*
In the Camp of the Sketching Brush *127*
In the Temple of the First King of Shu *143*
Inlaid Harp, The *125*
Inscribed in the Inn at T'ung Gate on an Autumn Trip to the Capital *94*
Inscribed in the Temple of the Wandering Genie *84*
Inscribed on the Wall of an Inn North of Ta-yü Mountain *172*

Jade Dressing-Table, The *83*
Jade Pool, The *123*

Letter to Censor Han, A 197
Lines 169
Lines 219
Long Climb, A 189
Looking at the Moon and Thinking of One Far Away 66
Looking Down in a Spring-Rain on the Course from Fairy-Mountain Palace
    to the Pavilion of Increase 223
Looking Toward an Inner Gate of the Great Wall 178
Lo-yu Tombs, The 122
Lute Song, A 102

Memories in Early Winter 153
Message, A 71
Message from Lake Tung-t'ing, A 150
Message from My Lodge at Wang-ch'üan, A 220
Message to Censor Tu Fu at His Office in the Left Court 174
Message to Commissioner Li at Tsu-choŭ, A 222
Message to Han Cho the Yang-chou Magistrate, A 207
Message to Mêng Hao-jan, A 109
Message to Secretary Ling-hu, A 122
Moon at the Fortified Pass, The 112
Moonlight Night, A 139
Mooring at Twilight in Yü-Yi District 234
Mooring on the Ch'in-huai River, A 206
Mooring Under North Fort Hill, A 217
Mount Chung-nan 221
Mountain-Stones 87
My Retreat at Mount Chung-nan 222

Nan-King Landscape, A 230
Near the Li-chou Ferry 236
New Year's at Ch'ang-sha 136
Night Abroad, A 187
Night at a Tavern, A 208
Night in the Watch-Tower 190
Night-Mooring at Wu-ch'ang, A 147
Night-Mooring Near Maple Bridge, A 62
Night-Mooring on the Chien-tê River, A 150
Night Thought on Terrace Tower, A 230
Night-Vigil in the Left Court of the Palace, A 185
North Among Green Vines 125
Not Finding Lu Hung-chien at Home 168

Note Left for an Absent Recluse, A 75
Note on a Rainy Night to a Friend in the North, A 122

Of One in the Forbidden City 69
Old Air, An 101
Old Fisherman, An 142
Old War-Song, An 105
On a Gate-Tower at Yu-chou 73
On a Walk in the Early Spring 209
On a Moonlight Night 184
On Climbing in Nan-king to the Terrace of Phœnixes 110
On Climbing Orchid Mountain in the Autumn 153
On Climbing Yen Mountain with Friends 151
On Hearing a Flute at Night from the Wall of Shou-hsiang 133
On Hearing a Lute-Player 134
On Hearing An Wan-shan Play the Reed-Pipe 104
On Hearing Chün the Buddhist Monk from Shu Play His Lute 110
On Hearing Her Play the Harp 132
On Hearing Tung Play the Flageolet 103
On Leaving Kiu-kiang Again 136
On Leaving the Tomb of Premier Fang 187
On Ma-wêi Slope 74
On Meeting a Messenger to the Capital 174
On Meeting Li-Kuêi-nien Down the River 184
On Meeting My Friend Fêng Chu in the Capital 234
On New Year's Eve 182
On Parting with the Buddhist Pilgrim Ling-ch'ê 134
On Passing Chia Yi's House in Ch'ang-sha 137
On Returning at the Year's End to Chung-nan Mountain 151
On Seeing the Snow-Peak of Chung-nan 178
On Seeing Wang Leave for the South 135
On the Border 64
On the Eve of Government Examinations 82
On the Festival of the Moon 88
On the Gate-Tower at Yo-chou 188
On the Mountain Holiday 219
On the Terrace of Assembled Angels 69
One-Hearted 218
Orchid and Orange 66
Over the Border 211

Palace of the Suêi Emperor, The 126
Palace Poem, A 96

Palace Poem, A 100
Parting 207
Parting, A 218
Parting at a Wine-Shop in Nan-king 116
Passing Through Hua-yin 180
Peach-Blossom River 68
Poem, A 140
Poem on the Stone Drums, A 90
Poem to a Taoist Hermit on Ch'üan-chiao Mountain, A 233
Political Prisoner Listening to a Cicada, A 145
Poor Girl, A 79

Reading Buddhist Classics with Ch'ao at His Temple in the Early Morning 141
Remembering My Brothers on a Moonlight Night 186
Returning at Night to Lu-mên Mountain 155
River-Snow 141

Seeing Li Po in a Dream 193
Setting Sail on the Yang-tsze 233
She Sighs on Her Jade Lute 236
She Sings an Old Song 69
Sigh from a Staircase of Jade, A 107
Sigh in the Court of Perpetual Faith, A 211
Sigh in the Spring Palace, A 205
Solitary Wildgoose, A 182
Song at Wêi-ch'êng, A 219
Song of an Old Cypress, A 198
Song of an Old General, A 227
Song of a Girl from Lo-yang, A 227
Song of a Guitar, The 164
Song of a Painting, A 196
Song of a Prince Deposed, A 203
Song of a Pure-Hearted Girl, A 149
Song of an Autumn Midnight, A 112
Song of an Autumn Night, A 219
Song of Ch'ang-kan, A 113
Song of Ch'ang-kan, A 179
Song of Dagger-Dancing, A 199
Song of Fair Women, A 201
Song of Liang-chou, A 215
Song of Lu Mountain, A 114
Song of Peach-Blossom River, A 228

Song of Pure Happiness, A *108*
Song of Running-Horse River, A *176*
Song of Sobbing by the River, A *202*
Song of the Palace, A *82*
Song of the Palace, A *158*
Song of the Southern River, A *133*
Song of the Spring Palace, A *210*
Song of the Yen Country, A *98*
Song of Unending Sorrow, A *159*
Song of War-Chariots, A *200*
Song of Wheel Tower, A *176*
Song of White Snow, A *177*
Spring Heart-Break *139*
Spring Morning, A *150*
Spring Rain *128*
Spring Sigh, A *78*
Spring Song, A *143*
Spring Thoughts *97*
Spring View, A *185*
Staying at the General's Headquarters *190*
Stopping at a Friend's Farm-House *152*
Stopping at a Temple on Hêng Mountain I Inscribe This Poem in the Gate-
   Tower *89*
Suêi Palace, The *123*
Suggestion to My Friend Liu, A *158*
Summer Palace, The *238*

Taking Leave of Friends on My Way to Hua-chou *185*
Taking Leave of Wang Wêi *153*
Temple of Su Wu, The *237*
Temple of the Premier of Shu, The *188*
There Is Only One *122*
Thinking of a Friend Lost in the Tibetan War *63*
Thoughts in the Cold *125*
Thoughts of Old Time *191*
Thoughts of Old Time at West Fort Mountain *144*
Thoughts of Old Time from a Night-Mooring Under Mount Niu-chu *110*
Thoughts of Old Time on the Ch'u River *148*
Through the Yang-tsze Gorges *108*
T'ien-mu Mountain Ascended in a Dream *115*
To a Friend Bound East *236*
To a Friend Bound North After the Rebellion *170*
To Ch'i-wu Ch'ien Bound Home After Failing in an Examination *225*

To Li Po at the Sky's End 186
To My Brothers and Sisters Adrift in Troubled Times This Poem of the
    Moon 159
To My Daughter on Her Marriage into the Yang Family 235
To My Friend at the Capital 77
To My Friends Li Tan and Yüan Hsi 232
To My Retired Friend Wêi 192
To One Unnamed 126
To One Unnamed 127
To One Unnamed 128
To One Unnamed 128
To the Moon Goddess 123
To the Tax Collectors After the Bandits' Retreat 240
To Vice-Prefects Li and Wang Degraded and Tranferred to Hsia-chung
    and Ch'ang-sha 98
Toward the Temple of Heaped Fragrance 221
Traveller's Song, A 149
Trooper's Burden, A 138
Turkestan 72

Under a Border-Fortress 212

View of T'ai-shan, A 192
View of the Han River, A 222
View of the Wilderness, A 189

When Lu Lun My Cousin Comes for the Night 170
While Visiting on the South Stream the Taoist Priest Ch'ang 135
Wind and Rain 124
With My Brother at the South Study 211

Yellow Crane Terrace, The 179

INDEX OF FIRST LINES

A bell in the mountain-temple sounds the coming of night 155
A bridge flies away through a wild mist 68
A cold light shines on the gathering dew 148
A cold wind blows from the far sky 186
A cool-matted silvery bed; but no dreams 236
A faint phœnix-tail gauze, fragrant and doubled 128
A fisherman is drifting, enjoying the spring mountains 228
A girl of the Lu clan who lives in Golden-Wood Hall 169
A hundred mountains and no bird 141
A lady of the palace these twenty years 69
A light wind is rippling at the grassy shore 187
A morning-rain has settled the dust in Wêi-ch'êng 219
A seafaring visitor will talk about Japan 115
A slip of the moon hangs over the capital 112
A wanderer hears drums portending battle 186
A wind, bringing willow-cotton, sweetens the shop 116
After rain the empty mountain 220
After the shower at Pa-shang 148
After these ten torn wearisome years 133
Against the City of the Yellow Dragon 169
All alone in a foreign land 219
Along the wall of the Capital a white-headed crow 203
An old fisherman spent the night here, under the western cliff 142
As I walk in the cool of the autumn night 231
As the holiday approaches, and grasses are bright after rain 61
As the seasons have dealt with this ancient terrace 134
As the years go by, give me but peace 221
At a little grass-hut in the valley of the river 76
At this lofty tower where the town ends, wilderness begins 141
Away from home, I was longing for news 106

Bamboo from the southern hills was used to make this pipe 104
Beside the Temple of the Great Premier stands an ancient cypress 198
Boundless grasses over the plain 158

By my old gate, among yellow grasses *147*
By this wall that surrounds the three Ch'in districts *216*

Can drifting clouds and white storks *134*
Chang handed me this tracing, from the stone drums *90*
China's Emperor, craving beauty that might shake an empire *159*
Cicadas complain of thin mulberry-trees *212*
Cock-crow, the Purple Road cold in the dawn *174*
Covet not a gold-threaded robe *183*

Dare I, at my age, accept my summons *136*
Down the blue mountain in the evening *111*
Drink, my horse, while we cross the autumn water *212*
Drive the orioles away *78*

Even in this good reign, how can I serve *206*
Even in this world the spirit of a hero *143*

Far off in Fu-chou she is watching the moonlight *184*
Far off in the clouds stand the walls of Han-yang *147*
Far through the night a harp is sighing *230*
Farther and farther from the three Pa Roads *182*
Finches flash yellow through the Imperial Grove *77*
Finch-notes and swallow-notes tell the new year *97*
Flowers are shadowed, the palace darkens *185*
Flowers, as high as my window, hurt the heart of a wanderer *190*
For years, to guard the Jade Pass and the River of Gold *138*
Friend, I have watched you down the mountain *218*
From a pot of wine among the flowers *111*
From office confinement all year long *234*
From ten thousand valleys the trees touch heaven *222*
From the temple, deep in its tender bamboos *134*
From the walls of Po-ti high in the coloured dawn *108*
Furling my sail near the town of Huai *234*

Gone is the guest from the Chamber of Rank *124*
Grass has run wild now by the Bridge of Red-Birds *143*

Having to travel back now from this far place *187*
Her candle-light is silvery on her chill bright screen *207*
Her hands of white jade by a window of snow *132*
Her jade-green alcove curtained thick with silk *86*
Her jade-white staircase is cold with dew *107*

Her robe is a cloud, her face a flower 108
Her tears are spent, but no dreams come 158
Here, beside a clear deep lake 65
Here in the Eighth-month the waters of the lake 150
Here, where you spent your three years' exile 137
High above, from a jade chamber, songs float half-way to heaven 100
High beyond the thick wall a tower shines with sunset 224
His golden arrow is tipped with hawk's feathers 146
His Palace of Purple Spring has been taken by mist and cloud 126
How beautiful she looks, opening the pearly casement 107
How gladly I would seek a mountain 152

I am endlessly yearning 119
I am far from the clouds of Sung Mountain, a long way from trees
    in Ch'in 122
I am lying in a white-lined coat while the spring approaches 128
I am only an old woodsman, whispering a sob 202
I am sad. My thoughts are in Yo-chou 197
I am the madman of the Ch'u country 114
I awake light-hearted this morning of spring 150
I clean my teeth in water drawn from a cold well 141
I dismount from my horse and I offer you wine 224
I face, high over this enchanted lodge, the Court of the Five Cities
    of Heaven 84
I go in a dream to the house of Hsieh 71
I had always heard of Lake Tung-t'ing 188
I had so long been troubled by official hat and robe 142
I have sailed the River of Yellow Flowers 225
I left home young, I return old 93
I met you often when you were visiting princes 184
I petition no more at the north palace-gate 151
I ponder on the poem of The Precious Dagger 124
I still remember those days of peace 240
I was bidding a guest farewell, at night on the Hsün-yang River 164
I wonder why my inlaid harp has fifty strings 125
In a happy reign there should be no hermits 225
In a sharp gale from the wide sky apes are whimpering 189
In dangerous times we two came south 170
In gala robes she comes down from her chamber 143
In my bed among the woods, grieving that spring must end 151
In the faded old imperial palace 238
In the Fourth-month the south wind blows plains of yellow barley 102
In the pure morning, near the old temple 65

In the slant of the sun on the country-side 226
In twelve chambers the ladies, decked for the day 96
Is it raining on the river all the way to Ch'u 232
It is almost as hard for friends to meet 192
It's a long way home, a long way east 174
Its massive height near the City of Heaven 221

Knowing beauty my misfortune 205

Lakka-trees ripen two by two 149
Last night my girdle came undone 83
Last night, while a gust blew peach-petals open 210
Last year you went with your troops to Tibet 63
Leaning alone in the close bamboos 218
Line after line has flown back over the border 182
Living under a thatch roof, never wearing fragrant silk 79
Long divided by river and sea 170
Look how swift to the snowy sea races Running-Horse River 176
Lords of the capital, sharp, unearthly 180
Lying on a high seat in the south study 211

Master, I hail you from my heart 109
Mist veils the cold stream, and moonlight the sand 206
Monkeys and birds are still alert for your orders 127
Mountains cover the white sun 214
My hair had hardly covered my forehead 113
My heart has been heavy all day long 235
My heart in middle age found the Way 222
My heart sank when I headed north from Yen Country 178
My heritage lost through disorder and famine 159
My office has grown cold today 233

New Year's only deepens my longing 136
News at this far western station! The north has been recaptured 189
No ripples in the river, no mist on the islands 137
North of me, south of me, spring is in flood 188
Not knowing the way to the Temple of Heaped Fragrance 221
Now that a candle-shadow stands on the screen of carven marble 123
Now that the palace-gate has softly closed on its flowers 82
Now that the sun has set beyond the western range 154

O General, descended from Wêi's Emperor Wu 196
O master, how did the world repay 95
O youngest, best-loved daughter of Hsieh 238

Oh, but it is high and very dangerous 117
On a northern peak among white clouds 153
On a part of a spear still unrusted in the sand 206
On a road outreaching the white clouds 140
On the third day of the Third-month in the freshening weather 201
On the third day, taking my place to cook 213
On Wheel Tower parapets night-bugles are blowing 176
Only to wanderers can come 209
Our host, providing abundant wine to make the night mellow 102
Out go the great red wedding-chamber candles 82
Out of the east you visit me 234
Outside are insignia, shown in state 232

Petals of spring fly all through the city 84
Phoenixes that played here once, so that the place was named for them 110
Preparing me chicken and rice, old friend 152
Pure of heart and therefore hungry 124
Pure wine costs, for the golden cup, ten thousand coppers a flagon 120

Red leaves are fluttering down the twilight 94
Rough were the mountain-stones, and the path very narrow 87
Round a turn of the Ch'in Fortress winds the Wêi River 223

Sad wanderer, once you conquered the South 135
Sailing far off from Ching-mên Ferry 109
See How Chung-nan Mountain soars 178
See how the Yellow River's waters move out of heaven 120
She brings a broom at dawn to the Golden Palace doorway 211
She is slim and supple and not yet fourteen 207
Since beauty is honored all over the Empire 226
Since I married the merchant of Ch'ü-t'ang 133
Since Wang Chün brought his towering ships down from Yi-chou 144
Since yesterday had to throw me and bolt 116
Slow and reluctant, I have waited 153
Snow is white on the westward mountains and on three fortified towns 189
So bright a gleam on the foot of my bed 107
Solitary at the tavern 208
South go the wildgeese, for leaves are now falling 153
Stone-Fish Lake is like Lake Tung-t'ing 241
Stories of passion make sweet dust 208

Tell me, where do you live 179
Ten thousand ranges and valleys approach the Ching Gate 191

Tender orchid-leaves in spring 66
The autumn night is clear and cold in the lakka-trees of this courtyard 190
The bright moon lifts from the Mountain of Heaven 112
The fine clouds have opened and the River of Stars is gone 88
The five Holy Mountains have the rank of the Three Dukes 89
The Han Emperor Wên bequeathed us this terrace 181
The limpid river, past its bushes 220
The monk from Shu with his green silk lute-case 110
The moon goes back to the time of Ch'in, the wall to the time of Han 211
The moon, grown full now over the sea 66
The Mother of Heaven, in her window by the Jade Pool 123
The mountain-light suddenly fails in the west 154
The mountains are cold and blue now 220
The north wind rolls the white grasses and breaks them 177
The northeastern border of China was dark with smoke and dust 98
The old fort brims with yellow leaves 236
The pagoda, rising abruptly from earth 175
The red-capped Cock-Man has just announced morning 223
The sand below the border-mountain lies like snow 133
The Son of Heaven in Yüan-ho times was martial as a god 129
The stars of last night and the wind of last night 126
The sun has gone slanting over a lordly roof 69
The sun has set in the water's clear void 236
The thread in the hands of a fond-hearted mother 149
The Three Kingdoms, divided, have been bound by his greatness 184
The travellers' parting-song sounds in the dawn 101
The war-chariots rattle 200
The woods have stored the rain, and slow comes the smoke 224
There are faint green mountains and far green waters 207
There are sobs when death is the cause of parting 193
There is only one Carved-Cloud, exquisite always 122
There lived years ago the beautiful Kung-sun 199
There once was a man, sent on military missions 101
There seems to be no one on the empty mountain 218
There's a girl from Lo-yang in the door across the street 227
There's a gleam of green in an old bottle 158
There's a harp in the midnight playing clear 94
They say that wildgeese, flying southward 172
They sing, they drain their cups of jade 215
Thinking only of their vow that they would crush the Tartars 72
This constellation, with its seven high stars 156
This is the road by which I fled 185
This is where your comrade must leave you 187

This night to the west of the river-brim 110
This one-story inn at Nan-king ferry 70
Though a bugle breaks the crystal air of autumn 64
Though a country be sundered, hills and rivers endure 185
Though a shower bends the river-grass, a bird is singing 230
Though our envoy, Su Wu, is gone, body and soul 237
Though you think to return to this maze of mountains 157
Thoughtful elation has no end 81
Through the bright day up the mountain, we scan the sky for a war-torch 105
Throughout this dynasty no one had painted horses 195
Time was long before I met her, but is longer since we parted 128
To find you, moved beyond the city 168
To your hermitage here on the top of the mountain 80
Together we officials climbed vermilion steps 174
Too young to have learned what sorrow means 210
Toward a mist upon the water 135

Under blue mountains we wound our way 217
Under the crescent moon a light autumn dew 219

Walking along a little path 135
We met last among flowers, among flowers we parted 232
We used to be companions on the Kiang and the Han 231
What are you thinking as we part from one another 98
What shall I say of the Great Peak 192
When gaily the Emperor toured the south 123
When he was a youth of fifteen or twenty 227
When I questioned your pupil, under a pine-tree 75
When the Emperor came back from his ride, they had murdered Lady Yang 74
When the Emperor sought guidance from wise men, from exiles 123
When the moon has coloured half the house 139
When the moonlight, reaching a tree by the gate 69
When this melody for the flageolet was made by Lady Ts'ai 103
When those red berries came in springtime 218
Where a yellow river climbs to the white clouds 214
Where, before me, are the ages that have gone 73
Where is the temple of the famous Premier 188
Where long ago a yellow crane bore a sage to heaven 179
Where tender grasses rim the stream 231
Where the sun has entered western hills 125

While a cold wind is creeping under my mat 84
While I watch the moon go down, a crow caws through the frost 62
While my little boat moves on its mooring of mist 150
While the autumn moon is pouring full 173
While the year sinks westward, I hear a cicada 145
While the winter daylight shortens in the elemental scale 190
While worldly matters take their turn 151
Who is lovelier than she 193
Wistful, away from my friends and kin 233
With a blue line of mountains north of the wall 109
With its three southern branches reaching the Ch'u border 222
With monkeys whimpering on the shadowy mountain 152
With my wine-bottle, watching by river and lake 207
With no other neighbour but the quiet night 170
With this cold night-rain hiding the river, you have come into Wu 210
With twilight passing her silken window 139
With twilight shadows in my heart 122

You are gone. The river is high at my door 125
You ask me when I am coming. I do not know 122
You have left me behind, old friend, at the Yellow Crane Terrace 107
You said you would come, but you did not, and you left me with no other
    trace 127
You were foreordained to find the source 76
You who have come from my old country 219
Your northern grasses are as blue as jade 112
Your seven strings are like the voice 134

INTRODUCTION TO

The Way of Life

According to Laotzu

BY DAVID LATTIMORE

Of all his works, the two volumes that Witter Bynner translated from Chinese have remained his most successful with the public. Both *The Jade Mountain* and *The Way of Life According to Laotzu* have been repeatedly reissued, appearing over recent years in paperback as well as hardbound editions. The popularity of the two books owes something, of course, to the ever-recurring vogue of things Chinese, one of those exotic crazes of our culture parodied by Bynner himself, with Arthur Davison Ficke, in their celebrated *Spectra* hoax. But *The Jade Mountain* and *The Way of Life* have been admired, too, for reasons more substantial than those of fashion.

The Jade Mountain was and is the only complete rendering, in any Western language, of a standard Chinese anthology, the *Three Hundred Poems of the T'ang*. As such, and as a version combining readability and poetic feeling with better than average accuracy, it has enjoyed enduring favor in college courses devoted to world literature or to East Asian civilization. But its appeal is scarcely limited to the classroom. Tributes to it by Arthur Waley and Kenneth Rexroth have probably helped to maintain its position as an influence on modern Anglo-American poetry.

In comparison to *The Jade Mountain*, Bynner's second translation—*The Way of Life*—has sold more substantially (41,000 copies in its first two decades), a fact which probably indicates its greater currency as a trade book. Its popularity is the more remarkable in that, unlike *The Jade Mountain*, *The Way of Life* has had to compete with rival renditions of its source text. No Chinese book has been more frequently translated than the mysterious little work called the *Laotzu* (after its putative author) or *Tao-te-ching* (*The Classic of the Way and Its Virtue*). At least nine German and more than forty English translations of it have been published, besides one or more translations into Sanskrit, Jurchen, Manchu, Latin, Japanese, Russian, Polish, French, Italian, Esperanto, and doubtless other languages. The *Laotzu* is second only to the Bible in its number of English versions. A very few translations of the *Laotzu* are weighty works of philological scholarship. Retired missionaries, soldiers, and consular officials wrote many of the others, in some cases inspired by Laotzu's fancied references to the Trinity and the name of Yahweh, or by his real parallels to New Testament dicta and to Indian and Greek philosophy. Like Bynner's, one earlier American version, by Paul Carus, resorts at times to rhyme. Most are in prose or free verse. Two versions, by Arthur Waley and Lin Yutang, are the works of scholarly men of letters. But Bynner's alone is the creation of a distinguished original poet in English. More resolutely than any other, his translation sacrifices what can't in the interests of what can be conveyed directly, without explanatory footnote or paraphrase; the object being to re-create, at whatever cost in content, some of the simple forcefulness of the original. The result, if it does not always read like Laotzu, also does not read like a translation. We experience it more as an original book of wisdom in our own language, which to a degree it is. This is the most accessible *Laotzu*, if not the one in which Laotzu himself is most accessible. One constantly meets people who, while possessing and desiring no special knowledge of Asia, have nevertheless found in Bynner's work exactly what its title promises: a guide to life. And they have shared their discovery with their friends. In its appropriately simple typography by Robert Josephy, and at a cost (when first issued) of one dollar, this was surely among the worthiest of the perennial gift books.

The Jade Mountain and *The Way of Life According to Laotzu* are by no means products of a single phase of Witter Bynner's activity. Twenty-five years separated his commencement of *The Jade Mountain* in 1918 from his commencement of *The Way of Life* in 1943. The two Chinese texts were very different, and so were the circumstances under which Bynner translated them. Bynner devoted more than a decade to *The Jade Mountain*, less than a year to *The Way of Life*. Given the means at hand, Bynner probably could not have improved his *Laotzu* through a greater expenditure of time. Nevertheless, of the two books, *The Way of Life*, judged as a representation of the Chinese text, was by far the more hazardous undertaking.

The *Three Hundred Poems of the T'ang*, dating from the well-documented T'ang era (618–906), are works for the most part by known authors, preserved in satisfactory texts. While Bynner was not a scholar of Chinese, he fashioned his translations of the poems from drafts prepared for him by a learned collaborator, Kiang Kang-hu, and was able to revise his versions with advice at every stage from Dr. Kiang. When, on the other hand, Bynner began to translate the *Laotzu*, his friend Dr. Kiang, then in Japanese-occupied China, was living beyond reach of the wartime mails. Working in the provincial Mexican town of Chapala, Jalisco, Bynner seems to have lacked any direct assistance from a Chinese specialist. His only recourse was to distill his interpretation from previously published translations, of which, under difficult circumstances, he was able to assemble fourteen. Moreover, the text underlying these versions was far more refractory than that which had inspired *The Jade Mountain*. The *Laotzu* is a philosophical work, chiefly in gnomic verse, written at least a thousand years before the heyday of the T'ang poets, and handed down with many garbled and variant readings. Even in its imperfect state, we would understand it better if we knew more about the contemporary philosophical controversies in which it represented one of many conflicting positions. But in all likelihood the *Laotzu* was never meant to be generally understood. Although loosely retaining the conventions of the book of advice to monarchs, the *Laotzu* must, in the first instance, have been addressed to a circle of adepts, who preserved it along with a private tradition, probably oral, of its interpretation. Neither the Taoist sect nor its traditions survived intact the upheavals, including the great book burnings and immolations of scholars in 213 B.C., which attended the founding of the first unified

Chinese empire. Who Laotzu was, when he lived, what precisely he said, and what he meant by what he said, have in consequence remained the subjects of inconclusive debate throughout two millennia.

In view of the well-known difficulties surrounding the text, and considering his lack of any special means—other than native poetic intuition—for coping with those difficulties, Bynner might be thought to have acted unwisely in deciding to add yet another to the already long list of attempts to translate the *Laotzu*. But in fact his *Way of Life According to Laotzu* was not written in consequence of a carefully pondered decision. Even when the translation was well under way, Bynner believed that he was contributing to, or else that he had been momentarily distracted from, the composition of an entirely different book, referred to in his letters as *Chinese People and Poetry;* a book which, had he completed it, would indeed have represented the result of a rational and moral plan. But *The Way of Life* was to supplant *People and Poetry*, slipping into existence by a more spontaneous and, appropriately enough, a more Taoist process.

•

During 1942, the year following the Japanese surprise attack on Pearl Harbor, Witter Bynner, a long-time resident of Santa Fe, was serving as state chairman, for New Mexico, of United China Relief. The job was a demanding one, and no doubt frustrating as well. A number of specialized "causes"—Chinese Industrial Cooperatives, for example—whose supporters had, in many cases, banded together before Pearl Harbor, were now gathered under a single umbrella organization, with headquarters in New York. As yet, however, the entire responsibility for conducting an annual fund-raising campaign rested with Bynner and the other regional directors. Moreover, United China Relief, like the United States government, was finding it extremely difficult to deliver to the suffering Chinese people that limited aid which was available. Between June 1942 and January 1943, the momentum of battle, on front after front of the Second World War, was shifting in favor of the Allies. After Midway, El Alamein, and Stalingrad, the Axis powers began, slowly, to yield the territories that they had seized. China, however—weakened by a century of civil war and foreign intervention—was to remain on the defensive against the Japanese for some time to come. In April 1942, Japan had closed off the Burma Road. China now lacked access, either by land or by sea, to the Western democracies. Her only outside contacts lay through a very long truck route from the Soviet Union, and through a perilous airlift over the eastern Himalayan "hump."

While Bynner labored for United China Relief, his friend Robert Hunt, editor of his *Selected Poems*, was serving as a volunteer on the Santa Fe draft board. Both men were in mediocre health; Hunt had earlier received an honorable discharge from the U.S. Navy on medical grounds. In 1943, however, Hunt left Santa Fe for San Francisco, to take up more active war work as checker on a naval pier. Bynner, at his winter home in Chapala—his "retreat from a retreat," as he called it—was likewise thinking of other ways to aid the war effort. The increased centralization of United China Relief had made the state chairmanship a less challenging task than it had been the previous year, and Bynner was seeking to delegate the now-reduced responsibility. A letter of November 16, 1943, to Harriette Franchot, suggests that he had thought of returning to Santa Fe to replace Hunt on the draft board. His preference, however, was to remain in Chapala, making a more personal contribution in the form of a book. To Hunt he had written (on August 21) that "the book I plan, if I can make it what I plan, will be of more service to China eventually and to the U.S. as well than any extra shekels I might exhort out of people by being at home."

In fact, Bynner did remain at his house near Lake Chapala, a place to which—following a first visit there with D. H. Lawrence in 1923—he had returned almost every year. (Writing to Mrs. Franchot, he speaks of the house "Bob Hunt and I have carefully built . . . around us so that, huge though it is, it fits like a glove—or a chambered nautilus.") During the First World War Bynner had begun his earlier Chinese book, *The Jade Mountain;* now he would start another. (To Frederick Mortimer Clapp he would write on April 30, 1944: "Twice now the Chinese have kept me calm while the ramparts of the world have been burning.") "The one possible good positive outcome of the war," he said to Mrs. Franchot, "seems to me to be a bettering of race relations. So, for my own sake too, I am turning back, as I did during the other war, to the deepest of the live civilizations. . . ." During the two summers in which he had taught poetry at the Writers' Conference of the University of Colorado, and later also in New Mexico, Bynner had lectured on "Chinese People and Poetry." This lecture would form the nucleus of the book. In a letter to Hunt (August 23), he describes the method of composition as a "prying loose and reassembling [of] thousands of notes into their proper compartments,—a floor job, figuratively and literally both." He had completed a chapter and read it to a receptive audience of Chapala neighbors before August 21. But doubts about the delegation of the China Relief work were holding him back. And he was feeling another doubt, recurrent with him: "You might think that at sixty-two I'd have learned to write prose, but I haven't," he admitted to Mrs. Franchot.

What Bynner did not tell Mrs. Franchot in November, but what he had told Hunt as early as August 21, was that he had already become sidetracked from *People and Poetry:*

And now what do you suppose is happening? In tackling the chapter connecting religion with poetry, I found myself irritated by the feeble quality of Lin Yutang's translations of Laotzu—just as poor as any of the previous poor ones on which he tried to improve. I needed the Taoistic sayings in what I had at hand; and suddenly I realized that I'd have to make my own versions of them. And I've begun. In fact a tenth of the Tao-Teh-Ching already faces me in my own versions—and I see that they will make a chapter in themselves. So that's that.

In other words, now that I've made a start I'm going a hell of a pace. . . .

Later (August 28) he adds, to Hunt, "I have been working for nearly a week till four or five a.m. and rising at nine or ten." In April 1944, the completed manuscript was accepted by John Day. A letter to Barry Faulkner of July 24, 1944, mentions *Chinese People and Poetry* once again, and says: "Now I'm back at my prose and not very happy about it. Living with the great philosopher was better."

•

Of the "Three Teachings" so long perpetuated in China—Confucianism, Taoism, Buddhism—the first two are native products, while Buddhism in its best-known Chinese form, Ch'an (in Japanese, Zen) or "Meditation" Buddhism, is virtually a hybridization of Taoism with the imported Indian religion. Since its high points in the ages of Leibniz and Voltaire, the Occidental reputation of Confucianism has declined. Ezra Pound was a rare modern case of the self-proclaimed Confucian sympathizer. Few in the West would nowadays espouse a doctrine glorifying, as Confucianism does, the traditional Chinese clan, state, legendary history, and ritual etiquette. The one Confucian scripture with a current vogue is the *I-ching*, or *Book of Changes*, which in content, however, is hardly more Confucian than Taoist. With its non-theistic nature-mysticism, its doctrines of simplicity and relaxation, Taoism might have been expected to exert a greater fascination upon Occidentals than it has done. But philosophical Taoism in China, unlike its Zen offshoot in Japan, is today an isolated, moribund tradition, one that has never sent forth its own apostles to the West. The Atlantic world has experienced Taoism through its most prestigious and perhaps oldest scripture, the *Laotzu*; through its reflections in Chinese poetry and painting, and in Zen; and through certain elements of late-Taoist hygiene, such as acupuncture and the T'ai-chi systems of body exercise. Curiously little known in the West is the masterpiece of Taoist and indeed of Chinese prose, the *Chuang-tzu*, a work of about the same period as *Laotzu*. It has been translated by Burton Watson.

But while few of us are *professed* Confucians or Taoists, it is nevertheless the case, as Arthur Waley has said, that "both Confucianism and Taoism express attitudes to life with which we are familiar. We could even roughly divide our friends and acquaintances into Confucians and Taoists."* Some of us (the "Confucians") are primarily social and moral beings, some (the "Taoists") are primarily individual and imaginative. Of course we are all a little bit of both. Taoists in China have always liked to tease the Confucians for their supposed narrowness of interests and literal-mindedness. But on the whole, the two doctrines have coexisted remarkably amiably, both in the community and in the inner lives of individuals. A Chinese might be Confucian by training, Taoist by inclination; Confucian when in office, Taoist when out of office; Confucian in the responsible prime of life, Taoist in youth and old age. As an American patriot and (adoptively) as a Chinese patriot, Witter Bynner showed his Confucian side; as translator of *Laotzu*, living in his "retreat from a retreat," his Taoist character emerged, probably in more ways than he realized.

To understand Bynner's translation as itself a Taoist act (or, as Taoists would prefer to say, an "inaction"), we may best begin by considering two Taoist principles: *tzu-jan* (pronounced *dz-ran*, in two equally accented syllables) and *wu-wei* (pronounced *woo-way*).

Tzu-jan means, literally, "self-so"; that which is as it is spontaneously, naturally, of itself, and is thus in accord with the

---

* *Three Ways of Thought in Ancient China* (London: 1939), p. 164.

Tao (pronounced *dow*) or "Way," in the larger sense of that term—the Way, not of man or of certain men, but of the universe, of nature as a whole.

Wu-wei means, literally, "lacking action." But it does not refer to a condition of stasis; rather, it refers to the absence of willed human interference in natural processes (*tzu-jan*). This explains the paradox that Laotzu enjoins on us: "Act non-action, serve non-service, taste the flavorless"—or, as Bynner translates it:

> Men knowing the way of life
> Do without acting,
> Effect without enforcing,
> Taste without consuming. . . .
> (*Chapter 63*)

The *Chuang-tzu*, which sometimes clarifies the *Laotzu*, says: "He who learns would learn what he cannot learn, he who practices would practice what he cannot practice, he who discriminates would discriminate what he cannot discriminate" (chapter 23). Studied, practical-minded action, founded upon close analysis of a limited situation, is self-defeating. The laissez-faire Taoist teaching doubtless runs counter to common prudence, yet inculcates a higher prudence. For to calculate, to use foresight, to meddle with nature, is to court failure; to let nature take its course is to succeed. Bynner relinquished, first, an obviously useful and charitable activity—his war relief work; and, thereafter, a labor of intellect—his project for an informative, uplifting book (*Chinese People and Poetry*), which was to have been produced by carefully laid-out "floor work"; in favor of a task—the translation of *Laotzu*—that reasonable people would have judged at once impossible and redundant. Yet in so doing he acted immediately, on natural impulse, as he and Ficke had done in the case of *Spectra*. Yielding to inspiration, he worked night after night—with results very probably more enlightening, and indeed commercially successful, than *Chinese People and Poetry* could have had.

Another Taoist paradox can be seen in the translating of *The Way of Life*, although I do not believe that Bynner was aware of it. Why did Bynner wish to make his own translation of the *Laotzu*? Because Lin Yutang's version was "feeble," a failed attempt at improvement on equally "poor" predecessors; because Waley's was "culpably dull and, to a Westerner, unintelligible" (letter to Hunt, March 7, 1944); because "of fourteen English translations not one was fit to use" (letter to Barry Faulkner, July 24, 1944). But what materials had he from which to fashion his own translation? Precisely those fourteen translations; nothing else whatsoever. I call this not only a paradox but a Taoist paradox, because it offers a striking analogy to—or, perhaps, an example of—the process by which the Taoist mystic, who (like the rest of us) has nothing before him but the shifting, broken-up appearances of things, is led to descry beneath them the eternally unitary Tao.

There is yet another way in which Bynner, in translating *Laotzu*, was himself performing a Taoist exercise. I have already suggested that *Laotzu* is difficult because its text is somewhat garbled, and because it represents a private and secret teaching to which we have lost the traditional key—the answers, so to speak, at the back of the book. Yet students are never supposed to consult the back of the book before they have made their own earnest attempt to solve the problems at the front of the book. A book may be difficult not only in consequence of the accidents of time—through damage to the text, or to our knowledge of its context—but on purpose and for good reason. The text may be difficult because the author wants to challenge and engage us, disrupt our passivity, bestir our minds and open them to change, even at the risk that, within allowable limits, each mind, forced to work out its own *Laotzu*, will produce a version differing from others. Indeed the *Laotzu* is trying to teach us something—loosely called Tao, or "eternal Tao," or simply "the great" (chapter 25; for Bynner, "the fullness of life")—which lies beyond words:

> Those who know do not tell,
> Those who tell do not know.
> (*Chapter 56*)

If Laotzu himself "knew," then why, it is often asked, did he choose to "tell" us in a text of more than five thousand words? But in fact Laotzu withholds more than he tells. In particular, he withholds references to context. There are no proper names in *Laotzu*, no people or places or dates, no exemplary ancient sages, no quotations, indeed no stories, no conversations. Words, facts, break up and categorize experience. The Tao, properly speaking nameless, unites. Each of us, in interpreting Laotzu's cryptically minimal words, must construe them by setting them into our own experience, on the way back to that truth which lies beyond words. That is why so many foreigners have been teased into translating the *Laotzu*, and why there exist so many more *Laotzus* in Chinese—the *Laotzos* of philosophical and of magical Taoism, of Buddhism and of neo-Confucianism, of modern liberalism and Marxism, and, finally, of modern philology and intellectual history. Even Bynner, in writing what he called an "American Version" of the *Laotzu*, was not by definition playing outside the rules. Only we ourselves can make the *Laotzu* that is right for us. At the same time, all interpretations, as well as the text itself, are more or less wrong, in that any verbal representation of the Tao is a makeshift, a compromise. The question is whether or to what extent Bynner's American *Laotzu* is needlessly and confusingly remote from Laotzu's *Laotzu*, in so far as that is knowable.

·

Bynner's introduction gives us our first impression of his *Laotzu*. His treatment of the legends concerning Laotzu is properly noncommittal. An essay by Kiang Kang-hu is cited, which puts forth a still somewhat popular semi-traditional position: the *Laotzu* derives from a personage named Laotzu of the sixth century B.C., as tradition maintains, but owes its present form to editors of the third century. All we can really say to this is that the *Laotzu*, as we have it, bears upon arguments—about the nature of words or "names," about humanity and righteousness —which belong to the third century. Any text of the third century must at the same time reflect ideas that had been developing since the sixth (and indeed earlier) centuries. Whether some of these ideas are owed to a real sixth-century person named Laotzu is unprovable, and unlikely, given the common occurrence, in Taoist materials, of fancifully named sages, who are simply jokes at the expense of Confucian literal-mindedness and deference to precedent—especially sages who, like "Laotzu" (perhaps meaning "Mr. Old"), are supposed to have been elders of Confucius, and to have bested him in argument. Self-effacement is both a Confucian and a Taoist virtue. But Taoism does not share the reverence of Confucianism for literary accomplishment and for a good name to bequeath to posterity. The author of the *Laotzu* did not want to be known. "Mr. Old" may well have begun as the jocular answer given to a Confucian who inappropriately inquired into the authorship of the work; it wouldn't be the only Taoist joke that Confucians took seriously.

In a letter to Frederick Mortimer Clapp (April 30, 1944), Bynner said that Laotzu "is just as much I as I am, which could be my answer to those who ask, 'But why aren't you doing your own work?' " Bynner's introduction to *The Way of Life* gives further evidence of the manner in which he, like any imaginative and sympathetic translator, has created a Laotzu in his own image. In what follows, my own judgments are added in parentheses. Laotzu, unlike Confucius, is a mystic (true), but not a hermit or one who addresses himself solely to hermits (true). He has a sense of humor (true), opposes pedantry (true), and is anticlerical (a plausible *argumentum ex silentio;* Laotzu says nothing about organized religion or theistic belief). He also opposes war (partly true; he deplores war but supports *wu-wei* tactics of defense). And he is a democrat. The last point is the most questionable, reflecting a widespread exaggeration in the 1940's of the traditionally democratic attitudes of the Chinese. In fact, the Chinese have never—at least in historical times— enslaved and therefore despised their people; they have even regarded popular approval or disapproval of the monarch as indicators of heaven's mandate, the divine sanction—always provisional—of his rule. But an essential of democracy is surely an informed electorate, whereas the Taoist sage "empties their minds and fills their bellies . . . he always causes the people to lack knowledge and desire" (chapter 3), a point which Bynner glosses over; in his version, "empties their minds" becomes "to open people's hearts," while "causes the people to lack knowledge" becomes, even more arbitrarily, "to clarify their thoughts."

Aside from a few such wishful misrepresentations as the foregoing, Bynner's translation is most questionable in its very free and variable treatment of the terminology which provides the framework of thought in *Laotzu*. Here Bynner was following a fashion of the 1940's, best exemplified by F. M. Cornford's translation of Plato's *Republic*, in which, for example, "*logos* combined with *musike*" becomes "a thoughtful and cultivated mind."* Paraphrase of this sort may be desirable in translating fiction or *belles lettres*, but is dangerous in translating philosophy. Even Laotzu's poetic and mystical philosophy at one level is, like other philosophies, a set of terms and of relations among terms. Although sometimes almost unavoidable, the obscuring of terms by translating them inconsistently tends to dissolve the philosophy or to create a different philosophy.

In Bynner's *Way of Life*, the greatest offense occurs, unfortunately, in his treatment of the central term, which is Tao or "Way." Every Chinese philosophy inculcates some "way" of life—the proper course of conduct for all men, or for the king.

---

* D. J. Furley, "Translation from Greek Philosophy," in *Aspects of Translation*, The Communication Research Centre, University College, London, Studies in Communication, 2 (1958), p. 53.

In addition, it was possible to speak of a "way of heaven." The humanism of Confucius concerned itself strictly with man's way, that is, his actions and trends of thought; Confucius would not even discuss the abstract question of man's nature, let alone the nature of the universe or of the spirit world. A disciple of Confucius said: "We cannot hear the Master speaking of man's nature or the way of heaven" (*Analects*, 5.12). Laotzu went in the other direction. He spoke not only of the ways of heaven and earth but of an "eternal way" that existed before these, created them, and gave life to all things. Although he considered the "eternal way" undefinable, indeed invisible, inaudible, untouchable (as well as inexhaustible, all-encompassing, omnipresent), he nevertheless, paradoxically, thought it all-important that we, or the ruler, should "grasp" it and "cleave to" it; the ruler who can do this will command universal loyalty. Laotzu makes no explicit distinction between a universal and a human way; for him, the right way for men to live is the same way that holds the stars in their courses. This identification of the universal, natural process or way with human morality is (so far as we know) original with Laotzu, and distinguishes his from all other ancient Chinese philosophies; it gives the notion of the "way" an importance in his philosophy that it has in no other, and is the reason why we call that philosophy "Taoism." But Bynner conceals this identification from us by translating Tao as "existence" or "life" when universal Tao seems to be the foremost topic, and as "the way of life" when human conduct seems to be more at issue. Thus the universal ceases to be a Way, and man's way loses universality. Like Cornford, Bynner has varied the term with the context, so as to render each passage more clearly, idiomatically, and compellingly, but in so doing he has obscured the continuity of ideas *between* passages, and thus some of the beauty of the whole.

Of course we cannot in translation reproduce a terminology without distortion, because the vocabularies of any two languages join and separate pieces of experience along different lines. Translators have known this at least since Hellenistic times (see, for example, the prologue to Ecclesiasticus). Many languages describe a course of life metaphorically as a way or road or path; here English and Chinese coincide. The Chinese Tao has one sense, however, which is strange to us. While as a noun Tao means a way or Way, tao can also function as a verb, meaning to clear a way, to open communication, to point or tell the way to someone, or simply to tell about or say. The famous first line of the *Laotzu* says, literally, that "The tao which one can tao is not the eternal Tao"—that is, the way that can be told of is not the eternal Way. Here a rhetorical device to which the word "antimetathesis" is sometimes applied—the repetition in one sentence of the same word with a different meaning—is used in the Chinese but cannot be reproduced in English. Consequently, the paradox is also lost, in which the eternal Way, although ineffable, is nevertheless called by a name meaning "to say."

In the first chapter of *Laotzu*, this thought introduces a linkage of ideas—those we call "thing," "name," and "desire"—which is crucial to the whole philosophy. The function of a name is to discriminate the thing (or category, or quality) named from all other things (or categories, or qualities). "Table" distinguishes the table from—and therefore, also, implies the existence of—all that is not a table, just as "long" implies the existence of "short," and so on. An object of desire must also be a thing, category, or quality distinct from others not desired. Exactly because language and desire discriminate, we cannot effectively apply them to the Way, because there is no non-Way from which the Way is to be told apart. Nevertheless, things are fragments, as it were, of the Way from which they derive. Instead of naming, categorizing, coveting, and hoarding these fragments, we should contemplate them nonverbally and unemotionally, erasing superficial distinctions, going back, in our mind, to their subtle and minute beginnings (*miao* or *wei*) which existed potentially in the infinite potentiality of Tao.

No translator, in all probability, could convey this nexus of ideas unless he added to his translation an extensive commentary, which would then confront the reader with an intellectual distraction from the philosopher's own voice, just the sort of un-Taoist pedantry that Bynner was trying to avoid. It must be said that Bynner has done damage to the verbal structure of Laotzu's thought. But then, is not the breakdown of verbal distinctions exactly what Laotzu advocates? Here is another Taoist paradox. If Bynner erred, he did so partly in being too Taoist. There are poets—Pound, for example, and Confucius—whose passion is the word; and poets—Bynner, for example, and Laotzu—enamored of something that forever escapes the word. Yet Laotzu was also, as much as anything else, a linguistic philosopher. Bynner was not.

Bynner's *Way of Life* nevertheless contains some of his best poetry. Poets of Bynner's generation had lived through enormous changes in mores and literary diction. Unlike the classical Chinese poets, and unlike some of the poets of today, they were still —in most cases—at a loss, or groping, for a way to transmute personal experience into what they could regard as poetry. It is likely that in the constraints of the adopted persona—whether that of Laotzu or that of the imaginary Emanuel Morgan in *Spectra*—Bynner found (by yet another paradox) a poetic freedom superior to that which he otherwise enjoyed. The Laotzu persona was one that he would again assume; see, for example, his poems entitled "A Taoist" and "Unbroken Flight," in *Take Away the Darkness* (1947).

•

To Bynner's great distress, Alfred A. Knopf, his publisher for many years, declined *The Way of Life According to Laotzu*. This was, for the Knopfs, an unusual business mistake. Bynner next sent his manuscript to Richard Walsh, Jr., president of the John Day Company, which issued many books on Asian subjects. Walsh's wife was Pearl Buck, a winner of the Nobel Prize for Literature, among whose best-selling novels with Chinese locales was *The Good Earth*. The Walshes were enthusiastic. In a letter to Robert Hunt (April 24, 1944), Bynner quoted Richard Walsh, who had written that he and his wife took "the exactly contrary opinion to that expressed by Mrs. Knopf—we think that what Laotzu has to say is of particular importance to the world right now." "This is much better," Bynner added, "than to have let the Knopfs publish it without heart, as they would have done if I had insisted."

The first printing sold out within three weeks and met a warm response from critics and friends. Arthur Davison Ficke— often "mildly disposed toward my verse," as Bynner conceded —called it "the seal and summit of your life-work—a major triumph" (quoted in a letter of Bynner's to Walter Leuba, November 7, 1944). The *New Yorker* review said: "A fresh simplicity and humane common sense prevail here . . . and the poems provide a delightful coolness for present disordered times." John Haynes Holmes, who sent a copy of *The Way of Life* to Gandhi, wrote: "The 81 sayings in this volume shine like gems cut clear and beautiful in every facet . . . this translation will stand as the perfect rendering of a classic work." Oliver St. John Gogarty gave a copy to his Irish compatriot, the well-known biographer Francis Hackett, who read it to his wife as, already prepared for the operating room, she awaited for four hours the arrival of a tardy surgeon; "I did not suffer at all," she later wrote Bynner.

Bynner's greatest disappointment must have been the book's reception by the esteemed and prolific British translator from Chinese and Japanese, Arthur Waley, with whom Bynner had corresponded for twenty years. Waley had expressed himself "delighted" at the first appearance of *The Jade Mountain* (letter of December 27, 1929) and had submitted a long list of corrections, which Bynner received with gratitude, adopting all of them in later issues of the work. Waley's response to *The Way of Life* (December 26, 1944) was much cooler. "I confess when I saw it was an 'American version' I thought it would be in the highly-coloured and vigorous idiom that now pervades our streets and villages, a speech to which we have become deeply attached," Waley wrote. "I find much in your version that is not in the original, but nothing that would seem to be American. My general criticism would be that your version is flat, easy and smooth. It does not startle or jolt one as the original does."

Waley's own *Laotzu*, entitled *The Way and Its Power*, had appeared ten years earlier. It is curious that the two men stated such similar reasons for disliking each other's version: Waley's was "dull" to Bynner, Bynner's "flat" to Waley. The simplest explanation is that they were looking for different things. Both distrusted organized religion. But Waley had sought to descripturalize the *Laotzu*, stripping away centuries of sectarian interpretation and exposing the more primitive beliefs that he thought it had originally reflected—beliefs that he overconfidently felt himself able to reconstruct, partly from anthropological analogies. Naturally he was disappointed that Bynner had not appreciated his scholarly findings. Bynner, on the other hand, was seeking, precisely, a scripture—a book to get one through 3 a.m. depressions—although a non-theological scripture. Like Ezra Pound, Amy Lowell, and all other translators with little or no knowledge of Chinese, he vastly overestimated the fidelity of his version, since he could not see the possible alternatives to his interpretations, and did not understand the context of the text; the fact, for example, that many of a philosopher's statements are primarily (if inexplicitly) denials of contrary statements by other philosophers. The translator in this position always feels—sometimes unjustly—that his learned critics are pedantic carpers. In translating the *Laotzu* Bynner had had no Kiang Kang-hu to forewarn him of errors, and his fourteen published sources had not been able to answer him back.

Burton Watson, in his introduction to *The Jade Mountain* contained in the present volume, has mentioned the two "Noble Truths" of all translators: that a translation should be faithful, and that it should itself read like a genuine work of literature. In conclusion, I should like to propose two further Noble Truths.

The first is that the translator should care very much about what he is doing. He should, perhaps, "identify" with the author. He should certainly feel that the text has something uniquely and preeminently important to say, something worth conveying at whatever cost in labor or even danger. For English-speakers, the foremost exemplar of this Truth, and martyr to it, is William Tyndale, who—knowingly working in the shadow of the stake —made the greatest single contribution to what would become the Authorized Version of the Bible.

My second Noble Truth is that languages as well as texts are translated; languages change through translation of texts into them; the greatest translator is he who translates not only a text but a language. The translator does this who believes—correctly, in the case of great poetic works—that the truth of the text lies in the very fiber of the language in which it is written; that the fiber of the language into which one translates may properly and profitably be bent to the pattern of the language from which one translates. Oral languages, linguists believe, are chiefly changed by children. Written languages are changed by translators. Here the exemplary figure once more is Tyndale. Our language has vastly increased its resources in consequence of his assumption that English should be made more like Hebrew and Greek, the language of the angels and the language of the evangelists.

Bynner did not and could not exemplify my second Truth, since he couldn't himself make out and follow the Chinese verbal fiber. In disagreement with Waley, I think that Bynner's *Way of Life* was too characteristically American. Other translators have reshaped poetic English (or American) by making it more Chinese. Bynner did not know how to do this. Probably he was well advised not to try; the result would have been merely a chinoiserie.

But Witter Bynner was a splendid exemplar of my first Noble Truth. He cared greatly about the Chinese. He believed in his Laotzu, labored over him, drew sustenance from him. And this is the secret behind the enduring charm of *The Way of Life*. As Bynner had written to Clapp, "He is magnificent. He tears the veil or, rather, sees its significance. And he's just as much I as I am."

THE WAY OF
LIFE

According to Laotzu

AN AMERICAN
VERSION BY

Witter Bynner

To

my collaborator for a decade (1918–1929) on *The Jade Mountain*, who finally received a copy of my *The Way of Life* in a Nanking prison in 1948 and wrote me before his death in 1954 in a Shanghai prison this reassurance:

> . . . *It is impossible to translate it without an interpretation. Most of the translations were based on the interpretations of commentators, but you chiefly took its interpretation from your own insight. It was your "fore-nature" understanding—or in Chinese,* hsien-t'ien—*that rendered it so simple and yet so profound. So the translation could be very close to the original text even without knowledge of the words. I am rather shameful that I could not assist you in any way.*

"The way to do is to be."

Laotzu

· ❧❀☙ ·

Legends as to Laotzu are more or less familiar.

Immaculately conceived to a shooting-star, carried in his mother's womb for sixty-two years and born, it is said, white-haired, in 604 B.c., he became in due time keeper of imperial archives at Loyang, an ancient capital in what is now the Chinese province of Honan.

Speaking wisdom which attracted followers, he had refused to the end of his life to set it down: considering the way of life and the ways of the world, he had decided that a great deal was done and said in the world which might better be spared. His choice, however, was not, as has been widely assumed, vacant inaction or passive contemplation. It was creative quietism. Though he realized the fact that action can be emptier than inaction, he was no more than Walt Whitman a believer in abstention from deed. He knew that a man can be a doer without being an actor and by no means banned being of use when he said that "the way to do is to be." Twenty-five centuries before Whitman, he knew the value of loafing and inviting one's soul; and the American poet, whether or not consciously, has been in many ways one of the Chinese poet's more eminent Western disciples, as Thoreau has been also, with his tenet, "Be it life or death, we seek only reality." But Whitman and Thoreau loved written words, whereas Laotzu felt that written words by defining, by limiting, could have dubious effects. Aware of the dangers inherent in dogma, he was reluctant to leave a set record of his own spoken belief, lest it become to followers an outer and formal rather than an inner and natural faith, an outside authority rather than intuition. He laid down no rigid laws for behavior: men's conduct should depend on their instinct and conscience. His last wish would have been to create other men in his own image; but he gently continued in life, by example presumably and by spoken word, suggesting to his neighbors and his emperor how natural, easy and happy a condition it is for men to be members of one another.

How do I know this integrity?
Because it could all begin in me.

One who recognizes all men as members of his own body
Is a sound man to guard them.

Legendary or true, it is told that Confucius, impressed by Laotzu's influence on people, visited him once to ask advice, ironically enough, on points of ceremonial etiquette. Baffled by the answers of the older man, to whom etiquette meant hypocrisy and nonsense, Confucius returned to his disciples and told them: "Of birds I know that they have wings to fly with, of fish that they have fins to swim with, of wild beasts that they have feet to run with. For feet there are traps, for fins nets, for wings arrows. But who knows how dragons surmount wind and cloud into heaven? This day I have seen Laotzu and he is a dragon."

The end of the life legend is that, saddened by men's tragic perversity, their indisposition to accept "the way of life," to use life with natural goodness, with serene and integral respect, Laotzu rode away alone on a water-buffalo into the desert beyond the boundary of civilization, the great wall of his period. It is narrated that when he arrived at one of its gates, a warden there, Yin Hsi, who had had a dream of the sage's coming, recognized him from the dream and persuaded him to forego his reluctance and to record the principles of his philosophy. The result is said to have been the *Tao Teh Ching*, tao meaning the way of all life, teh the fit use of life by men and ching a text or classic. And from the gate-house or from somewhere, this testament of man's fitness in the universe, this text of five thousand words, comprising eighty-one sayings, many of them in verse, has come down through the centuries.

In written history there is little basis for these legends. Record of the philosopher appears first—a brief account ending, "No one knows where he died"—in the annals of Ssu Ma Ch'ien, born five hundred years after Laotzu; and some Western scholars, like some of their Eastern predecessors, have believed that long-lived Laotzu was a myth and that the sayings attributed to him were a compilation of the sayings of a number of men who lived during the next two or three hundred years. Gowen and Hall in their *Outline History of China* say that the *Tao Teh Ching* "is very probably the work of a later age, perhaps of the second century B.C., but is generally regarded as containing many of the sayings of the sage." In an essay accompanying the Buddhist-minded translation by Waitao and Dwight Goddard, Dr. Kiang Kang-hu is more specific. "Three Taoist sages," he writes, "who lived two or three hundred or more years apart, according to history, are commonly believed to be the same man, who by his wisdom had attained longevity . . . The simpler and more probable solution of the confusion is to accept the historicity of all three but to give credit for the original writing to Laotzu and consider the others as able disciples and possibly editors. The book in its present form might not have been written until the third century B.C. . . . for it was engraved on stone tablets soon after that time." It might, he thinks, have contained verses by later Taoists "without detracting from the larger credit that belongs to Laotzu." The earliest known manuscript dates from the T'ang Dynasty, a thousand years later. In *A Criticism of Some Recent Methods of Dating Laotzu*, Dr. Hu Shih has shown that the methods of internal evidence used to impugn the authenticity of Laotzu's writings might have cast similar doubt on the writings of Confucius or of almost anyone. Mark Twain's comment that *Hamlet* was written by Shakespeare or by some one else of the same name is pertinent. The *Tao Teh Ching* is a book, an important and coherent book; and its value comes not from the outward identity or identities but from the inward and homogeneous identity of whoever wrote it.

More relevant is a divergence of judgment as to the book's value. Herbert Giles, the able, pioneering British sinophile, tender toward Confucian orthodoxy and finding in Laotzu "direct antagonism to it," wrote in his *Chinese Literature* published at the turn of the century that "scant allusion would have been made" to the *Tao Teh Ching*, "were it not for the attention paid to it by several more or less eminent foreign students of the language."

Perhaps pedantic Giles was annoyed by the fact that Laotzu could speak of scholars as a corrupting nuisance. Other scholars more imaginative than Giles have differed with him; and current tendency gives the mystical ethics of Laotzu a surer place in import for the world than the practical properties of Confucius. Certainly *Tao* has had profound influence on a great part of the world's population. Apart from the superstitious and the misled who have taken over the name for religious sects and have perverted its meaning into alchemy, geomancy, occultism, church tricks generally, a majority in the Oriental world has been fundamentally informed by Taoist quietism, whether or not they realize the source of the patience, forbearance and fortitude which characterize them. Not only has Laotzu's creative quietism been the foundation of China's agelong survival; what was originally good in Japanese Shintaoism has also derived from him. And the Western world might well temper its characteristic faults by taking Laotzu to heart.

Herrymon Maurer in postscript to *The Old Fellow*, his fictional portrait of Laotzu, notes how closely the use of life according to Laotzu relates to the principles of democracy. Maurer is right that democracy cannot be a successful general practice unless it is first a true individual conviction. Many of us in the West think ourselves believers in democracy if we can point to one of its fading flowers even while the root of it in our own lives is gone with worms. No one in history has shown better than Laotzu how to keep the root of democracy clean. Not only democracy but all of life, he points out, grows at one's own doorstep. Maurer says, "Laotzu is one of our chief weapons against tanks, artillery and bombs." I agree that no one has bettered the ancient advice:

"Conduct your triumph as a funeral."

•

"In this life," reflected Sarah, Duchess of Marlborough, in an eighteenth-century letter to her granddaughter, "I am satisfied there is nothing to be done but to make the best of what cannot be helped, to act with reason oneself and with a good conscience. And though that will not give all the joys some people wish for, yet it will make one very quiet." Laotzu's quietism is nothing but the fundamental sense commonly inherent in mankind, a common-sense so profound in its simplicity that it has come to be called mysticism. Mysticism or not, it seems to me the straightest, most logical explanation as yet advanced for the continuance of life, the most logical use yet advised for enjoying it. While most of us, as we use life, try to open the universe to ourselves, Laotzu opens himself to the universe. If the views of disciples or commentators have sifted into his text, the original intent and integrity shine through nonetheless. All the deadening paraphernalia wished on him by priests and scholars cannot hide him. He remains as freshly and as universally alive as childhood. Followers of most religions or philosophies, feeling called upon to follow beyond reason, follow only a little way. Laotzu's logical, practical suggestions are both reasonable and simple.

However, if metaphysical or scholarly terms seem necessary for understanding, Dr. I. W. Heysinger relates Laotzu's basic concept to that of Roames, Darwin's pupil and co-worker: "the integrating principle of the whole—the Spirit, as it were, of the universe—instinct with contrivance, which flows with purpose"; and to the philosophy of Lamarck. I myself have found Socrates and Plato in it, Marcus Aurelius and Tolstoi.

More modernly it is at the heart of Mrs. Eddy's doctrines or of Bergson's creative evolution. Many a contemporary cult would do well to stop fumbling at the edges of Tao, to forget its priests who invented the ouija board and to go to its center.

Concerned with this center, Dr. Lin Yutang says in *The Wisdom of India and China:* "If there is one book in the whole of Oriental literature which should be read above all the others, it is, in my opinion, Laotzu's *Book of Tao* . . . It is one of the profoundest books in the world's philosophy . . . profound and clear, mystic and practical."

He says this in the preface to his own English version of *The Book of Tao*. I had hoped that this version would be enough clearer than others in English to explain for me the influence of Laotzu on many of the T'ang poets, with whom I had become acquainted through Dr. Kiang Kang-hu's literal texts. With all admiration for Dr. Lin's Chinese spirit and English prose, I found myself little better satisfied with his presentation of Laotzu in Western free verse than I have been with other English versions, most of which have seemed to me dry and stiff, pompous and obscure. And that is why I have been led to make my own version.

Though I cannot read Chinese, two years spent in China and eleven years of work with Dr. Kiang in translating *The Jade Mountain* have given me a fair sense of the "spirit of the Chinese people" and an assiduity in finding English equivalents for idiom which literal translation fails to convey. And now, through various and varying English versions of the *Tao Teh Ching*, I have probed for the meaning as I recognize it and have persistently sought for it the clearest and simplest English expression I could discover. Above all I have been prompted by hope to acquaint Western readers with the heart of a Chinese poet whose head has been too much studied.

I have used, incidentally, even when I quote in this preface from those who use other orthography, the spellings Laotzu and *Tao Teh Ching* as preferable for the English or American ear and eye. And perhaps I shall be taken to task for using two or three times an unorthodox interpretation of text. But might not Laotzu's expression, for example, to "stand below other people," usually translated to "humble oneself below them," have been an ancient origin of our own word, "to understand"?

"There can be little doubt," says Walter Gorn Old, "that any translation from the Chinese is capable of extreme flexibility and license, of which, indeed, the translator must avail himself if he would rightly render the spirit rather than the letter of the text; and the spirit, after all, is the essential thing, if we follow the teaching of Laotzu. It is safe to say that the more literal the translation may be the more obscure its meaning." Some of the *Tao Teh Ching* sayings, I am told, jingle repetitively with a surface lightness like that of nursery rhymes; and I have now and then ventured such effects, besides using rhyme whenever it felt natural to the sense and stayed by the text. Dr. Heysinger, deft and honest though his version is, sometimes lets the exactions of prosody dilate and dilute his writing. Dr. Lin Yutang's faithfulness, on the other hand, like Arthur Waley's, stays by expressions significant to Eastern but not to Western readers; and Laotzu should, I am convinced, be brought close to people in their own idiom, as a being beyond race or age.

As to other translations, Walter Gorn Old's has been popular in England and its comparatively direct wording is accompanied by brief friendly essays of both Buddhist and Christian tinge, Arthur Waley's is painstakingly accurate and scholarly but difficult for any but scholars to follow, and there are several which are overcolored with Buddhism. Despite some fourteen offerings, and despite the fact that "the wording of the original," according to Dr. Lionel Giles, keeper of Oriental manuscripts in the British Museum, "is extraordinarily vigorous and terse," Westerners have not yet, in my judgment, been given a sufficiently intelligible version of Laotzu. Now that East and West have met, I suspect that every coming generation of Westerners will, in its own turn, in its own preferred words, try to express Laotzu's conception of the way and use of life.

Though he himself said that words cannot express existence, he himself trespassed into them for his own generation.

Together with this absence of a forthright and congenial English translation, there are two other principal reasons why Laotzu has not as yet endeared himself to many Westerners. As religion on the one hand, as philosophy on the other, Taoism has been adulterated and complicated by its Oriental adherents. "The Taoist religion," writes Dr. Kiang, "is an abuse of Taoist philosophy. We find nothing essentially in common between them and, in many respects, they are conflicting." He elaborates upon this abuse, as he might have done upon ecclesiastical abuse of the philosophy of Jesus; but he does not, in my Occidental judgment, sufficiently emphasize the disservice done Laotzu by academicians. As the master himself said of the sensible man he commended,

> The cultured might call him heathenish,
> This man of few words, because his one care
> Is not to interefre but to let nature renew
> The sense of direction men undo

and as he said also,

> False teachers of the life use flowery words
> And start nonsense.

Even Laotzu's most famous disciple, Chuangtzu, playfully complicated his master's firm, calm teaching; and the do-nothing idea has been so stressed a misreading as to alienate or puzzle many a Westerner who, seeing Laotzu steadily and whole, would have understood him and responded. Quakers, for instance, would be better Quakers for knowing Tao. Not all Westerners are natural addicts of the strenuous life.

But finally Dr. Kiang is right. Worse than the disservice done the sensible master by some of his scholarly followers has been the wrong done him by the religionists who have preempted him.

Laotzu knew that organization and institution interfere with a man's responsibility to himself and therefore with his proper use of life, that the more any outside authority interferes with a man's use of life and the less the man uses it according to his own instinct and conscience, the worse for the man and the worse for society. The only authority is "the way of life" itself; a man's sense of it is the only priest or prophet. And yet, as travelers have seen Taoism in China, it is a cult compounded of devils and derelicts, a priest-ridden clutter of superstitions founded on ignorance and fear. As an organized religion, its initial and main sect having been established in the first century A.D. by a Pope named Chang Tao-lin, Taoism has even less to do with its founder than most cults have to do with the founders from whom they profess derivation. Even in modern China a Taoist papacy is paid to exorcise demons out of rich homes. To symbolize the patches of a beggar's cloak in Buddhistic ritual, fine brocades are cut into squares and then pieced together again in aesthetically broken design; Christ's cross has been made the pattern for palatial temples; and Laotzu's faith in the naturally and openly beneficent flow of life has been distorted into a commanding but hidden breath of dragons, his simple delighted awareness of the way of life has been twisted into a quest for the philosopher's stone. Thus men love to turn the simplest and most human of their species into complex and superhuman beings; thus everywhere men yearn to be misled by magicians; thus priests and cults in all lands and under virtuous guise make of ethics a craft and a business.

Confucius had the wisdom to forbid that a religion be based on his personality or codes; and his injunction against graven images has fared better than a similar injunction in the Ten Commandments. Hence Confucius continues unchanged as a realistic philosopher, an early pragmatist, while Laotzu and Jesus, his ethical fellows, have been tampered with by prelates, have been more and more removed from human living and relegated as mystics to a supernatural world.

Confucius prescribed formalized rather than spontaneous

conduct for the development of superior men in their relation not only to the structure of society but to themselves. Laotzu, with little liking for organized thought or recruited action, no final faith in any authority but the authority of the heart, suggests that if those in charge of human affairs would act on instinct and conscience there would be less and less need of organized authority for governing people or, at any rate—and here he is seen as the realist he remains, as a man aware of necessarily gradual steps—less need for "superior men" to show. In our own time we have had evidence of the tragic effects of showy authority. In this dislike of show, rather than in any fundament of ethics, lay most of what Giles considered Laotzu's "direct antagonism" to Confucian orthodoxy. The trouble was that Confucius so ritualized his ethical culture that conduct of life took on forms similar to those of religion, whereas Laotzu spurned both religious and civil ceremony as misleading and harmful spectacle, his faith and conduct depending upon no outward prop but upon inner accord with the conscience of the universe.

Faith of this sort is true mysticism. Yet nothing could be further from the realistic core of Laotzu's way of life than Wilder Hobson's description of it as "that great mystical doctrine which holds that by profound, solitary meditation men may obtain knowledge of the Absolute."

Laotzu was concerned, as man must ever be, with the origin and meaning of life but knew and declared that no man's explanation of it is absolute. His book opens,

> Existence is beyond the power of words
> To define:
> Terms may be used
> But are none of them absolute.

In at all considering the origin of life he was a mystic, as anyone must be, theist or atheist, who ventures either positive or negative guess concerning what is beyond the mind of man to know; and insofar as Laotzu's sayings probe this region he differed again from Confucius who, contentedly agnostic, restricted his philosophy to known nature and empirical bound. Laotzu, on the other hand, fused mysticism and pragmatism into a philosophy as realistic as that of Confucius but sweetened by the natural and sufficient intuition of rightness with which he believed all men to be endowed and by which he believed all men could discover their lives to be peaceful, useful and happy. He was by no means the solitary, unneighborly hermit, occult with meditation. He was as natural, as genial, as homely as Lincoln. Having a sense of proportion, he had a sense of humor and, as much as any man who has lived, was the everlasting neighbor. At least this is my reading of him from the one record by which he may be appraised.

It is worthy of note, moreover, that his philosophy anticipated and contained the humanitarian philosophies which have succeeded it, conflicting with none of them, deepening them all. It is a fair guess that neither the great Indian nor the great Jew would have found anything unacceptable in Laotzu's mystical uses, which have been made no more mystical by the one, no more useful by the other. Connecting not only mystically but practically with the springs and ends of our action, our thought, our being, it is a fundamental expression of everything in the heart and mind of men which respects, enjoys and serves the individual good by respecting, enjoying and serving the common good.

Though without the help this time of Dr. Kiang, who is beyond reach in China, and though mindful of Arthur Waley's distinction between scriptural and historical translation, I wait no longer to offer my reading of a poet whom I trust other readers will find with me to be neither occult nor complex but open and simple, neither pontifical nor archaic but lay and current, in his calm human stature.

Witter Bynner

Chapala, Jalisco, Mexico
June 15, 1944

THE WAY OF LIFE

1

Existence is beyond the power of words
To define:
Terms may be used
But are none of them absolute.
In the beginning of heaven and earth there were no
      words,
Words came out of the womb of matter;
And whether a man dispassionately
Sees to the core of life
Or passionately
Sees the surface,
The core and the surface
Are essentially the same,
Words making them seem different
Only to express appearance.
If name be needed, wonder names them both:
From wonder into wonder
Existence opens.

2

People through finding something beautiful
Think something else unbeautiful,
Through finding one man fit
Judge another unfit.
Life and death, though stemming from each other,
      seem to conflict as stages of change,
Difficult and easy as phases of achievement,
Long and short as measures of contrast,

High and low as degrees of relation;
But, since the varying of tones gives music to a voice
And what is is the was of what shall be,
The sanest man
Sets up no deed,
Lays down no law,
Takes everything that happens as it comes,
As something to animate, not to appropriate,
To earn, not to own,
To accept naturally without self-importance:
If you never assume importance
You never lose it.

3

It is better not to make merit a matter of reward
Lest people conspire and contend,
Not to pile up rich belongings
Lest they rob,
Not to excite by display
Lest they covet.
A sound leader's aim
Is to open people's hearts,
Fill their stomachs,
Calm their wills,
Brace their bones
And so to clarify their thoughts and cleanse their needs
That no cunning meddler could touch them:
Without being forced, without strain or constraint,
Good government comes of itself.

4

Existence, by nothing bred,
Breeds everything.

Parent of the universe,
It smooths rough edges,
Unties hard knots,
Tempers the sharp sun,
Lays blowing dust,
Its image in the wellspring never fails.
But how was it conceived?—this image
Of no other sire.

5

Nature, immune as to a sacrifice of straw dogs,
Faces the decay of its fruits.
A sound man, immune as to a sacrifice of straw dogs,
Faces the passing of human generations.
The universe, like a bellows,
Is always emptying, always full;
The more it yields, the more it holds.
Men come to their wit's end arguing about it
And had better meet it at the marrow.

6

The breath of life moves through a deathless valley
Of mysterious motherhood
Which conceives and bears the universal seed,
The seeming of a world never to end,
Breath for men to draw from as they will:
And the more they take of it, the more remains.

7

The universe is deathless,
Is deathless because, having no finite self,
It stays infinite.

A sound man by not advancing himself
Stays the further ahead of himself,
By not confining himself to himself
Sustains himself outside himself:
By never being an end in himself
He endlessly becomes himself.

8

Man at his best, like water,
Serves as he goes along:
Like water he seeks his own level,
The common level of life,
Loves living close to the earth,
Living clear down in his heart,
Loves kinship with his neighbors,
The pick of words that tell the truth,
The even tenor of a well-run state,
The fair profit of able dealing,
The right timing of useful deeds,
And for blocking no one's way
No one blames him.

9

Keep stretching a bow
You repent of the pull,
A whetted saw
Goes thin and dull,
Surrounded with treasure
You lie ill at ease,
Proud beyond measure
You come to your knees:
Do enough, without vying,
Be living, not dying.

10

Can you hold the door of your tent
Wide to the firmament?
Can you, with the simple stature
Of a child, breathing nature,
Become, notwithstanding,
A man?
Can you continue befriending
With no prejudice, no ban?
Can you, mating with heaven,
Serve as the female part?
Can your learned head take leaven
From the wisdom of your heart?
If you can bear issue and nourish its growing,
If you can guide without claim or strife,
If you can stay in the lead of men without their knowing,
You are at the core of life.

11

Thirty spokes are made one by holes in a hub
By vacancies joining them for a wheel's use;
The use of clay in moulding pitchers
Comes from the hollow of its absence;
Doors, windows, in a house,
Are used for their emptiness:
Thus we are helped by what is not
To use what is.

12

The five colors can blind,
The five tones deafen,
The five tastes cloy.

The race, the hunt, can drive men mad
And their booty leave them no peace.
Therefore a sensible man
Prefers the inner to the outer eye:
He has his yes,—he has his no.

13

Favor and disfavor have been called equal worries,
Success and failure have been called equal ailments.
How can favor and disfavor be called equal worries?
Because winning favor burdens a man
With the fear of losing it.
How can success and failure be called equal ailments?
Because a man thinks of the personal body as self.
When he no longer thinks of the personal body as self
Neither failure nor success can ail him.
One who knows his lot to be the lot of all other men
Is a safe man to guide them,
One who recognizes all men as members of his own body
Is a sound man to guard them.

14

What we look for beyond seeing
And call the unseen,
Listen for beyond hearing
And call the unheard,
Grasp for beyond reaching
And call the withheld,
Merge beyond understanding
In a oneness
Which does not merely rise and give light,
Does not merely set and leave darkness,

But forever sends forth a succession of living things as mys-
   terious
As the unbegotten existence to which they return.
That is why men have called them empty phenomena,
Meaningless images,
In a mirage
With no face to meet,
No back to follow.
Yet one who is anciently aware of existence
Is master of every moment,
Feels no break since time beyond time
In the way life flows.

15

Long ago the land was ruled with a wisdom
Too fine, too deep, to be fully understood
And, since it was beyond men's full understanding,
Only some of it has come down to us, as in these sayings:
'Alert as a winter-farer on an icy stream,'
'Wary as a man in ambush,'
'Considerate as a welcome guest,'
'Selfless as melting ice,'
'Green as an uncut tree,'
'Open as a valley,'
And this one also, 'Roiled as a torrent.'
Why roiled as a torrent?
Because when a man is in turmoil how shall he find peace
Save by staying patient till the stream clears?
How can a man's life keep its course
If he will not let it flow?
Those who flow as life flows know
They need no other force:
They feel no wear, they feel no tear,
They need no mending, no repair.

16

Be utterly humble
And you shall hold to the foundation of peace.
Be at one with all these living things which, having arisen and
    flourished,
Return to the quiet whence they came,
Like a healthy growth of vegetation
Falling back upon the root.
Acceptance of this return to the root has been called 'quietism,'
Acceptance of quietism has been condemned as 'fatalism.'
But fatalism is acceptance of destiny
And to accept destiny is to face life with open eyes,
Whereas not to accept destiny is to face death blindfold.
He who is open-eyed is open-minded,
He who is open-minded is open-hearted,
He who is open-hearted is kingly,
He who is kingly is godly,
He who is godly is useful,
He who is useful is infinite,
He who is infinite is immune,
He who is immune is immortal.

17

A leader is best
When people barely know that he exists,
Not so good when people obey and acclaim him,
Worst when they despise him.
'Fail to honor people,
They fail to honor you';
But of a good leader, who talks little,
When his work is done, his aim fulfilled,
They will all say, 'We did this ourselves.'

18

When people lost sight of the way to live
Came codes of love and honesty,
Learning came, charity came,
Hypocrisy took charge;
When differences weakened family ties
Came benevolent fathers and dutiful sons;
And when lands were disrupted and misgoverned
Came ministers commended as loyal.

19

Rid of formalized wisdom and learning
People would be a hundredfold happier,
Rid of conventionalized duty and honor
People would find their families dear,
Rid of legalized profiteering
People would have no thieves to fear.
These methods of life have failed, all three,
Here is the way, it seems to me:
Set people free,
As deep in their hearts they would like to be,
From private greeds
And wanton needs.

20

Leave off fine learning! End the nuisance
Of saying yes to this and perhaps to that,
Distinctions with how little difference!
Categorical this, categorical that,
What slightest use are they!
If one man leads, another must follow,

How silly that is and how false!
Yet conventional men lead an easy life
With all their days feast-days,
A constant spring visit to the Tall Tower,
While I am a simpleton, a do-nothing,
Not big enough yet to raise a hand,
Not grown enough to smile,
A homeless, worthless waif.
Men of the world have a surplus of goods,
While I am left out, owning nothing.
What a booby I must be
Not to know my way round,
What a fool!
The average man is so crisp and so confident
That I ought to be miserable
Going on and on like the sea,
Drifting nowhere.
All these people are making their mark in the world,
While I, pig-headed, awkward,
Different from the rest,
Am only a glorious infant still nursing at the breast.

21

The surest test if a man be sane
Is if he accepts life whole, as it is,
Without needing by measure or touch to understand
The measureless untouchable source
Of its images,
The measureless untouchable source
Of its substances,
The source which, while it appears dark emptiness,
Brims with a quick force
Farthest away
And yet nearest at hand

From oldest time unto this day,
Charging its images with origin:
What more need I know of the origin
Than this?

22

'Yield and you need not break':
Bent you can straighten,
Emptied you can hold,
Torn you can mend;
And as want can reward you
So wealth can bewilder.
Aware of this, a wise man has the simple return
Which other men seek:
Without inflaming himself
He is kindled,
Without explaining himself
Is explained,
Without taking credit
Is accredited,
Laying no claim
Is acclaimed
And, because he does not compete,
Finds peaceful competence.
How true is the old saying,
'Yield and you need not break'!
How completely it comes home!

23

Nature does not have to insist,
Can blow for only half a morning,
Rain for only half a day,
And what are these winds and these rains but natural?

If nature does not have to insist,
Why should man?
It is natural too
That whoever follows the way of life feels alive,
That whoever uses it properly feels well used,
Whereas he who loses the way of life feels lost,
That whoever keeps to the way of life
Feels at home,
Whoever uses it properly
Feels welcome,
Whereas he who uses it improperly
Feels improperly used:
'Fail to honor people,
They fail to honor you.'

24

Standing tiptoe a man loses balance,
Walking astride he has no pace,
Kindling himself he fails to light,
Acquitting himself he forfeits his hearers,
Admiring himself he does so alone.
Pride has never brought a man greatness
But, according to the way of life,
Brings the ills that make him unfit,
Make him unclean in the eyes of his neighbor,
And a sane man will have none of them.

25

Before creation a presence existed,
Self-contained, complete,
Formless, voiceless, mateless,
Changeless,
Which yet pervaded itself
With unending motherhood.

Though there can be no name for it,
I have called it 'the way of life.'
Perhaps I should have called it 'the fullness of life,'
Since fullness implies widening into space,
Implies still further widening,
Implies widening until the circle is whole,
In this sense
The way of life is fulfilled,
Heaven is fulfilled,
Earth fulfilled
And a fit man also is fulfilled:
These are the four amplitudes of the universe
And a fit man is one of them:
Man rounding the way of earth,
Earth rounding the way of heaven,
Heaven rounding the way of life
Till the circle is full.

26

Gravity is the root of grace,
The mainstay of all speed.
A traveler of true means, whatever the day's pace,
Remembers the provision-van
And, however fine prospect be offered, is a man
With a calm head.
What lord of countless chariots would ride them in vain,
Would make himself fool of the realm,
With pace beyond rein,
Speed beyond helm?

27

One may move so well that a foot-print never shows,
Speak so well that the tongue never slips,

Reckon so well that no counter is needed,
Seal an entrance so tight, though using no lock,
That it cannot be opened,
Bind a hold so firm, though using no cord,
That it cannot be untied.
And these are traits not only of a sound man
But of many a man thought to be unsound.
A sound man is good at salvage,
At seeing that nothing is lost.
Having what is called insight,
A good man, before he can help a bad man,
Finds in himself the matter with the bad man.
And whichever teacher
Discounts the lesson
Is as far off the road as the other,
Whatever else he may know.
That is the heart of it.

28

'One who has a man's wings
And a woman's also
Is in himself a womb of the world'
And, being a womb of the world,
Continuously, endlessly,
Gives birth;
One who, preferring light,
Prefers darkness also
Is in himself an image of the world
And, being an image of the world,
Is continuously, endlessly
The dwelling of creation;
One who is highest of men
And humblest also
Is in himself a valley of the world,
And, being a valley of the world,

Continuously, endlessly
Conducts the one source
From which vessels may be usefully filled;
Servants of the state are such vessels,
To be filled from undiminishing supply.

29

Those who would take over the earth
And shape it to their will
Never, I notice, succeed.
The earth is like a vessel so sacred
That at the mere approach of the profane
It is marred
And when they reach out their fingers it is gone.
For a time in the world some force themselves ahead
And some are left behind,
For a time in the world some make a great noise
And some are held silent,
For a time in the world some are puffed fat
And some are kept hungry,
For a time in the world some push aboard
And some are tipped out:
At no time in the world will a man who is sane
Over-reach himself,
Over-spend himself,
Over-rate himself.

30

One who would guide a leader of men in the uses of life
Will warn him against the use of arms for conquest.
Weapons often turn upon the wielder,
An army's harvest is a waste of thorns,
Conscription of a multitude of men

Drains the next year dry.
A good general, daring to march, dares also to halt,
Will never press his triumph beyond need.
What he must do he does but not for glory,
What he must do he does but not for show,
What he must do he does but not for self;
He has done it because it had to be done,
Not from a hot head.
Let life ripen and then fall,
Force is not the way at all:
Deny the way of life and you are dead.

31

Even the finest arms are an instrument of evil,
A spread of plague,
And the way for a vital man to go is not the way of a soldier.
But in time of war men civilized in peace
Turn from their higher to their lower nature.
Arms are an instrument of evil,
No measure for thoughtful men
Until there fail all other choice
But sad acceptance of it.
Triumph is not beautiful.
He who thinks triumph beautiful
Is one with a will to kill,
And one with a will to kill
Shall never prevail upon the world.
It is a good sign when man's higher nature comes forward,
A bad sign when his lower nature comes forward,
When retainers take charge
And the master stays back
As in the conduct of a funeral.
The death of a multitude is cause for mourning:
Conduct your triumph as a funeral.

32

Existence is infinite, not to be defined;
And, though it seem but a bit of wood in your hand, to carve as
    you please,
It is not to be lightly played with and laid down.
When rulers adhered to the way of life,
They were upheld by natural loyalty:
Heaven and earth were joined and made fertile,
Life was a freshness of rain,
Subject to none,
Free to all.
But men of culture came, with their grades and their distinctions;
And as soon as such differences had been devised
No one knew where to end them,
Though the one who does know the end of all such differences
Is the sound man:
Existence
Might be likened to the course
Of many rivers reaching the one sea.

33

Knowledge studies others,
Wisdom is self-known;
Muscle masters brothers,
Self-mastery is bone;
Content need never borrow,
Ambition wanders blind:
Vitality cleaves to the marrow
Leaving death behind.

34

Bountiful life, letting anyone attend,
Making no distinction between left or right.

Feeding everyone, refusing no one,
Has not provided this bounty to show how much it owns,
Has not fed and clad its guests with any thought of claim;
And, because it lacks the twist
Of mind or body in what it has done,
The guile of head or hands,
Is not always respected by a guest.
Others appreciate welcome from the perfect host
Who, barely appearing to exist,
Exists the most.

35

If the sign of life is in your face
He who responds to it
Will feel secure and fit
As when, in a friendly place,
Sure of hearty care,
A traveler gladly waits.
Though it may not taste like food
And he may not see the fare
Or hear a sound of plates,
How endless it is and how good!

36

He who feels punctured
Must once have been a bubble,
He who feels unarmed
Must have carried arms,
He who feels belittled
Must have been consequential,
He who feels deprived
Must have had privilege,
Whereas a man with insight

Knows that to keep under is to endure.
What happens to a fish pulled out of a pond?
Or to an implement of state pulled out of a scabbard?
Unseen, they survive.

37

The way to use life is to do nothing through acting,
The way to use life is to do everything through being.
When a leader knows this,
His land naturally goes straight.
And the world's passion to stray from straightness
Is checked at the core
By the simple unnamable cleanness
Through which men cease from coveting,
And to a land where men cease from coveting
Peace comes of course.

38

A man of sure fitness, without making a point of his fitness,
Stays fit;
A man of unsure fitness, assuming an appearance of fitness,
Becomes unfit.
The man of sure fitness never makes an act of it
Nor considers what it may profit him;
The man of unsure fitness makes an act of it
And considers what it may profit him.
However a man with a kind heart proceed,
He forgets what it may profit him;
However a man with a just mind proceed,
He remembers what it may profit him;
However a man of conventional conduct proceed, if he be not
    complied with
Out goes his fist to enforce compliance.

Here is what happens:
Losing the way of life, men rely first on their fitness;
Losing fitness, they turn to kindness;
Losing kindness, they turn to justness;
Losing justness, they turn to convention.
Conventions are fealty and honesty gone to waste,
They are the entrance of disorder.
False teachers of life use flowery words
And start nonsense.
The man of stamina stays with the root
Below the tapering,
Stays with the fruit
Beyond the flowering:
He has his no and he has his yes.

39

The wholeness of life has, from of old, been made manifest in its
    parts:
Clarity has been made manifest in heaven,
Firmness in earth,
Purity in the spirit,
In the valley conception,
In the river procreation;
And so in a leader are the people made manifest
For wholeness of use.
But for clarity heaven would be veiled,
But for firmness earth would have crumbled,
But for purity spirit would have fumbled,
But for conception the valley would have failed,
But for procreation the river have run dry;
So, save for the people, a leader shall die:
Always the low carry the high
On a root for growing by.
What can stand lofty with no low foundation?
No wonder leaders of a land profess

Their stature and their station
To be servitude and lowliness!
If rim and spoke and hub were not,
Where would be the chariot?
Who will prefer the jingle of jade pendants if
He once has heard stone growing in a cliff!

40

Life on its way returns into a mist,
Its quickness is its quietness again:
Existence of this world of things and men
Renews their never needing to exist.

41

Men of stamina, knowing the way of life,
Steadily keep to it;
Unstable men, knowing the way of life,
Keep to it or not according to occasion;
Stupid men, knowing the way of life
And having once laughed at it, laugh again the louder.
If you need to be sure which way is right, you can tell by their
     laughing at it.
They fling the old charges:
'A wick without oil,'
'For every step forward a step or two back.'
To such laughers a level road looks steep,
Top seems bottom,
'White appears black,'
'Enough is a lack,'
Endurance is a weakness,
Simplicity a faded flower.
But eternity is his who goes straight round the circle,
Foundation is his who can feel beyond touch,

Harmony is his who can hear beyond sound,
Pattern is his who can see beyond shape:
Life is his who can tell beyond words
Fulfillment of the unfulfilled.

42

Life, when it came to be,
Bore one, then two, then three
Elements of things;
And thus the three began
—Heaven and earth and man—
To balance happenings:
Cool night behind, warm day ahead,
For the living, for the dead.
Though a commoner be loath to say
That he is only common clay,
Kings and princes often state
How humbly they are leading,
Because in true succeeding
High and low correlate.
It is an ancient thought,
Which many men have taught,
That he who over-reaches
And tries to live by force
Shall die thereby of course,
And is what my own heart teaches.

43

As the soft yield of water cleaves obstinate stone,
So to yield with life solves the insoluble:
To yield, I have learned, is to come back again.
But this unworded lesson,
This easy example,
Is lost upon men.

44

Which means more to you,
You or your renown?
Which brings more to you,
You or what you own?
And which would cost you more
If it were gone?
The niggard pays,
The miser loses.
The least ashamed of men
Goes back if he chooses:
He knows both ways,
He starts again.

45

A man's work, however finished it seem,
Continues as long as he live;
A man, however perfect he seem,
Is needed as long as he live:
As long as truth appears falsity,
The seer a fool,
The prophet a dumb lout,
If you want to keep warm keep stirring about,
Keep still if you want to keep cool,
And in all the world one day no doubt
Your way shall be the rule.

46

In a land where the way of life is understood
Race-horses are led back to serve the field;
In a land where the way of life is not understood
War-horses are bred on the autumn yield.

Owning is the entanglement,
Wanting is the bewilderment,
Taking is the presentiment:
Only he who contains content
Remains content.

47

There is no need to run outside
For better seeing,
Nor to peer from a window. Rather abide
At the center of your being;
For the more you leave it, the less you learn.
Search your heart and see
If he is wise who takes each turn:
The way to do is to be.

48

A man anxious for knowledge adds more to himself every min-
ute;
A man acquiring life loses himself in it,
Has less and less to bear in mind,
Less and less to do,
Because life, he finds, is well inclined,
Including himself too.
Often a man sways the world like a wind
But not by deed;
And if there appear to you to be need
Of motion to sway it, it has left you behind.

49

A sound man's heart is not shut within itself
But is open to other people's hearts:

I find good people good,
And I find bad people good
If I am good enough;
I trust men of their word,
And I trust liars
If I am true enough;
I feel the heart-beats of others
Above my own
If I am enough of a father,
Enough of a son.

50

Death might appear to be the issue of life,
Since for every three out of ten being born
Three out of ten are dying.
Then why
Should another three out of ten continue breeding death?
Because of sheer madness to multiply.
But there is one out of ten, they say, so sure of life
That tiger and wild bull keep clear of his inland path,
Weapons turn from him on the battle-field,
No bull-horn could tell where to gore him,
No tiger-claw where to tear him,
No weapon where to enter him.
And why?
Because he has no death to die.

51

Existence having borne them
And fitness bred them,
While matter varied their forms
And breath empowered them,

All created things render, to the existence and fitness they de-
pend on,
An obedience
Not commanded but of course.
And since this is the way existence bears issue
And fitness raises, attends,
Shelters, feeds and protects,
Do you likewise:
Be parent, not possessor,
Attendant, not master,
Be concerned not with obedience but with benefit,
And you are at the core of living.

52

The source of life
Is as a mother.
Be fond of both mother and children but know the mother dearer
And you outlive death.
Curb your tongue and senses
And you are beyond trouble,
Let them loose
And you are beyond help.
Discover that nothing is too small for clear vision,
Too insignificant for tender strength,
Use outlook
And insight,
Use them both
And you are immune:
For you have witnessed eternity.

53

If I had any learning
Of a highway wide and fit,

Would I lose it at each turning?
Yet look at people spurning
Natural use of it!
See how fine the palaces
And see how poor the farms,
How bare the peasants' granaries
While gentry wear embroideries
Hiding sharpened arms,
And the more they have the more they seize,
How can there be such men as these
Who never hunger, never thirst,
Yet eat and drink until they burst!
There are other brigands, but these are the worst
Of all the highway's harms.

54

'Since true foundation cannot fail
But holds as good as new,
Many a worshipful son shall hail
A father who lived true.'
Realized in one man, fitness has its rise;
Realized in a family, fitness multiplies;
Realized in a village, fitness gathers weight;
Realized in a country, fitness becomes great;
Realized in the world, fitness fills the skies.
And thus the fitness of one man
You find in the family he began,
You find in the village that accrued,
You find in the country that ensued,
You find in the world's whole multitude.
How do I know this integrity?
Because it could all begin in me.

55

He whom life fulfills,
Though he remains a child,
Is immune to the poisonous sting
Of insects, to the ravening
Of wild beasts or to vultures' bills.
He needs no more bone or muscle than a baby's for sure hold.
Without thought of joined organs, he is gender
Which grows firm, unfaltering.
Though his voice should cry out at full pitch all day, it would
    not rasp but would stay tender
Through the perfect balancing
Of a man at endless ease with everything
Because of the true life that he has led.
To try for more than this bodes ill.
It is said, 'there's a way where there's a will';
But let life ripen and then fall.
Will is not the way at all:
Deny the way of life and you are dead.

56

Those who know do not tell,
Those who tell do not know.
Not to set the tongue loose
But to curb it,
Not to have edges that catch
But to remain untangled,
Unblinded,
Unconfused,
Is to find balance,
And he who holds balance beyond sway of love or hate,
Beyond reach of profit or loss,
Beyond care of praise or blame,
Has attained the highest post in the world.

57

A realm is governed by ordinary acts,
A battle is governed by extraordinary acts;
The world is governed by no acts at all.
And how do I know?
This is how I know.
Act after act prohibits
Everything but poverty,
Weapon after weapon conquers
Everything but chaos,
Business after business provides
A craze of waste,
Law after law breeds
A multitude of thieves.
Therefore a sensible man says:
If I keep from meddling with people, they take care of them-
    selves,
If I keep from commanding people, they behave themselves,
If I keep from preaching at people, they improve themselves,
If I keep from imposing on people, they become themselves.

58

The less a leader does and says
The happier his people,
The more a leader struts and brags
The sorrier his people.
Often what appears to be unhappiness is happiness
And what appears to be happiness is unhappiness.
Who can see what leads to what
When happiness appears and yet is not,
When what should be is nothing but a mask
Disguising what should not be? Who can but ask
An end to such a stupid plot!
Therefore a sound man shall so square the circle

And circle the square as not to injure, not to impede:
The glow of his life shall not daze,
It shall lead.

59

To lead men and serve heaven, weigh the worth
Of the one source:
Use the single force
Which doubles the strength of the strong
By enabling man to go right, disabling him to go wrong,
Be so charged with the nature of life that you give your people
 birth,
That you mother your land, are the fit
And ever-living root of it:
The seeing root, whose eye is infinite.

60

Handle a large kingdom with as gentle a touch as if you were
 cooking small fish.
If you manage people by letting them alone,
Ghosts of the dead shall not haunt you.
Not that there are no ghosts
But that their influence becomes propitious
In the sound existence of a living man:
There is no difference between the quick and the dead,
They are one channel of vitality.

61

A large country is the low level of interflowing rivers.
It draws people to the sea-end of a valley
As the female draws the male,

Receives it into absorbing depth
Because depth always absorbs.
And so a large country, inasfar as it is deeper than a small coun-
     try,
Absorbs the small—
Or a small country, inasfar as it is deeper than a large country,
Absorbs the large.
Some countries consciously seek depth into which to draw others.
Some countries naturally have depth into which to draw others:
A large country needs to admit,
A small country needs to emit,
And so each country can naturally have what it needs
If the large country submit.

62

Existence is sanctuary:
It is a good man's purse,
It is also a bad man's keep.
Clever performances come dear or cheap,
Goodness comes free;
And how shall a man who acts better deny a man who acts worse
This right to be.
Rather, when an emperor is crowned, let the three
Ministers whom he appoints to receive for him fine horses and
     gifts of jade
Receive for him also the motionless gift of integrity,
The gift prized as highest by those ancients who said,
'Only pursue an offender to show him the way.'
What men in all the world could have more wealth than they?

63

Men knowing the way of life
Do without acting,

Effect without enforcing,
Taste without consuming;
'Through the many they find the few,
Through the humble the great';
They 'respect their foes,'
They 'face the simple fact before it becomes involved.
Solve the small problem before it becomes big.'
The most involved fact in the world
Could have been faced when it was simple,
The biggest problem in the world
Could have been solved when it was small.
The simple fact that he finds no problem big
Is a sane man's prime achievement.
If you say yes too quickly
You may have to say no,
If you think things are done too easily
You may find them hard to do:
If you face trouble sanely
It cannot trouble you.

64

Before it move, hold it,
Before it go wrong, mould it,
Drain off water in winter before it freeze,
Before weeds grow, sow them to the breeze.
You can deal with what has not happened, can foresee
Harmful events and not allow them to be.
Though—as naturally as a seed becomes a tree of arm-wide
    girth—
There can rise a nine-tiered tower from a man's handful of earth
Or here at your feet a thousand-mile journey have birth,
Quick action bruises,
Quick grasping loses.
Therefore a sane man's care is not to exert
One move that can miss, one move that can hurt.

Most people who miss, after almost winning,
Should have 'known the end from the beginning.'
A sane man is sane in knowing what things he can spare,
In not wishing what most people wish,
In not reaching for things that seem rare.
The cultured might call him heathenish,
This man of few words, because his one care
Is not to interfere but to let nature renew
The sense of direction men undo.

65

Sound old rulers, it is said,
Left people to themselves, instead
Of wanting to teach everything
And start the people arguing.
With mere instruction in command,
So that people understand
Less than they know, woe is the land;
But happy the land that is ordered so
That they understand more than they know.
For everyone's good this double key
Locks and unlocks equally.
If modern man would use it, he
Could find old wisdom in his heart
And clear his vision enough to see
From start to finish and finish to start
The circle rounding perfectly.

66

Why are rivers and seas lords of the waters?
Because they afford the common level
And so become lords of the waters.
The common people love a sound man

Because he does not talk above their level,
Because, though he lead them,
He follows them,
He imposes no weight on them;
And they in turn, because he does not impede them,
Yield to him, content:
People never tire of anyone
Who is not bent upon comparison.

67

Everyone says that my way of life is the way of a simpleton.
Being largely the way of a simpleton is what makes it worth
     while.
If it were not the way of a simpleton
It would long ago have been worthless,
These possessions of a simpleton being the three I choose
And cherish:
To care,
To be fair,
To be humble.
When a man cares he is unafraid,
When he is fair he leaves enough for others,
When he is humble he can grow;
Whereas if, like men of today, he be bold without caring,
Self-indulgent without sharing,
Self-important without shame,
He is dead.
The invincible shield
Of caring
Is a weapon from the sky
Against being dead.

68

The best captain does not plunge headlong
Nor is the best soldier a fellow hot to fight.
The greatest victor wins without a battle:
He who overcomes men understands them.
There is a quality of quietness
Which quickens people by no stress:
'Fellowship with heaven,' as of old,
Is fellowship with man and keeps its hold.

69

The handbook of the strategist has said:
'Do not invite the fight, accept it instead,'
'Better a foot behind than an inch too far ahead,'
Which means:
Look a man straight in the face and make no move,
Roll up your sleeve and clench no fist,
Open your hand and show no weapon,
Bare your breast and find no foe.
But as long as there be a foe, value him,
Respect him, measure him, be humble toward him;
Let him not strip from you, however strong he be,
Compassion, the one wealth which can afford him.

70

My way is so simple to feel, so easy to apply,
That only a few will feel it or apply it.
If it were not the lasting way, the natural way to try,
If it were a passing way, everyone would try it.
But however few shall go my way
Or feel concerned with me,
Some there are and those are they

Who witness what they see:
Sanity is a haircloth sheath
With a jewel underneath.

71

A man who knows how little he knows is well,
A man who knows how much he knows is sick.
If, when you see the symptoms, you can tell,
Your cure is quick.
A sound man knows that sickness makes him sick
And before he catches it his cure is quick.

72

Upon those who defy authority
It shall be visited,
But not behind prison walls
Nor through oppression of their kin;
Men sanely led
Are not led by duress.
To know yourself and not show yourself,
To think well of yourself and not tell of yourself,
Be that your no and your yes.

73

A man with outward courage dares to die,
A man with inward courage dares to live;
But either of these men
Has a better and a worse side than the other.
And who can tell exactly to which qualities heaven objects?
Heaven does nothing to win the day,
Says nothing—

Is echoed,
Orders nothing—
Is obeyed,
Advises nothing—
Is right:
And which of us, seeing that nothing is outside the vast
Wide-meshed net of heaven, knows just how it is cast?

74

Death is no threat to people
Who are not afraid to die;
But even if these offenders feared death all day,
Who should be rash enough
To act as executioner?
Nature is executioner.
When man usurps the place,
A carpenter's apprentice takes the place of the master:
And 'an apprentice hacking with the master's axe
May slice his own hand.'

75

People starve
If taxes eat their grain,
And the faults of starving people
Are the fault of their rulers.
That is why people rebel.
Men who have to fight for their living
And are not afraid to die for it
Are higher men than those who, stationed high,
Are too fat to dare to die.

76

Man, born tender and yielding,
Stiffens and hardens in death.
All living growth is pliant,
Until death transfixes it.
Thus men who have hardened are 'kin of death'
And men who stay gentle are 'kin of life.'
Thus a hard-hearted army is doomed to lose.
A tree hard-fleshed is cut down:
Down goes the tough and big,
Up comes the tender sprig.

77

Is not existence
Like a drawn bow?
The ends approach,
The height shortens, the narrowness widens.
True living would take from those with too much
Enough for those with too little,
Whereas man exacts from those with too little
Still more for those with too much.
Now what man shall have wealth enough to share with all men
Save one who can freely draw from the common means?
A sane man needs no better support, no richer reward,
Than this common means,
Through which he is all men's equal.

78

What is more fluid, more yielding than water?
Yet back it comes again, wearing down the rigid strength
Which cannot yield to withstand it.
So it is that the strong are overcome by the weak,

The haughty by the humble.
This we know
But never learn,
So that when wise men tell us,
'He who bites the dust
Is owner of the earth,
He who is scapegoat
Is king,'
They seem to twist the truth.

79

If terms to end a quarrel leave bad feeling,
What good are they?
So a sensible man takes the poor end of the bargain
Without quibbling.
It is sensible to make terms,
Foolish to be a stickler:
Though heaven prefer no man,
A sensible man prefers heaven.

80

If a land is small and its people are few,
With tenfold enough to have and to do,
And if no one has schooled them to waste supply
In the country for which they live and would die,
Then not a boat, not a cart
Tempts this people to depart,
Not a dagger, not a bow
Has to be drawn or bent for show,
People reckon by knots in a cord,
Relish plain food on the board,
Simple clothing suits them well,
And they remain content to dwell

In homes their customs can afford.
Though so close to their own town another town grow
They can hear its dogs bark and its roosters crow,
Yet glad of life in the village they know,
Where else in the world shall they need to go?

81

Real words are not vain,
Vain words not real;
And since those who argue prove nothing
A sensible man does not argue.
A sensible man is wiser than he knows,
While a fool knows more than is wise.
Therefore a sensible man does not devise resources:
The greater his use to others
The greater their use to him,
The more he yields to others
The more they yield to him.
The way of life cleaves without cutting:
Which, without need to say,
Should be man's way.